ZEN IN ENGLISH LITERATURE
AND ORIENTAL CLASSICS

ZEN IN
ENGLISH LITERATURE
AND ORIENTAL CLASSICS

BY

R. H. BLYTH

𝕿𝖔𝖐𝖞𝖔

THE HOKUSEIDO PRESS

PRINTED IN JAPAN

Dedicated to
Kayama Taigi,
Rôshi of Myoshinji Betsu-In, Keijô, Chôsen,
but for whom I should have known
nothing of Zen,

And to
Imamura Jûzo,
of Kichijôji, Tôkyô.

PREFACE

Zen is the most precious possession of Asia. With its beginnings in India, development in China, and final practical application in Japan, it is today the strongest power in the world. It is a world-power, for in so far as men *live* at all, they live by Zen. Wherever there is a poetical action, a religious aspiration, a heroic thought, a union of the nature within a man and the Nature without, there is Zen.

Speaking generally, in world culture we find Zen most clearly and significantly in the following: in the ancient worthies of Chinese Zen, for instance, Enô and Unmon; in the practical men of affairs of Japan, Hôjô Tokimune, for example, and in the poet Bashô; in Christ; in Eckehart, and in the music of Bach; in Shakespeare and Wordsworth. *Zen in English Literature* embraces the literature of Zen in Chinese and Japanese, the Chinese and Japanese Classics, and the whole extent of English Literature, with numerous quotations from German, French, Italian and Spanish Literatures. Don Quixote has a chapter all to himself; he is for the first time, I believe, satisfactorily explained. He is the purest example, in the whole of world literature, of the man who lives by Zen; but Sancho Panza also is not so far from the Kingdom of Heaven as perhaps even his author supposed.

Of the Chinese poets, Tôenmei and Hakurakuten, with

their feeling for *things,* for everyday life, are nearest to Zen;
the "poetical" poets, Ritaihaku and Toho, are far behind.
The question then arises: if Zen and poetry are taken as
roughly interchangeable words, how it is possible to rate a
lesser poet as having more Zen? The answer is: there is a
confusion here between the two allied meanings of poetry (a
life in accord with reality; and the writing of poetry,) and of
Zen (a religious system, that is, a certain way of thinking about
life; and living in accord with reality). In the meaning of
"poetry" as used in *Zen in English Literature,* Bashô is the
world's greatest poet. In such a poem as the following, over-
praised as it is,

> Along the mountain path,
>> The scent of plum-blossoms,—
>>> And, on a sudden, the rising sun!

梅 が 香 に の つ と 日 の 出 る 山 路 か な

a great deal must of course be supplied by the reader, but not
in the sense that he "fills in the picture," not that the poem
"suggests" something which the poem is not long enough to
say, not that the poem is in any sense symbolic; it presupposes
that the reader is living, at least in fits and starts, a poetical
life, a life of Zen.

In English Literature we find expression of the Zen attitude
towards life most consistently and purely in Shakespeare,
Wordsworth, Dickens and Stevenson. Arnold says, "The
strongest part of our religion today is its unconscious poetry,"
and this is true of any religion at any time in the history of
the world. The word "unconscious" implies that the poetry
is taken unawares, that it is unrecognised as such, as, for example, in Dickens; that what is believed *is* the poetry, and not
the intellectual concepts involved in it. It is of the essence of

poetry that it points to Something, just as (to use a favourite
Buddhist simile,) the finger points to the moon.   This something, though instantly recognised, is not to be defined.

> We say amisse
> This or that is;
> Thy word is all, if we could spell.

For Buddhism or Christianity, the "word" (Zen) of both is the
same.   On the one hand, it is the attainment of freedom, a
state in which we can say, as Beatrice said to Virgil,

> Io son fatta da Dio, sua mercè, tale,
> Che la vostra miseria non mi tange,
> Nè fiamma d'esto incendio non m'assale.
> > *Inferno,* II, 91-93.

> I am made of God, through His Grace,
> Such that your misery touches me not,
> Nor does flame of that burning assail me.

On the other hand, it is the salvation of mankind by our
vicarious suffering:

> She sees her Son, her God,
> Bow with a load of borrowed sins; and swim
> In woes that were not made for him.

Literature, especially poetry, has this same double, paradoxical nature as religion, and it is the main theme of *Zen in
English Literature,* that where there is religion there is poetry,
where there is poetry there is religion; not two things in close
association, but one thing with two names.   "Zen in English
Literature" means Zen in English Poetry, that is, Poetry as
English Zen.   The false religious and the false poetical life are
equally one: a wallowing in God, a vague and woolly pantheism, nightingales and roses.   If anything in so-called poetry,

if anything in Buddhism or Christianity will not stand the test
of reality, the test of Zen,

> What will not hold Perfection, let it burst!

Look, for example, at Cowper's verse:

> Can a woman's tender care
> Cease toward the child she bare?
> Yes, she may forgetful be,
> Yet will I remember thee.

When we read this, we know, with the immediacy that is the
hall-mark of absolute knowledge, that it is true.

> Truth is the trial of itself,
> And needs no other touch.

But who or what is this "I" that never forgets, that numbers
the hairs of our heads and turns them white with the years,
that "loves" us all without discrimination, that brings us into
being and then, sooner or later, murders us?   Zen alone can
answer such a question.   The answer is,

> Can a woman's tender care
> Cease toward the child she bare?
> Yes, she may forgetful be,
> Yet will I remember thee.

Do you understand?

It is to be feared that this book may fall between two (or
more) stools, since it is addressed, on the one hand, to English
readers who know much of English Literature and nothing of
Zen, and on the other, to Japanese readers who know a little
of both.   For the sake of the latter, quotations are longer and
more numerous than necessary for the former, but this is profitable for the English reader also, for I have endeavoured to
attain to that definition of a teacher given by Confucius,

A true teacher is one who knows (and makes known) the New, by revitalising the Old.

溫 故 而 知 新， 可 以 爲 師 矣。 (論語、二、十一)

In other words, the English reader is to look once more at English Literature, from the standpoint of Zen.

I have asked and received no help from anyone in the writing of this book; the mistakes, especially in the translations, will be ample evidence of this. But like the snow on Sotôba's hat, these errors are light, being mine own.

我 雪 と 思 へ ば 輕 し 笠 の 上   其 角

However, my indebtedness to Taisetz Suzuki's books on Zen will be apparent to all; if I venture to criticise him, it is only biting the hand that fed me. In addition, I have referred often to Asatarô Miyamori's *An Anthology of Haiku, Ancient and Modern;* I thank him deeply and sincerely for his labour of love. Another book I wish to recommend is Harold Gould Henderson's *The Bamboo Broom, An Introduction to Japanese Haiku,* a little masterpiece. Even his talk of " Bashô's eternal concentration on the beauties of the Absolute," which is the antithesis of Zen and the spirit of *haiku,* may be (temporarily) necessary for those who find *haiku* thin and tasteless.

In conclusion, I wish to thank Mrs. Saeko Kobayashi of Tôkyô for the Zen she displayed in typing the manuscript,— much more than I in the writing of it.

Kanazawa,
May 1941.

CONTENTS

CHAPTER I

WHAT IS ZEN?

Consider the lives of birds and fishes. Fish never weary of the water; but you do not know the true mind of a fish, for you are not a fish. Birds never tire of the woods; but you do not know their real spirit, for you are not a bird. It is just the same with the religious, the poetical life: if you do not live it, you know nothing about it.

魚鳥の有様を見よ。 魚は水にあかず。 魚に
あらざれば、その心を知らず。鳥は林を顧ふ。
鳥にあらざれば、その心を知らず。 閑居の氣
味も亦かくの如し。 住まずして誰か悟らむ。

This that Chômei says in the *Hôjôki*[1] is true of the life of Zen, which is the real religious, poetical life. But, as Mrs. Browning says in *Aurora Leigh,*

> The cygnet finds the water, but the man
> Is born in ignorance of his element.

Dôgen, (1200-1253) founder of the Sôtô Sect of Zen in Japan, expresses this more poetically:

> The water-bird
> Wanders here and there
> Leaving no trace,
> Yet her path
> She never forgets.

水鳥の往くも還るも跡たえて
　　されども道は忘れざりけり

[1] 1212 A.D.

1

Zen, though far from indefinite, is by definition indefinable, because it is the active principle of life itself.

> The sun passeth through pollutions and itself remains as
> pure as before,[1]

so Zen passes through all our definings and remains Zen as before. As we think of it, it seems dark, but "dark with excessive light." It is like Alice in The Looking Glass, the more we run after it the farther away we get. Yet we read books on Zen, and more books, hoping to find on some page, in some sentence or other, the key to a door which is only a hallucination. Zen says "Walk in!" Never mind the key or the bolt or the massive-seeming door. Just walk in! Goethe's revised version of the beginning of the Gospel of St. John, comes nearest:

> Im Anfang war die Tat,

for action cannot be defined. In *The Anticipation* Traherne says,

> His name is Now ...
> His essence is all Act.

Milton describes its unnoticed universality in *Comus:*

> A small unsightly root,
> The leaf was darkish, and had prickles on it,
> But in another country, as he said,
> Bore a bright golden flow'r, but not in this soil;
> Unknown, and like esteem'd, and the dull swain
> Treads on it daily with his clouted shoon.

It is seen selected for our admiration in art, music and poetry. The difference between Zen in actual life and Zen in Art, is that Art is like a photograph (and music like a film), that can be looked at whenever we please. Or, we may say, just as

[1] Bacon: *The Advancement of Learning.*

Goethe called architecture frozen music,[1] art is frozen Zen. Truth is everywhere, but is more *apparent* in science. Beauty is in dustbins and butcher's shops as well, but is more visible in the moon and flowers. Religion is in every place, at every moment, but as Johnson says in his *Journey to the Western Islands,*

> That man is little to be envied whose patriotism would not gain force upon the plain of Marathon, or whose piety would not grow warmer among the ruins of Iona.

We need not wait a moment, we need not stir a foot, to see Zen, but it is more evident in *some* acts, *some* works of art, *some* poems. In this book I have chosen examples from those which have a special meaning for me. Emerson says,

> It is as difficult to appropriate the thoughts of others as to invent.

I have tried to appropriate them as far as lay in my power.

Here is an example from *Oliver Twist.* The Artful Dodger, having been arrested, appears in court:

> It was indeed Mr. Dawkins, who, shuffling into the office with the big coat sleeves tucked up as usual, his left hand in his pocket, and his hat in his right hand, preceded the jailer, with a rolling gait altogether indescribable, and, taking his place in the dock, requested in an audible voice to know what he was placed in that 'ere disgraceful sitivation for.
> "Hold your tongue, will you?" said the jailer.
> "I'm an Englishman, ain't I?" rejoined the Dodger. "Where are my priwileges?"
> "You'll get your privileges soon enough," retorted the jailer, "and pepper with 'em."

---

[1] Gespräche mit Goethe, Montag, den 23. März, 1829. "Ich habe unter meinen Papieren ein Blatt gefunden," sagte Goethe heute, "wo ich die Baukunst eine erstarrte Musik nenne."

"We'll see wot the Secretary of State for the Home Affairs has got to say to the beaks, if I don't," replied Mr Dawkins. "Now then! Wot is this here business? I shall thank the madg'strates to dispose of this here little affair, and not to keep me while they read the paper, for I've got an appointment with a genelman in the City, and as I'm a man of my word, and wery punctual in business matters, he'll go away if I ain't there to my time, and then pr'aps there won't be an action for damage against them as kep me away. Oh no, certainly not!"

At this point, the Dodger, with a show of being very particular with a view to proceedings to be had thereafter, desired the jailer to communicate "the names of them two files as was on the bench."

(A witness is called who testifies to the Dodger's pickpocketing.)

"Have you anything to ask this witness, boy?" said the magistrate.

"I wouldn't abase myself by descending to hold no conversation with him," replied the Dodger.

"Have you anything to say at all?"

"Do you hear his worship ask if you've anything to say?" inquired the jailer, nudging the silent Dodger with his elbow.

"I beg your pardon," said the Dodger, looking up with an air of abstraction, "Did you redress yourself to me, my man?"

"I never see such an out-and-out young wagabond, your worship," observed the officer with a grin. "Do you mean to say anything, you young shaver?"

"No," replied the Dodger, "not here, for this ain't the shop for justice; besides which, my attorney is a breakfasting with the Wice President of the House of Commons; but I shall have something to say elsewhere, and so will he, and so will a wery numerous and 'spectable circle of acquaintances as 'll make them beaks wish they'd never been born, or that they'd got their footmen to hang 'em up to their own hat-pegs, 'afore they let 'em come out this morning to try it on me. I'll——"

"There! He's fully committed!" interposed the clerk. "Take him away."

"Come on," said the jailer.

"Oh, ah! I'll come on," replied the Dodger, brushing his hat with the palm of his hand. "Ah! (to the Bench) it's no use your looking frightened; I won't show you no mercy, not a ha'porth of it. *You'll* pay for this, my fine fellers. *I wouldn't be you for something! I wouldn't go free, now, if you was to fall down on your knees and ask me. Here, carry me off to prison! Take me away!"*

The Artful Dodger is "the chameleon poet that shocks the virtuous philosophers" on the bench. Notice how what seems to be at first mere impudence, rises with influx of energy, into an identification of himself with the whole machinery of the Law. He attains, for moment, to "Buddhahood, in which all the contradictions and disturbances caused by the intellect are entirely harmonised in a unity of higher order."[1] Someone to whom I related the above, said to me, "I suppose the case of Mata Hari, the celebrated woman spy, was similar. When she was being executed she refused to have her eyes bandaged." This is not so. Courage may and does often have Zen associated with it, but Zen is not courage. A thief running away like mad from a ferocious watch-dog may be a splendid example of Zen. Bashô gazing at the moon, is an example of Zen; eating one's dinner, yawning —— where is the courage in these?

Here is an example, similar to that of Dickens, but taken from real life. I was walking along a lonely mountain road with my wife and we were talking about her elder sister, who had died the year before. She said, "When we were young we would often come back from town at night along this very road. I am a coward, and was always afraid even though we

[1] Prof. Suzuki's definition of Zen.

were together, but my sister said, 'I would like to whiten my face and put on a white kimono, and stand over there in the shadow of the pine-trees.'" Once again, it is not the courage, but the willing identification of self, the subject, with the ghost, the object of fear, that has in it the touch of Zen. Here is another example of a different kind, in which there is no trace of ordinary courage; it consists in entire engrossment, conscious and unconscious, in what one is doing. This requires, of course, that one's work at the moment should be thoroughly congenial to one's nature, that is to say, it must be like the swimming of a fish or the flying of a bird. In his *Conversations with Goethe,* under Tuesday, April 22nd, 1830, Eckermann notes the following:

> I was much struck by a Savoyard boy, who turned a hurdy-gurdy, and led behind him a dog, on which a monkey was riding. He whistled and sang to us, and for a long time tried to make us give him something. We threw him down more than he could have expected, and I thought he would throw us a look of gratitude. However he did nothing of the kind, but pocketed his money, and immediately looked after others to give him more.

What struck Eckermann? Was it the ingratitude of the boy? I think not. It was the complete absorbtion of the boy in the work he was doing to get money. Other people had no existence for him. Three days after, a very similar thing struck Eckermann.

> At dinner, at the table d'hôte, I saw many faces, but few expressive enough to fix my attention. However, the head waiter interested me highly, so that my eyes constantly followed him and all his movements: and indeed he was a remarkable being. The guests who sat at the long table were about two hundred in number, and it seems almost incredible when I say that nearly the whole of the atten-

dance was performed by the head waiter, since he put on and took off all the dishes, while the other waiters only handed them to him and received them from him. During all this proceeding, nothing was spilt, no one was incommoded, but all went off lightly and nimbly, as if by the operation of a spirit. Thus, thousands of plates and dishes flew from his hands upon the table, and again from the table to the hands of the attendants behind him. Quite absorbed in his vocation, the whole man was nothing but eyes and hands, and he merely opened his closed lips for short answers and directions. Then he not only attended to the table but took the orders for wine and the like, and so well remembered everything, that when the meal was over, he knew everybody's score and took the money.

This is a splended example of Zen, which Eckermann calls "comprehensive power, presence of mind and strong memory." We may call it "presence of Mind," or "absence of mind." The memory, as Freud would say, is a matter of the will. We forget because we will (wish) to forget, and remember because we will to remember. "The whole man was nothing but eyes and hands." Turner was nothing but a paint-brush, Michael Angelo nothing but a chisel. There is no greater pleasure in ordinary life, so-called, than to see a bus-conductor, a teacher, anybody, really engrossed in his work, with no thought of its relative or absolute value, with no thought of its interest or profit to himself or others.

A similar example is given in Dickens' *Martin Chuzzlewit*. Mr. Pecksniff and his daughters are dining at Todger's, but the really interesting thing about the hilarious and convivial proceedings is Bailey, the boy who cleans the boots and is temporarily serving at table. He has "life more abundantly," with no self-consciousness or "choosing" or judging or attachment; equal to all circumstances, master of every situation. And be it noted that just as Eckermann's head waiter shows his Zen by doing his work so well, to perfection, so Dickens' boy shows his Zen by doing practically nothing at all, *to perfection,* in similar circumstances.

> Their young friend Bailey sympathised [with the two Miss Pecksniffs] in these feelings to the fullest extent, and abating nothing of his patronage, gave them every encouragement in his power: favouring them, when the general attention was diverted from his proceedings, with many nods and winks and other tokens of recognition, and occasionally touching his nose with a corkscrew, as if to express the Bacchanalian character of the meeting.   In truth perhaps even the spirits of the two Miss Pecksniffs, and the hungry watchfulness of Mr. Todgers, were less worthy of note than the proceedings of this remarkable boy, whom nothing disconcerted or put out of his way. If any piece of crockery, a dish or otherwise, chanced to slip through his hands (which happened once or twice) he let it go with perfect good breeding, and never added to the painful emotions of the company by exhibiting the least regret.   Nor did he, by hurrying to and fro, disturb the repose of the assembly, as many well-trained servants do; on the contrary, feeling the hopelessness of waiting upon so large a party, he left the gentlemen to help themselves to what they wanted, and seldom stirred from behind Mr. Jenkins's chair: where, with his hands in his pockets, and his legs planted pretty wide apart, he led the laughter, and enjoyed the conversation.

This perfection, which we see always in inanimate things, usually in animals, so seldom in human beings, almost never in ourselves, is what Christ urges us to attain:

Be ye perfect, as your Father which is in Heaven is perfect.

Many people will no doubt be surprised that Mark Tapley is not used as an example of Zen. His desire "to come out strong" in the most difficult circumstances may seem evidence of this, but actually it is evidence of the opposite. Zen is essentially unconscious, unselfconscious, even unSelfconscious. Notice further that, as Mrs. Lupin says, he is "a good young man." Sad to relate, we can find Zen in Mr. Pecksniff, Mrs. Gamp, Bailey Junior, that is, in hypocrisy, vulgarity, and impudence, more readily than in the conscious unselfishness of Mark Tapley. This is why the latter has something thin, unreal, out-of-joint about him. He is not equal to all circumstances, only to the worst.

There are two fables by Stevenson, *The Sinking Ship*, which shows Zen on its destructive side, and *The Poor Thing*, which illustrates its constructive working. Here is *The Sinking Ship*:

"Sir," said the first lieutenant, bursting into the Captain's cabin, "the ship is going down."

"Very well, Mr. Spoker," said the Captain; "but that is no reason for going about half-shaved. Exercise your mind a moment, Mr. Spoker, and you will see that to the philosophic eye there is nothing new in our position: the ship (if she is to go down at all) may be said to have been going down since she was launched."

"She is settling fast," said the first lieutenant, as he returned from shaving.

"Fast, Mr. Spoker?" asked the Captain. "The expression is a strange one, for time (if you will think of it) is only relative."

"Sir," said the lieutenant, "I think it is scarcely worth while to embark in such a discussion when we shall all be in Davy Jones's Locker in ten minutes."

"By parity of reasoning," returned the Captain gently, "it would never be worth while to begin any inquiry of importance; the odds are always overwhelming that we must die before we shall have brought it to an end. You have not considered, Mr. Spoker, the situation of man," said the Captain, smiling, and shaking his head.

"I am much more engaged in considering the position of the ship," said Mr. Spoker.

"Spoken like a good officer," replied the Captain, laying his hand on the lieutenant's shoulder.

On deck they found the men had broken into the spirit room, and were fast getting drunk.

"My men," said the Captain, "there is no sense in this. The ship is going down, you will tell me, in ten minutes: well, and what then? To the philosophic eye, there is nothing new in our position. All our lives long, we may have been about to break a blood-vessel or to be struck by lightning, not merely in ten minutes, but in ten seconds; and that has not prevented us from eating dinner, no, nor from putting money in the Savings Bank. I assure you, with my hand on my heart, I fail to comprehend your attitude."

The men were already too far gone to pay much heed.

"This is a very painful sight, Mr. Spoker," said the Captain.

"And yet to the philosophic eye, or whatever it is," replied the first lieutenant, "they may be said to have been getting drunk since they came aboard."

"I do not know if you always follow my thought, Mr. Spoker," returned the Captain gently. "But let us proceed."

In the powder magazine they found an old salt smoking his pipe.

"Good God," cried the Captain, "what are you about?"

"Well, sir," said the old salt, apologetically, "they told me as she were going down."

"And suppose she were?" said the Captain. "To the philosophic eye, there would be nothing new in our position. Life, my old shipmate, life, at any moment and in any view, is as dangerous as a sinking ship; and yet it is man's handsome fashion to carry umbrellas, to wear india-rubber over-shoes, to begin vast works, and to conduct himself in every way as if he might hope to be eternal. And for my own poor part I should despise the man who, even on board a sinking ship, should omit to take a pill or to wind up his watch. That, my friend, would not be the human attitude."

"I beg pardon, sir," said Mr. Spoker. "But what is precisely the difference between shaving in a sinking ship and smoking in a powder magazine?"

"Or doing anything at all in any conceivable circumstances?" cried the Captain. "Perfectly conclusive; give me a cigar!"

Two minutes afterwards the ship blew up with a glorious detonation.

It is very amusing to see how the Captain adopts the absolute position in, "the ship may be said to have been going down since she was launched," and, "time is only relative," and then, descending to the relative in reproving the men for drunkenness, is caught up by the first lieutenant. The "philosophic eye," is the eye of God, which sees shaving in a sinking ship (where the shaving and the sinking have no immediate connection) and smoking in a powder magazine (where the smoking is the cause of the ship's blowing up) as the same.[1] When we have the eye of God we are released from cause and effect ("He that loseth his life shall find it") from space ("If ye shall say unto this mountain, Be thou removed, and be thou cast into the sea; it shall be done,") and from time ("A thousand years in Thy sight are but as yesterday when it is past").

[1] Speaking of superstition, William James points out that "to the philosophic eye," everything is both the cause and effect of everything else. People connect a man's death with his having been one of thirteen at a dinner, the fall of a sparrow with some occurrence in the Milky Way.

"Were the intelligence investigating the man's or the sparrow's death omniscient or omnipresent, able to take in the whole of time and space at a single glance, there would not be the slightest objection to the Milky Way or the fatal feast being invoked among the sought-for causes. Such divine intelligence would see instantaneously all the infinite lines of convergence towards a given result, and it would, moreover, see impartially: it would see the fatal feast to be as much a condition of the sparrow's death as of the man's; it would see the boy with the stone to be as much a condition of the man's fall as of the sparrow's."

Compare Lyly, of the skylark:
> Now at heaven's gates she claps her wings,
> *The morn not waking till she sings.*

"Doing anything at all in any conceivable circumstances," is the freedom of Zen. A man must be able (that is, willing) to do anything on any occasion whatever. Hundreds of verses in the writings of Zen express this perfect freedom, which alone allows us to act perfectly. Here are some from the *Zen-rinkushū* (禪林句集).

> Stones rise up into the sky;
> Fire burns down in the water.

石 從 空 裏 立、 火 向 水 中 焚。

> Ride your horse along the edge of a sword;
> Hide yourself in the middle of the flames.

劍 双 上 走 馬、 火 焰 裏 藏 身。

> Blossoms of the fruit-tree bloom in the fire;
> The sun rises in the evening.

桃 李 火 中 開、 黃 昏 後 日 出。

But the most important word in the fable is "glorious." Glorious means Good, as distinguished from good. The word 'good' is a relative word opposed to 'bad.' The word "Good" is absolute and has no contrary. In the same way we may distinguish, in writing, but not in speaking, 'happy' and 'Happy.' Stephen being stoned to death was Happy; he was certainly not happy. Again, Love is what makes the world go round; love is quite another thing. So as I say, glorious means Good; we have the Glorious Inferno of Dante, the Glorious deafness of Beethoven, the Glorious sun that Blake saw. The revolt of Lucifer, the career of Nero, the crucifixion of Christ——all these were Glorious, like the detonation that sent hundreds of souls into eternity. "Nothing is Glorious, but thinking makes it so."

Just at this point another fable of Stevenson is relevant perhaps, *The Reader*. Let me insert it here:

"I never read such an impious book," said the reader, throwing it on the floor.

"You need not hurt me," said the book; "You will only get less for me second-hand, and I did not write myself."

"That is true," said the reader, "My quarrel is with your author."

"Ah, well," said the book, "you need not buy his rant."

"That is true," said the reader. "But I thought him such a cheerful writer."

"I find him so," said the book.

"You must be differently made from me," said the reader.

"Let me tell you a fable," said the book. "There were two men wrecked upon a desert island; one of them made believe he was at home, the other admitted . . ."

"Oh, I know your kind of fable," said the reader. "They both died."

"And so they did," said the book. "No doubt of that. And every body else."

"That is true," said the reader. "Push it a little further for this once. And when they were all dead?"

"They were in God's hands, the same as before," said the book.

"Not much to boast of, by your account," cried the reader.

"Who is impious, now?" said the book, and the reader put him on the fire.

> The coward crouches from the rod,
> And loathes the iron face of God.

Most religious people are impious, far more so than the irreligious. They always tell you, "God wouldn't do that." "The universe couldn't be made like that." "Good is good and bad is bad, and never the twain shall meet." Impiety means ingratitude, not being thankful for what God gives, but wanting, nay, demanding something else, requiring the uni-

verse to be different from what it is.   Before we are born, all
our life, and for all eternity after, we are in God's hands;
whether our life continues, or whether it fizzles out, we are to
say "Thank God!"

The other fable is *The Poor Thing,* which shows Zen
working, as it so often does, in a man of "little lore."   This
simplicity of mind, which we see and envy in children and
idiots, is essential if we would become the real master of our
fate, the captain of our soul.   Bashô, in his *Oku no Hosomichi*
quotes with approval Confucius' saying, that firmness, resolute-
ness, simplicity and slowness of speech, are not far from virtue,

剛毅木訥の仁に近きたぐひ、氣稟の清質最も尊ぶべし。

and Theseus, in *A Midsummer Night's Dream,*

> Never anything can be amiss
> When simpleness and duty tender it.

THE POOR THING

There was a man in the islands who fished for his
bare bellyful and took his life in his hands to go forth
upon the sea between four planks.   But though he had
much ado, he was merry of heart; and the gulls heard him
laugh when the spray met him.   And though he had little
lore, he was sound of spirit; and when the fish came to his
hook in the mid-waters, he blessed God without weighing.
He was bitter poor in goods and bitter ugly of countenance,
and he had no wife.

It fell at the time of the fishing that the man awoke
in his house about the midst of the afternoon.   The fire
burned in the midst, and the smoke went up and the sun
came down by the chimney.   And the man was aware of
the likeness of one that warmed his hands at the red peat
fire.

"I greet you," said the man, "in the name of God."

"I greet you," said he that warmed his hands, "but not in the name of God, for I am none of His; nor in the name of Hell, for I am not of Hell. For I am but a bloodless thing, less than wind and lighter than a sound, and the wind goes through me like a net, and I am broken by a sound and shaken by the cold."

"Be plain with me," said the man, "and tell me your name and of your nature."

"My name," quoth the other, "is not yet named, and my nature not yet sure. For I am part of a man; and I was a part of your fathers, and went out to fish and fight with them in the ancient days. But now is my turn not yet come; and I wait until you have a wife, and then shall I be in your son, and a brave part of him, rejoicing manfully to launch the boat into the surf, skilful to direct the helm, and a man of might where the ring closes and the blows are going."

"This is a marvellous thing to hear," said the man; "and if you are indeed to be my son, I fear it will go ill with you; for I am bitter poor in goods and bitter ugly in face, and I shall never get me a wife if I live to the age of eagles."

"All this have I come to remedy, my Father," said the Poor Thing; "for we must go this night to the little isle of sheep, where our fathers lie in the dead-cairn, and tomorrow to the Earl's Hall, and there shall you find a wife by my providing."

So the man rose and put forth his boat at the time of the sunsetting; and the Poor Thing sat in the prow, and the spray blew through his bones like snow, and the wind whistled in his teeth, and the boat dipped not with the weight of him.

"I am fearful to see you, my son," said the man. "For methinks you are no thing of God."

"It is only the wind that whistles in my teeth," said the Poor Thing, "and there is no life in me to keep it out."

So they came to the little isle of sheep, where the surf burst all about it in the midst of the sea, and it was all green with bracken, and all wet with dew, and the moon enlightened it. They ran the boat into a cove, and set foot to land; and the man came heavily behind among the rocks in the deepness of the bracken, but the Poor Thing went before him like a smoke in the light of the moon. So they came to the deadcairn, and they laid their ears to the stones; and the dead complained withinsides like a swarm of bees: "Time was that marrow was in our bones, and strength in our sinews; and the thoughts of our head were clothed upon with acts and the words of men. But now are we broken in sunder, and the bonds of our bones are loosed, and our thoughts lie in the dust."

Then said the Poor Thing: "Charge them that they give you the virtue they withheld."

And the man said: "Bones of my fathers, greeting! for I am sprung of your loins. And now, behold, I break open the piled stones of your cairn, and I let in the noon between your ribs. Count it well done, for it was to be; and give me what I come seeking in the name of blood and in the name of God."

And the spirits of the dead stirred in the cairn like ants; and they spoke: "You have broken the roof of our cairn and let in the moon between our ribs; and you have the strength of the still-living. But what virtue have we? what power? or what jewel here in the dust with us, that any living man should covet or receive it? for we are less than nothing. But we tell you one thing, speaking with many voices like bees, that the way is plain before all like the grooves of launching. So forth into life and fear not, for so did we all in the ancient ages." And their voices passed away like an eddy in a river.

"Now," said the Poor Thing, "they have told you a lesson, but make them give you a gift. Stoop your hand among the bones without drawback, and you shall find their treasure."

So the man stooped his hand, and the dead laid hold upon it many and faint like ants; but he shook them off, and behold, what he brought up in his hand was the shoe of a horse, and it was rusty.

"It is a thing of no price," quoth the man, "for it is rusty."

"We shall see that," said the Poor Thing; "for in my thought it is a good thing to do what our fathers did, and to keep what they kept without question. And in my thought one thing is as good as another in this world; and a shoe of a horse will do."

Now they got into their boat with the horse-shoe, and when the dawn was come they were aware of the smoke of the Earl's town and the bells of the Kirk that beat. So they set foot to shore; and the man went up to the market among the fishers over against the palace and the Kirk; and he was bitter poor and bitter ugly, and he had never a fish to sell, but only a shoe of a horse in his creel, and it rusty.

"Now," said the Poor Thing," "do so and so, and you shall find a wife and I a mother."

It befell that the Earl's daughter came forth to go into the Kirk upon her prayers; and when she saw the poor man stand in the market with only the shoe of a horse, and it rusty, it came in her mind it should be a thing of price.

"What is that?" quoth she.

"It is a shoe of a horse," said the man.

"And what is the use of it?" quoth the Earl's daughter.

"It is for no use," said the man.

"I may not believe that," said she; "else why should you carry it?"

"I do so," said he, "because it was so my fathers did in the ancient ages; and I have neither a better reason nor a worse."

Now the Earl's daughter could not find it in her mind to believe him. "Come," quoth she, "sell me this, for I am sure it is a thing of price."

"Nay," said the man, "the thing is not for sale."

"What!" cried the Earl's daughter. "Then what make you here in the town's market, with the thing in your creel and nought beside?"

"I sit here," says the man, "to get me a wife."

"There is no sense in any of these answers," thought the Earl's daughter; "and I could find it in my heart to weep."

By came the Earl upon that; and she called him and told him all. And when he had heard, he was of his daughter's mind that this should be a thing of virtue; and charged the man to set a price upon the thing, or else be hanged upon the gallows; and that was near at hand, so that the man could see it.

"The way of life is straight like the grooves of launching," quoth the man. "And if I am to be hanged let me be hanged."

"Why!" cried the Earl, "will you set your neck against a shoe of a horse, and it rusty?"

"In my thought," said the man, "one thing is as good as another in this world; and a shoe of a horse will do."

"This can never be," thought the Earl; and he stood and looked upon the man, and bit his beard.

And the man looked up at him and smiled. "It was so my fathers did in the ancient ages," quoth he to the Earl, "and I have neither a better reason nor a worse."

"There is no sense in any of this," thought the Earl, "and I must be growing old." So he had his daughter on one side, and says he: "Many suitors have you denied, my child. But here is a very strange matter that a man should cling so to a shoe of a horse, and it rusty; and that he should offer it like a thing on sale, and yet not sell it; and that he should sit there seeking a wife. If I come not to the bottom of this thing, I shall have no more pleasure in bread; and I can see no way, but either I should hang or you should marry him."

"By my troth, but he is bitter ugly," said the Earl's daughter. "How if the gallows be so near at hand?"

"It was not so," said the Earl, "that my fathers did in the ancient ages. I am like the man, and can give you neither a better reason nor a worse. But do you, prithee, speak with him again."

So the Earl's daughter spoke to the man. "If you were not so bitter ugly," quoth she, "my father the Earl would have us marry."

"Bitter ugly am I," said the man, "and you as fair as May. Bitter ugly I am, and what of that? It was so my fathers——"

"In the name of God," said the Earl's daughter, "let your fathers be!"

"If I had done that," said the man, "you had never been chaffering with me here in the market, nor your father the Earl watching with the end of his eye."

"But come," quoth the Earl's daughter, "this is a very strange thing, that you would have me wed for a shoe of a horse, and it rusty."

"In my thought," quoth the man, "one thing is as good——"

"Oh, spare me that," said the Earl's daughter, "and tell me why I should marry."

"Listen and look," said the man.

Now the wind blew through the Poor Thing like an infant crying, so that her heart was melted; and her eyes were unsealed, and she was aware of the thing as it were a babe unmothered, and she took it to her arms, and it melted in her arms like the air.

"Come," said the man, "behold a vision of our children, the busy hearth, and the white heads. And let that suffice, for it is all God offers."

"I have no delight in it," said she; but with that she sighed.

"The ways of life are straight like the grooves of launching," said the man; and he took her by the hand.

"And what shall we do with the horseshoe?" quoth she.

"I will give it to your father," said the man; "and he can make a kirk and a mill of it for me."

It came to pass in time that the Poor Thing was born; but memory of these matters slept within him, and he knew not that which he had done. But he was a part of the eldest son; rejoicing manfully to launch the boat into the surf, skilful to direct the helm, and a man of might where the ring closes and the blows are going.

"Sound of spirit" and "merry of heart,"—to how few is it given to be this. It is a kind of natural Zen. "He blessed God without weighing." Long fish, short fish, fat fish, thin fish,

many fish, few fish, no fish — he thanked God for them all.
" The way is plain before all like the grooves of launching."[1]
In *Inscribed on the Believing Mind,* we have:

The Way is not difficult; but you must avoid choosing!

至 道 無 難、 唯 嫌 揀 擇。 (信 心 銘)

(" Avoid choosing " means " without weighing," " Judge
not that ye be not judged.")

Christians and Buddhists alike put their religion in some
other place, some other time; but we are all, with or without
religion, tarred with the same brush.   Like Mrs. Jelleby in
Bleak House, with her "impossible love of the blackamoors" [2]
and indifference to her own husband and children, we think
of our religion, our ideals, forgetting (on purpose) that the
Way is here and now, in what we are doing, saying, feeling,
reading, at this very moment.   Confucius says in *The Doctrine
of the Mean,*

The Way is not far from man; if we take the Way as
something superhuman, beyond man, this is not the real
Way.

子 曰 道 不 遠 人。 人 之 爲 道 而 遠 人。 不 可 以 爲 道。
                                    (中 庸 十 三、 一。)

Mencius is even closer to Stevenson:

The Way is near, but men seek it afar.   It is in easy
things, but men seek for it in difficult things.

道 在 爾 而 求 諸 遠。 事 在 易 而 求 諸 難。(孟 子、四、一、十 一。)

The Way is like a great highroad; there is no difficulty

---

[1] John Clare, in *Ploughman Singing,* says,
            O happiness, how single is thy track.
[2] Emerson.

whatever in recognising it. What is wrong with us is that we do not really search for it. Just go home, and plenty of people will point it out to you.

夫道若大路然。豈難知哉。人病不求耳。
子歸而求之有餘師。　　　　　　（孟子、六、二、二、七。）

The *Saikontan*[1] says,

> The Zen Sect tells us: When you are hungry, eat rice; when you are weary, sleep.

禪宗曰、饑來喫飯、倦來眠。（菜根譚）

That is all religion is: eat when you are hungry, sleep when you are tired. But to do such simple things properly is really the most difficult thing in the world. I remember when I began to attend lectures, at a Zen temple, on the *Mumonkan,* I was surprised to find that there were no lofty spiritual truths enunciated at all. Two things stuck in my head, because they were repeated so often, and with such gusto. One of them, emphasised with extreme vigour, was that you must not smoke a cigarette while making water. The other was that when somebody calls you (in Japanese " Oi!") you must answer (Hai!) at once, without hesitation. When we compare this with the usual Christian exhortatory sermon, we cannot help being struck by the difference. I myself heard the "Oi!" " Hai!" so many times I began to wait for it and look on it as a kind of joke, and as soon as I did this, I began to see a light, or " get warm," as the children say. It is like the grooves of launching. Release the blocks and the ship moves. One calls " Oi!" the other says " Hai!" There is nothing between.

"It is a good thing to do what our fathers did, and to keep what they kept without question." This is not a popular

[1] *Meditations on the Life of Simplicity,* by Kô-ji-sei (洪自誠) of the Ming Era.

doctrine nowadays. Old traditions are forgotten but new ones spring up like mushrooms everywhere. In the Zen temple, together with some unnecessary and old-fashioned customs, there is a vast body of essential religion preserved in the form of rules: regularity of life, celibacy, vegetarianism, poverty, unquestioning obedience, methodical destruction of self-full thinking and acting, complete control of mind and body,—all these systematised into a way of life in which work, we may say, Work, is the grand answer to the question, "What is man's element?"

"And in my thought, one thing is as good as another in this world." This states the absolute value of everything; all things have equal value, for all have infinite value. If you like this kind of mystical truth and can swallow it easily, well and good. If not, it does not matter, because it is only ordinary common sense. The value of a thing is in its use,[1] as Robinson Crusoe found out with regard to the pieces-of-gold on his desert island. It's no good playing the cello to a thirsty man. You can't light a fire with ice-cream. You may protest that things differ at least in their potential value; a drawing by Claude is not equal in value to a grain of sand. It may well be so. The financial, the artistic, the moral values may differ : the point is that the *absolute* value is the same. If you see infinity in a grain of sand and heaven in a wild flower, where is

[1] For example:

> I saw her read
> Her Bible on hot Sunday afternoons,
> And loved the book, when she had dropped asleep,
> And made of it a pillow for her head.   (*Prelude*, IV, 229)

and,

> The melons, which last year
>   I scolded him for eating,
>   I now offer to his spirit.   *Oemaru* (1719–1805)

去年まで叱つた瓜を手向けけり   (大伴大江丸)

the necessity for anything else? Everything depends on the mind of man;

There is nothing either good or bad but thinking makes it so.

So when the man was asked what was the use of his rusty horse-shoe, he answered, "It is for no use." This has exactly the same meaning as the 1st Case of the *Mumonkan.*

A monk said to Joshu, "Has this dog the Buddha-nature or not?" Joshu replied "No!"

趙州和尚、因僧問。 狗子還有佛性也無。 州云無。

Its absolute value is nil. It has the same value as a rusty horse-shoe. Has this rusty horse-shoe the Buddha nature? The answer is, Yes! If you can rise, just for a moment, beyond this No-Yes, you understand that one thing is as good (that is, as Good) as another in this world. "And let that suffice, for it is all God offers." What is happening to me, the writer, in this place, at this moment; to you, the reader, in your place, at the very moment of reading this, what you see and feel, your circumstances internal and external, — it is all that God offers. Do you want to be in some other place, in different circumstances? Take the present ones to your heart,[1] let them suffice, for it is all God offers. If you feel aggrieved with so little, remember that "one thing is as good as another." If your aim is comfort, only some things, some times, some places will do.

[1] Compare what Nietzsche says in connection with his doctrine of Eternal Recurrence (ewige Wiederkehr), giving a fine definition of the man who lives by Zen,

das Ideal des übermüthigsten, lebendigsten und *weltbejahendsten* Menschen, der sich nicht nur mit dem was war und ist, abgefunden und vertragen gelernt hat, sondern es, so wie es war und ist, wieder haben will, in alle Ewigkeit hinaus unersättlich *da capo* rufend. (*Jenseits von Gut und Böse,* par. 56)

If your aim is virtue (that is, Goodness, not goodness,) anything, any time, any place will suffice. When Confucius was
asked concerning the brothers Haku I and Shuku Sai, who
gave up the throne and their lives rather than do wrong,

"Had they any regrets?"

he answered,

"They sought for virtue; they got virtue: what was
there for them to regret?"

怨 乎。　曰、求 仁 而 得 仁、又 何 怨。
(論語、七、十四。)

CHAPTER II

RELIGION IS POETRY

Many people must have been struck by the fact that the most profoundly religious passages in the Bible are the most poetical.   When we think of such lines as,

> The morning stars sang together and all the sons of God shouted for joy.

> He maketh me to lie down in green pastures; he leadeth me beside the still waters.

> Her ways are ways of pleasantness, and all her paths are peace.

> How oft would I have gathered thy children together, even as a hen gathereth her chickens under her wings, and ye would not!

the religion and the poetry are not merely inseparable but identical.   The poetry may be analysed, but disappears in the process: the religious elements may be separated, but it is no longer religion.

With the Buddhist sutras it is quite otherwise.   Take for example *The Gospel of Buddha,* by Paul Carus, a collection of the most interesting and pregnant of the sayings of Buddha, or *A Buddhist Bible,* by Dwight Goddard, containing translations of the Diamond Sutra, the Lankavatara Sutra, the Surangana Sutra etc.   There is not a line of poetry, not a poetical thought in either of them.   Of the verbose and interminable repetitions of the *Sacred Books of The East* it is not necessary to speak. And this is not simply a question of the quality of the translation; in the Japanese, Chinese, German, French translations, the same is true. Must we say, then, that Truth is Truth and Poetry is Poetry, and never the twain shall meet? Is it impossible to reconcile the poetico-religiousness of the Bible with the prosaic truth of the sutras?

Throughout this book and throughout life itself, one thing must never be forgotten:

In the three worlds, everything depends on the mind,[1]

that is,

Nothing is either good or bad but thinking makes it so.

When we use the word "poetical," we can ascribe it to three different things: the poet, the subject of the poem, or the poem itself; Burns, the mouse, or the poem he wrote on it. Burns was a poet. By this we mean that above other men he saw the Life of life. He was also a poet in that he wrote poetry, that is, the latent power in him was expressed in what the 18th century called "tuneful numbers." But Burns in a vacuum is meaningless; he needed the mouse. The mouse was a poetical subject; what is not? Many ploughmen had overturned a mouse's nest before, with and without poetical thoughts and feelings, but Burns expressed them; not merely his own personal feelings but the feelings of man, that is, of God, towards the mouse. The mouse is all right, just as it is, but it is worked up, so to speak, as a poetical object for the mind. Some people prefer the mouse, some the poem on the mouse. This is a matter of taste, of temperament, and there is no disputing, and no odious comparisons to be made. This same difference of character, of approach to reality, is the basis of the difference

---

[1] Hôjôki: それ三界はたゞ心一つなり。

between the Bible and the Sutras. This may be proved in an example. The most profound, the most religious utterance in the world is a sentence in the *Kongô Kyô*,

Awaken the mind without fixing it anywhere.[1]

應 無 所 住 而 生 其 心 （第 十 章）

This has no power to move us, it seems. If you can understand it, it reveals the secret of life, of living, but it has no cadence, no tone; it is too abstract, too vague; too cold, too inhuman. It lacks all the humanity, the emotion, the poetry, the religion, of

Come unto me, all ye that labour and are heavy laden, and I will give you rest. Take my yoke upon you, and learn of me; for I am meek and lowly of heart, and ye shall find rest unto your souls.

But everything depends on the mind. Nothing is poetical or unpoetical but thinking makes it so. E-Nô, a woodseller of Canton was selling firewood one day, in the local market. A man bought some wood and ordered it to be carried to his shop. E-Nô carried it there, received the money, and as he came out heard a priest reciting the Kongô Kyô. When he heard this sentence, "Awaken the mind without fixing it anywhere," he became enlightened (converted).

市 に 於 て 柴 を 賣 る。 時 に 一 客 有 つ て 柴 を 買 ひ、
使 令 し て 客 店 に 至 ら し め て、 客 收 め 去 ら し む、
慧 能、 錢 を 得 て 却 つ て 門 外 に 出 で て、 一 客 の 經
を 誦 す る を 見 る。 慧 能 一 た び 經 の 語 を 聞 い て、
心 即 ち 開 悟 す。 　　　　　　（六 祖 壇 經、第 一 章）

He received the robe and bowl from the 5th Patriarch, fled

1 For other translations, see Chapter 19, Non-attachment, II.

into the wilderness where he remained for 15 years, but later became so famous that he received a command from the Emperor Chūsô to come to the capital to preach, but excused himself on the grounds of ill-health. If it had not been for E-Nô, it is doubtful whether Zen would have made any further progress in China, and whether it would have ever arrived in Japan. What would Japanese culture have been without the stimulus of Zen? No tea ceremony, no Bushidô, no Nô, no Haiku — all this and more contained in the words, "Awaken the mind without fixing it anywhere." Further, *these words at bottom are identical with the words of Christ.* The "mind" of the Kongô Kyô is the "I" of Christ; "labour," "heavy laden" of the Bible is the "fixing" of the sutra. The object of both is *rest*. This was the object of the 2nd Patriarch; to Daruma he cried,

> "Please put my soul at rest!"

乞 師 安 心　(無門關第四十一則)

Just as some insects live on the dry wood of old furniture, and as many spiritual lives have been sustained on the most arid dogmas of Christian theology, so when E-Nô and hundreds of thousands of others read those words of the Kongô Kyô, all the deep-hidden, latent poetry and religion burst out of their hearts. From this central thought of rest through freedom from the illusion of a self come such lines as,

> The clear streams never cease their flowing;
> The evergreen trees never lose their green.

清 流 無 間 斷、碧 樹 不 曾 凋。

> The flowers abloom on the hill are like brocade;
> The brimming mountain lake is black as indigo.

山 花 開 似 錦、澗 水 湛 如 藍。　(碧巖錄、八十二)

The poetry, the religion of these you bring with yourself; there
is no spoon-feeding here.   A more extreme example is,

> Day after day the sun rises in the east;
> Day after day it sets in the west.

日 日 日 東 出、 日 日 日 西 沒。 (譚林句集)

which is more striking in the original.   This seems very tame,
but is as full of tragedy as Macbeth's

> Tomorrow and tomorrow and tomorrow,
> Creeps in this petty pace from day to day.

It is as full of hope as Wordsworth's *Stepping Westward,*

> with the thought
> Of travelling through the world that lay
> Before me in my endless way.

Coming to Japanese literature, we have,

> Because of Spring,
> This morning a nameless hill
> Is veiled with mist.

春 な れ や 名 も な き 山 の 朝 霞

> The first snow:
> The leaves of the daffodils
> Are bending.

初 雪 や 水 仙 の 葉 の た は む ま で

> Gazing at the flowers
> Of the morning glory,
> I eat my breakfast.

あ さ が ほ に 我 は 飯 く ふ を と こ 哉

all by Bashô, all poetical in the sense of crying aloud for a
poetical reader; all religious, though with no mention of God
or Buddha, Heaven or Hell, and no thought of them.

This austerity of feeling is in no way due to lack of poetry
or religion but to precisely the opposite; beauty is in the eye
of the beholder.   This was the basis of Wordsworth's plea for
the abolition of poetic diction and the choice of the simplest
subjects from daily life.   Nevertheless, we do not wish to
fall into the opposite error of neglecting the poetical.   For
example, when we read *Christianity and Buddhism,* by T.
Sterling Berry, we find prejudice and cant, no love of truth, no
understanding of Buddhism, and, a natural corollary, no real
understanding of Christianity itself, but suddenly he ends a
chapter,

> We are the children of God, called to glorify Him on earth
> by lives of lowly service and of willing obedience, and des-
> tined hereafter to see Him as He is, and to be made like
> unto Him in His eternal and everlasting Glory,

and we cannot help feeling, in these echoes of the majesty of
the Bible, that he has proved his case after all.

Do not distrust this feeling: hold fast to it.   All our troubles
come from disregarding the still small voice that speaks so
often, and so often in vain.   We read *Martin Chuzzlewit* and
find Mrs. Gamp irresistible, unforgettable, overwhelming, but
dismiss her as a mere comic character.   So here, these resound-
ing words, taken literally and unpoetically, are nonsense, un-
scientific, impossible.   But they are not empty rhetoric.   Their
real meaning is that of the dryest and most prosaic sutra.

But poetry, by creating, through words, a new world of
the imagination, is in great danger of forgetting the real world.
This is the Way of Poetry for Keats.

> Fade far away, dissolve, and quite forget
>   What thou amongst the leaves hast never known,
> The weariness, the fever, and the fret
>   Here, where men sit and hear each other groan.

These four lines are bad poetry and bad religion. It is a way that leads nowhere, except

> back from thee to my sole self.

Yet Keats had an instinct that religion was to be found in poetry, poetry in religion, expressed in the line, hackneyed out of almost all meaning,

> Beauty is truth, truth beauty.

Taken unpoetically, unreligiously, the line is a manifest falsehood. What Keats meant was that the further into beauty we go, the more we make it our own, the more our life is immersed in beauty, the nearer we are to reality. Thus a mathematician will speak of a "beautiful proof" of a theorem in algebra or geometry, and this overlapping of the aesthetic and scientific realms is an indication of their ultimate and fundamental identity. When therefore we say that religion is poetry and poetry is religion, we mean that it is so whether we realise it or not, and that from the beginning, these two being one, our distinction of Reality into Religion and Beauty is both baseless in fact and destructive to both. One drys up into lifeless dogmas, the other vapours into groundless phantasies. In the history of Buddhism and Christianity, we see the same thing; the one too rarefied, too true for acceptance by ordinary people, the other overlaid with so much emotion and symbolism that the true and the false were inextricably mixed. In this sense Zen is essentially aristocratic; it calls for asceticism in all the human activities. For Zen, Peter Bell is in the right and Wordsworth in the wrong.

> A primrose by a river's brim
> A yellow primrose was to him,
> And it was nothing more.

To a poet, the primrose is enough, just as it is, without pluck-
ing the flower out of the crannied wall, without thinking about
what God is and what man is; the yellow primrose on the bank
of the river is what it is and nothing more whatever.   But for
Wordsworth, in his weakest, most unpoetic, most insincere
moments, the flower was nothing in itself :

> To me the meanest flower that blows can give
> Thoughts that do often lie too deep for tears.

Christ did not say any thing like this, partly because he was a
greater poet than Wordsworth, partly because he was not trying to compose poetry.

> Consider the lilies of the field, how they grow.

Just look at them, that is enough.   Buddha went one better
than Christ, he only held up the flower in silence before the
congregation.   (This silence is paralleled by Christ's silence
before Pilate, the two great silences in the history of the world.)

These thoughts *about* things, this colouring of things by
the emotions, that is, the desires and antipathies of the mind,
— this is what Zen wishes us, above all things, to do away with.
Is then the aim of Zen to see things as God sees them?   This
postulates three separate entities, I, God, the flower.   We may
say that this Trinity is a Unity, we may *say* so, but it gets us
no 'forrader.'   Coleridge's very unpoetical definition of poetry
as " the best words in the best order "[1] is pertinent here, for
religion may be defined as " the best actions in the best manner."   By the " best actions," we mean the best under those
circumstances, such as Nansen's killing of the kitten (see end
of Chap. 21.) Christ's cursing the fig tree, and so on.   But the

[1] Stolen, like much of Coleridge: this is Swift's "Proper words in
proper places" (*Definition of a Good Style*)

essence of religion is contained in the words, "in the best manner." Manner is the outward expression of our state of mind.[1] The poetical and the religious are identical states of mind, in which every thing is seen to have its real value, that is, an absolute value, which cannot be compared to that of any other thing. To the religious, all things are poetical—eating, drinking, sleeping, going to the lavatory—not one more than another. To the poetical, all things are religious, every blade of grass, every stick and stone, the butterfly and the intestinal worms. The surgeon and the doctor achieve this condition in their own sphere. To them no part of the body is clean, no part is dirty, all have equal interest. To the musician there is the same universality of outlook; the second violin is just as important as the first, the drum and the piccolo no whit inferior to any other instrument. This is beautifully expressed in the following lines (the translation is very poor):

In the scenery of spring nothing is better, nothing worse;
The flowering branches are some long, some short.

春 色 無 高 下 花 枝 自 短 長　(譚林句集)

But even if we admit that religion is poetry in some sense or other, what about the statement that poetry is religion? Instead of arguing about this *in vacuo,* let us take some poems and consider to what extent this statement is true. In a later chapter, "Religious Poetry," poems whose subject is definitely some religious aspect of life, are dealt with. Here we wish to consider poems which have no ostensible connection with re-

[1] Compare Emerson's description of an odd friend of his, in *Society and Solitude:*

He had a remorse running to despair, of social gaucheries, and walked miles and miles to get the twitching out of his face, the starts and shrugs out of his arms and shoulders. 'God may forgive sins' he said, 'but *awkwardness has no forgiveness in heaven or earth.'*

ligion whatever, poems which seem to be pure poetry, poetry
for poetry's sake. Actually, of course, such a poem as *Paradise
Lost* would be the hardest example to take.   To show that
Paradise Lost has any connection with real religion would be
a difficult task indeed.   But what we are attempting to show
here is that *the poetry of Paradise Lost and of Don Juan is religion,* equally, because absolutely: irrespective of subject, because all subjects are equally poetical, all things equally religious;

> For the good God who loveth us,
> He made and loveth all.

Remembering that religion means the finite become the infinite,[1]
not in any vague and wooly sense, but in actual literal fact
(since the finite and the infinite are originally[2] one) that it
means in other words, a unifying of oneself with each thing
and all things, or rather, the realisation that the thought and
feeling of separation from things is the Great Illusion, — let us
look at the following :

> The youth of green savannahs spake,
> And many an endless, endless lake
> With all its fairy crowds
> Of islands, that together lie
> As quietly as spots of sky
> Among the evening clouds.

Without the flowing streams and rolling waters, without the
depths of the sky and vast horizons, how could man ever have
conceived of his eternity, his infinity?

Ever onwards to where the waters have an end;
Waiting motionless for when the white clouds shall arise.

[1] Compare the definition of religion given above, " the way we do
things."   It is the infinite way we do finite things.
[2] This, of course, has not a temporal meaning here.

行 到 水 窮 處、 坐 看 雲 起 時。 (禪林句集)

Look again at Marlowe's famous lines, apparently at the very antipodes of religion :

> Was this the face that launch'd a thousand ships,
> And burnt the topless towers of Ilium?
> O thou art fairer than the evening air
> Clad in the beauty of a thousand stars.

But Dante understands Marlowe.   Beatrice says,

> Io veggio ben sì come già risplende
>   Nello intelletto tuo l'eterna luce,
>   Che, vista sola, sempre amore accende ;
> E s'altra cosa vostro amor seduce,
>   Non è, se non di quella alcun vestigio
>   Mal conosciuto, che quivi traluce.

> I clearly see how the Eternal Light
>   Shines in your mind,
>   So that, upon its mere sight, love is enkindled.
> And if some other (earthly) thing draw your love away,
>   Naught is it but a vestige of the Light,
>   Half-understood, which shines through that thing.
>   (Paradiso, V, 7)

Hakuin Zenji in his *Zazenwasan* tells us that

In all song and dance[1] is heard the voice of the Law.

謠 ふ も 舞 ふ も 法 の 聲

All beauty, all music, all religion, all poetry, is a dancing of the mind.   Without this dancing of the spirit there is no true Zen. This joyful dancing before the Lord, is Beethoven's 9th Symphony ; it is expressed by Nietzsche in *Am Mitternacht.*

---

[1] This means, ' all activities,' but are not song and dance, even of the Moulin Rouge, activities of the Eternal Mind?
> And God fulfils himself in many ways,
> Lest one good custom should corrupt the world.

Eins! O Mensch, gib acht!
Zwei! Was spricht die tiefe Mitternacht?
Drei! Ich schlief, ich schlief—
Vier! Aus tiefem Traum bin ich erwacht!
Fünf! Die Welt ist tief—
Sechs! Und tiefer, als der Tag gedacht.
Sieben! Tief ist ihr Weh,
Acht! Lust—tiefer noch als Herzeleid!
Neun! Weh spricht: Vergeh!
Zehn! Doch alle Lust will Ewigkeit—
Elf! Will tiefe, tiefe Ewigkeit!
Zwölf!

Christ took upon himself our humanity, but according to the dogmas of the Church, a perfect humanity. Kwannon, in a similar, but more universal way, becomes Cleopatra, Helen of Troy, Guinevere (see Suzuki's Essays in Zen, IIIrd Series, page 370) She is, like Paul, "all things to all men," in order to save, in a myriad different forms, the erring multitudes. Goethe shares in this belief and in the last lines of *Faust* says,

Das Ewig-Weibliche
Zieht uns hinan.

Here is another example, from *Measure for Measure*, to prove, that is, to test the rule of the identity of poetry and religion (I hope I am getting credit from the reader for choosing the most difficult examples).

Take, O, take those lips away,
    That so sweetly were forsworn;
And those eyes, the break of day,
    Lights that do mislead the morn:
But my kisses bring again, bring again;
Seals of love, but sealed in vain, sealed in vain.

The music of the verse, its rhythm and cadence, touches the heart like a symphony of Mozart, of which Schubert said that in it you could hear the angels singing.   The thought expressed is of the unrequited love of Mariana.   If this emotion of unavailing regret, of wasted hours and broken promises, of desire for the impossible, for days that are no more, is nothing to you, you are only saying,

> What's Hecuba to me, or me to Hecuba,
> That I should weep for her?

What are you to Stephen, or Stephen to you, that you should weep for his being stoned to death?   Whether your hopes and fears are for Mariana or Stephen or Hecuba or Christ, griefs and hopes are one.   So Wordsworth says,

> My hopes must no more change their name.

Another example, from *The Tempest:*

> Where the bee sucks, there suck I,
> In a cowslip's bell I lie.

> Merrily merrily shall I live now,
> Under the blossom that hangs on the bough.

In Zen writings we have the same Ariel, Puck-like, amoral, absolute freedom, expressed in similar images:

> We sleep with both legs stretched well out;
> For us, no truth, no error exists.

> 長 伸 兩 脚 睡、 無 僞 亦 無 眞。 (禪林句集)

> For long years a bird in a cage;
> Now, flying along with the clouds of heaven.

> 多 年 籠 中 鳥、 今 日 負 雲 螢。 (禪林句集)

Puck says,

> I'll put a girdle round about the earth
> In forty minutes.

but the Master of Zen can do better than this.

> He holds the handle of the hoe, but his hands are empty;
> He rides astride the water-buffalo, but he is walking.

空手把鋤頭、步行騎水牛。

This world is more wonderful than the Hexenküche of *Faust:*

> The stones rise up into the sky;
> Fire burns down into the water.

石從空裏立、火向水中焚。 (禪林句集)

Enough examples have been taken, perhaps, to show that the degree of poetry is the degree of religion and *vice-versa.* This degree depends in practice to some extent upon the subject, for

> ogni dove
> In cielo è Paradiso, e sì la grazia
> Del sommo ben d'un modo non vi piove.
>
> (Paradiso, III, 88.)

"Every place in Heaven is Paradise, but the Highest Good does not rain down in one same fashion." Take the following, by a modern poet:

> A piece of wood —
> Bobbity, bobbity it floats down
> The spring river.

流木やたぶりたぶりと春の川　　嗚 雪

You must repress any possible tendency to make this symbolise human life. It is the thing as it is, following its own nature, with something in it unwontedly akin to the mildness and tranquillity of a spring day. The same sun shines, the same breeze blows in Buson's untranslatable

春の海ひねもすのたりのたり哉

  (The spring sea;
    Gently rising and falling
     The whole day long.)

When the subject is vaster, as in Bashô's

  A wild sea,
    And the Galaxy stretching out over
     The Island of Sado.

  荒海や佐渡によこたふ天の川

the poetry, the religion, is deeper; deeper still when man enters:

  Beneath the cherry blossoms
    There are no
     Strangers.

  花の陰あかの他人はなかりけり　　一　茶

  It is evening, autumn;
    I think only
     Of my parents.

  父母の事のみ思ふ秋の暮　　　　蕪　村

and deepest of all when we contemplate the gods. At Nikkô:

  Ah, how glorious
    The young leaves, the green leaves,
     Glittering in the sunshine!

  あらたふと青葉若葉の日の光　　芭　蕉

At the Shrine of Isé:

  The fragrance of some
    Unknown blossoming tree
     Filled all my soul!

  何の木の花とは知らず匂ひ哉　　芭　蕉

The gods in Japan are never far from the leaves and the flowers, but like them, and like the piece of wood floating down the river, like the waves of the sea and the stars of the Milky Way, they obey the law of their being. The net of the Law catches all the fish, big and little, not one can escape. Thus the difference is of quantity, not quality; of potentiality, not absolute worth; of use, not of essence. The world, a grain of sand, eternity, an hour, — to see these as the same, is religion, is poetry. But in the next chapter we shall see that religion and poetry are identical in that they are both common sense, everyday life, reality, the fact, the thing as it is.

CHAPTER III

POETRY IS EVERY-DAY LIFE

From Aristotle down to Arnold it was considered that a great subject was necessary to the poet. Arnold says that the plot is everything. It is useless for the poet

> to imagine that he has everything in his own power; that he can make an intrinsically inferior action equally delightful with a more excellent one by his treatment of it.

Wordsworth stands outside this tradition by instinct and by choice. He chooses the aged, the poor, the idiot, the vagrant, but does not endeavour to make them "delightful" at all. "Nothing is inferior or superior, delightful or repugnant, but thinking makes it so." What becomes, then, of the great subject? The answer is that on the one hand it is a concession to human weakness, which sees the house afire over the way as more thrilling than the flames of the sun, a toothache as more tragic than an earthquake or pestilence. On the other hand, the great subject is in its nature richer if only by mere quantity and mass. The fact that Lear is a King, Hamlet a Prince, Othello a General, and Cæsar an Emperor, adds to the tragic force of the action, though *intrinsically,* to borrow Arnold's word, they are no more tragic than Jesus the Carpenter's son. Nevertheless, size is not meaningless. Even Sôshi, the arch-absolutist, points out that a cup cannot float in the quantity of water that will support a poppy seed.

覆杯水於土幼堂之上、則芥爲之舟、置杯焉則膠。

But it is the poet, the man, who decides the meaning, the relation of quality to quantity.   Thus Paul was converted by a
supernatural light from Heaven and the voice of the ascended
Christ; Kyôgen, (香嚴) by the sound of a stone striking a bamboo.

To return to Wordsworth.   Critics have often pointed out
his inconsistency of practice and precept in regard to diction,
but there are other contradictions more worthy of note.   In
the Preface to *Lyrical Ballads* he has the following notorious
sentence:

> The principal object, then, proposed in these poems
> was to choose incidents and situations from common life,
> and to relate or describe them, throughout, as far as was
> possible, in a selection of language really used by men,
> and, at the same time, *to throw over them a certain colour-
> ing of the imagination,* whereby ordinary things should be
> presented to the mind in an unusual aspect; and further,
> and above all, *to make these incidents and situations inter-
> esting* by tracing in them, truly though not ostentatiously,
> the primary laws of our nature.

"To throw over them a certain colouring of the imagination"!
This is a phrase that must have worked incalculable harm to
English poetry during the next century and a half, though it
is directly opposed to Wordsworth's actual practice.   Look at
the two following extracts and find if you can, "the colouring
of the imagination" which is thrown over them:

> No motion has she now, no force;
>   She neither hears nor sees;
> Rolled round in earth's diurnal course
>   With rocks and stones and trees!

This and the following are the greatest lines Wordsworth ever
wrote:

> She died, and left to me
> This heath, this calm and quiet scene;

> The memory of what has been,
> And never more will be.

Wordsworth looks steadily at the object, and this is his greatness, as it is also Shakespeare's.   Again, what an unfortunate phrase, "to make these incidents and situations interesting." It suggests a cook adding condiments, a little bit of alliteration here, a bit of onomatopoeia there, some personification, a paradox or two, and an unexpected, brilliant last line for the critics to quote.[1]   Wordsworth himself not only never does this (or almost never; the *Immortality Ode* is rather suspicious in places, and though successful, is still a *tour de force*) but himself says,

> O Reader! had you in your mind
> Such stores as silent thought can bring,
> O gentle Reader! you would find
> A tale in everything,

that is, poetry everywhere. Let us take *Michael* as an example.

In this poem of four hundred and eighty two lines, there are five or six lines of what is ordinarily termed poetry (quoted in a succeeding chapter), which might be overlooked, or rather, taken with the rest, by an earnest and careful reader. This so-called poem, then, is a piece of everyday country life, just as Dickens' novels are descriptions of everyday life and everyday city people.   Two hard-working people had a son who was a failure and fled abroad.   They died.   This is not merely the whole story, there is no account of their despair and grief,

---

[1] It is both amusing and heartening to see how Matthew Arnold, to the confusion of the critics, suddenly throws overboard all his theories and principles of art in an essay on Tolstoy.

The truth is we are not to take *Anna Karenine* as a work of art; we are to take it as a piece of life. . . .   The author saw it all happening so—Saw it, and therefore relates it; and *what his novel in this way loses in art it gains in reality.*

not a word of it. Wordsworth avoids what would be called the chances which the story offers to wring the reader's feelings. Yet we feel the majesty, the dignity of man more than in Hamlet's most tragic speeches. Othello at his most poetic, Lear at his most pathetic, Macbeth at his most desperate, have not the grandeur of the old shepherd who

> still looked up to sun and cloud,
> And listened to the winds.

Why is this? It is because the true poetic life is the ordinary everyday life.

Of the Chinese poets Hakkyo-i (Po Chū-i) that is, Haku-rakuten, and Tô-en-mei (Tao Yüan-ming) understood this fact best of all. Ritaihaku (Li Po) Toho (Tu Fu) and most of the lesser poets of the Tô (T'ang) dynasty, as represented in the Tôshisen, are "poetical" poets. The following is by Hakurakuten:

> I take your poems in my hand and read them beside the
> candle;
> The poems are finished: the candle is low: dawn not yet
> come.
> With sore eyes by the guttering candle still I sit in the
> dark,
> Listening to waves that, driven by the wind, strike the
> prow of the boat.[1]

把 君 詩 卷 燈 前 讀、 詩 盡 燈 殘 天 未 明。
眼 痛 滅 燈 猶 暗 坐、 逆 風 吹 浪 打 船 聲。

There is great art in the selection of facts presented, but no "colouring of the imagination"; the incidents and situations are chosen "from common life." This is true also of the first of a series of thirteen poems by Tôenmei, entitled *Reading the Book of the Seas and Mountains.*

[1] Waley's translation.

It is early summer: grass is rank, plants grow wildly,
And the trees round my house are in full leaf.
The birds rejoice in their nests here,
And I too love my dwelling-place as dearly as they.
I have ploughed my fields and sown them:
Now at last, I have time to sit at home and read my books!

The lanes are too narrow for fine carriages,
And even my old friends are often turned back.
Contentedly I pour out my wine,
And partake of the lettuce grown in my own garden.

Borne on a soft eastern wind,
Light showers come.
Unrolling the Book of the Seas and Mountains,
I read the story of the King of Shū:
Gazing at sky and earth while yet we live—
How otherwise shall we take our pleasure here?[1]

讀　山　海　經

孟夏草木長	遠屋樹扶疎	衆鳥欣有託
吾亦愛吾廬	既耕亦已種	時還讀我書
窮巷隔深轍	頗廻故人車	歡言酌春酒
摘我園中蔬	微雨從東來	好風與之俱
汎覽周王傳	流觀山海圖	俯仰終宇宙
不樂復何如		

In Ritaihaku the subject and treatment is always romantic;
the famous *Crows at Twilight* is typical:

Athwart the yellow clouds of sunset, seeking their nests
                              under the city wall,
The crows fly homeward.　Caw! Caw! Caw! they cry
                              among the branches.
At her loom sits weaving silk brocade, one like the Lady
                              of Shinsen:

[1] See Waley for a different translation. 歡言, in some versions, is
歡然, with the same meaning.

Their voices come to her through the window with its
                                    curtains misty-blue.
She stays the shuttle; grieving, she thinks of her far-
                                    distant lord:
In the lonely, empty room, her tears fall like rain.

烏　夜　啼

黃雲城邊烏欲棲　歸飛啞啞枝上啼
機中織錦秦川女　碧砂如煙隔牎語[1]
停梭悵然憶遠人　獨宿空房淚如雨

Ritaihaku had mystical leanings all his life, but especially in
his youth and old age. In the poem *Answering a Question in
the Mountains* he says,

I am asked why I live in the green mountains:
I smile but reply not, for my heart is at rest.
The flowing waters carry the image of the peach blossoms
                                    far, far away:
There is an earth, there is a heaven, unknown to men.

山　中　問　答

問余何意棲碧山　笑而不答心自閑
桃花流水杳然去　別有天地非人間

Compare this with Obata's translation in *Li Po the Chinese
Poet,* page 73.

Why do I live among the green mountains?
I laugh and answer not, my soul is serene:
It dwells in another heaven and earth belonging to no man.
The peach trees are in flower, and the water flows on. . . .

---

[1] If we take this 語 as referring to the woman and translate, "mur-
murs to herself," it is meaningless in the poem, spoils the connection, and
nullifies the title, which means literally, " Crows cawing at nightfall." It
is their cawing to each other which causes her tears to fall. Though 語
is a very long way from its subject, rather in the fashion of Ovid or
Horace, poetically speaking, this is the only possible interpretation, I think.
See Giles and Obata, and decide for yourself between them.

This is a translation by a Japanese, and, in a sense, better than the original, but his translation of the third line is hardly possible, I think. Also, 桃花 seems to have a reference to Tôenmei's 桃花源記 and means, withdrawn from this world, and living in another, spiritual world. (See Giles, *Gems of Chinese Literature,* Prose, page 104, The Peach-Blossom Fountain. The Earthly Paradise began where the river and the peach-trees left off.) "The peach trees are in bloom and the water flows on,"—this is in the spirit of Zen but it is not what the Chinese poet is thinking. Another title for this poem is 山中答俗人, *Answering an Ordinary Man in the Mountains.* Many are humble before God but proud before ordinary man. To Ritaihaku poetry was mysticism, Taoism, dreams, romance, glory. He would have sympathised with Spenser who lived in the same kind of age and had a similar view of life. He wished to live in a world of poetry that was not this world of toil and struggle. (且諸宿所好永願辭人間).

When we come to Japanese poetry, which means Bashô, we find "Poetry is everyday life" in its purest form. Bashô could and did write "poetical" poetry of the highest order. Scattered throughout this book will be found a great number of this kind of poem; here are a few more:

> The sea darkens:
>> Voices of the wild ducks
>>> Are dim and white.[1]

海くれて鴨の聲ほのかにしろし

> The autumn tempest!
>> It blows along
>>> Even wild boars!

1 Compare Gray's *Ode on the Spring:*
    Yet hark, how through the peopled air
    The busy murmur *glows.*

猪もともに吹かるる野分かな

The summer rains through the ages
Have left undimmed then,
The Hall of Gold.

五月雨の降りのこしてや光堂

I heard the unblown flute
In the deep summer shadows
Of the Temple of Suma.

須磨寺やふかぬ笛きく木下やみ

This remarkable poem with its similarity to Keats'

Heard melodies are sweet, but those unheard
Are sweeter: therefore ye soft pipes, play on;
Not to the sensual ear, but more endear'd,
Pipe to the spirit ditties of no tone.

had a not dissimilar origin and background.   Bashô visited
Sumadera in the summer and saw there the flute Atsumori
used to play in the castle before his death.   In his heart he
heard its thin melancholy notes.   There is the same thought in
the following:

Veil'd from sight today
In misty showers:
Still, Mt. Fuji!

霧しぐれふじを見ぬ日ぞおもしろき

Whiter than the stones
Of the Stony Mountain,
The wind of autumn!

石山の石より白し秋の風

The shell of a cicada:
It sang itself
Utterly away.

聲にみな鳴きしまふてや蟬の殻

The summer rains:
    All things hidden
        But the long bridge of Seta.

五月雨にかくれぬものや瀨田の橋

But where Bashô is at his greatest is where he seems most insignificant, the neck of a firefly, hailstones in the sun, the chirp of an insect, muddy melons, leeks, a dead leaf,—these are full of interest, meaning, value, that is, poetry, but *not as symbols of the Infinite, not as types of Eternity, but in themselves.* Their meaning is just as direct, as clear, as unmistakable, as complete and perfect, as devoid of reference to other things, as dipping the hand suddenly into boiling water. The mind is roused as with the sound of a trumpet. When you read one of the following it is just like opening a door and being confronted by a tiger. It is like suddenly seeing the joke of something. It is like being unexpectedly reprieved from the sentence of death.

The melons look cool,
    Flecked with mud
        From the morning dew.

朝露によごれて涼し瓜の土

Just washed,
    How chill
        The white leeks!

葱白く洗ひたてたるさむさ哉

The hail-stones
    Glance off the rocks
        Of the Stony Mountain.

石山の石にたばしるあられかな

By day-light
    The firefly has
        A neck of red.

畫見れば首筋赤き螢かな

On the mushroom
    Is stuck the leaf
        Of some unknown tree.

松茸やしらぬ木の葉のへばりつく

With every gust of wind,
    The butterfly changes its place
        On the willow.

吹く度に蝶の居なをる柳かな

Naturally, when the distinction between the poetical and unpoetical subject disappears, (to attain this state is the true practical aim of a poet) foul is fair and fair is foul, to the pure all things are pure, nothing is unclean.

The sound of someone
    Blowing his nose with his hand;
        The scent of the plum flowers!

手鼻かむ音さへ梅の匂ひ哉

The sound of the nose-blowing, the scent of the flowers, which is more beautiful? The first may remind us of a long-lost, beloved friend; the second, of the death of a child who fell from the bough of a plum-tree. Beethoven may have got the *motif* of the first movement of the Fifth Symphony from someone's blowing his nose. Underneath all our prejudices for and against things, we must be free of them. This same freedom from the idea of dignity, that there are vessels of honour and vessels of dishonour, is shown in the following, full of life and truth:

Look ! the dried rice cakes
   At the end of the verandah —
      The *uguisu* is pooping on them !

鶯や餅に糞する椽のさき

More certainly than many things written in the Gospels, Christ went to the lavatory. This action was no less holy and no more symbolical than the breaking of bread and drinking wine at the Last Supper. Wherever bread is eaten, Christ's body is broken. Wherever wine is drunk, His blood is shed. But because of the hardness of our hearts we are taught to remember the Sabbath day to keep it holy, Easter, Pentecost, Christmas, Buddha's birthday, the Commemoration of Entering into Nirvana, the Day of His Enlightenment. These symbols are only crutches to our weakness, milk for babes. For

Every day is a good day,

日 日 是 好 日 (碧巖錄、六)

as Unmon said, every day is the best day, every moment is the best moment, and thus,

Your every-day mind — that is the Way !

平 常 心 是 道 (無門關、十九)

From morning to night, walking, eating, sleeping, praying, living, dying,

Whatsoever thy hand findeth to do, do it with all thy might,

and again,

Whether therefore ye eat or drink or whatsoever ye do, do it all to the glory of God.

One eye on the work, and one eye on God, one eye on the

object, the finite, and the other on the Infinite — this is not the meaning. "With all thy might" equals "the glory of God," for as Blake says,

> Energy is Eternal Delight.

The distinction between ideal and real, man and God, individual and universal, poetry and matter of fact, ordinary life and religion — it is this illusory distinction that Zen seeks to break down. There is a saying attributed to Christ:

> Render unto Cæsar the things that are Cæsar's and unto God the things that are God's.

This has a fine eloquence, but leaves the mind unillumined and uninspired. The things of Cæsar *are* the things of God. Sweeping a room, Cæsar's room, is sweeping God's room. There is a thrilling story told of Stevenson in this connection:

> At Pillochry, in 1881, when he saw a dog being ill-treated, he at once interposed, and when the owner resented his interference and told him, "It's not your dog," he cried out, "It's God's dog and I'm here to protect it!"

In English literature the best examples of the kind of poetry which takes its material from the apparently trivial or disgusting, are Shakespeare's songs; for example,

> When icicles hang by the wall,
>   And Dick the shepherd blows his nail,
> And Tom bears logs into the hall,
>   And milk comes frozen home in pail;
> When blood is nipt, and ways be foul,
> Then nightly sings the staring owl
>   Tuwhoo!
> Tuwhit! Tuwhoo! A merry note!
> While greasy Joan doth keel[1] the pot.

[1] Cool, by stirring or otherwise.

> When all around the wind doth blow,
>   And coughing drowns the parson's saw,
> And birds sit brooding in the snow,
>   And Marian's nose looks red and raw;
> When roasted crabs hiss in the bowl—
> Then nightly sings the staring owl
>   Tuwhoo!
> Tuwhit! Tuwhoo! A merry note!
> While greasy Joan doth keel the pot.

The last line, the refrain, is particularly noteworthy, because it is an epitome of "natural" poetry, of the whole truth in art, where selection and arrangement is everything and the material indifferent, because all equally good and useful. Look at another example from *Martin Chuzzlewit:*

"I think, young woman," said Mrs. Gamp to the assistant chambermaid, in a tone expressive of weakness, "that I could pick a little bit of pickled salmon, with a nice little sprig of fennel, and a sprinkling of white pepper. I takes new bread, my dear, with jest a little pat of fresh butter, and a mossel of cheese. In case there should be such a thing as a cowcumber in the 'ous, will you be so kind as to bring it for I'm rather partial to 'em, and they does a world of good in a sick room. If they draws the Brighton Old Tipper here, I takes *that* ale at night, my love; it bein' considered wakeful by the doctors. And whatever you do, young woman, don't bring more than a shilling's-worth of gin and water-warm when I rings the bell a second time; for that is always my allowance, and I never takes a drop beyond!"

To explain the Zen, the religion, the poetry of this would be as difficult as to explain the humour of it: you either see it or not. Mrs. Gamp would be a match for any of the Ancient Worthies such as Rinzai, Ôbaku, or Unmon, because *she is herself,* she is true to herself and therefore not false to anything; she cannot be defeated by God, Nature, Circumstance, or their vice-regents, those who live by Zen. Mrs. Gamp is not divided from the pickled salmon or the bottle which she asks may be left

> "on the chimley-piece, and let me put my lips to it when I am so dispoged,"

as other people are by their notions of what is refined and vulgar, the distinction of material and spiritual. From this comes the gusto that is the hall-mark of Zen, of abundant life. Look at one more of Mrs. Gamp's speeches, flattering the undertaker's wife with eternal youth:

> "There are some happy creeturs" Mrs. Gamp observed, "as time runs back'ards with, and you are one, Mrs. Mould; not that he need do nothing except use you in his most owldacious way for years to come, I'm sure; for young you are and will be. I says to Mrs. Harris," Mrs. Gamp continued, "only t'other day; the last Monday evening fortnight as ever dawned upon this Piljian's Projiss of a mortal wale; I says to Mrs. Harris when she says to me, 'Years and our trials, Mrs. Gamp, sets marks upon us all.'—'Say not the words Mrs. Harris, if you and me is to be continual friends, for sech is not the case. Mrs. Mould,' I says, making so free, I will confess, as use the name" (she curtseyed here) "is one of them that goes agen the obserwation straight; and never, Mrs. Harris, whilst I've a drop of breath to draw, will I set by, and not stand up, don't think it."

Compare the words of this dirty, drunken, ghoulish, self-seeking, garrulous, greedy creature, with those of the refined, educated, idealistic poet William Butler Yeats:

> Though leaves are many the root is one;
> Through all the lying days of my youth
> I swayed my leaves and flowers in the sun;
> Now I may wither into the truth.

Which of the two has more life, more guts, more Zen? Whose
view of old age and death is truer, those people who talk about

> Reality as a number of great eggs laid by the Phoenix
> and that these eggs turn inside out perpetually without
> breaking the shell,[1]

or those who like Mrs. Gamp and Falstaff and Gargantua, say
with Dr. Johnson,

> I look upon it that he who does not mind his belly,
> will hardly mind anything else.

We eat hypocritically, wive in shame and stealth, talk of ideals,
fritter our half-lives away. Mrs. Gamp shows us up, but we
laugh to hide our feelings from ourselves; we laugh, as Byron
said, that we may not weep. It is worth noting, by the way,
that she comes into the story after about 400 pages; not as an
afterthought, but, like life itself, when it happens. She grew
as naturally out of Dickens' soul, as a yellow crocus comes out
of the black earth in spring.

To return to Shakespeare. One of his songs,

> Full fathom five thy father lies,
>   Of his bones are coral made;
> Those are pearls that were his eyes:
>   Nothing of him that doth fade
> But doth suffer a sea-change
> Into something rich and strange.
> Sea-nymphs hourly ring his knell:
> Hark! now I hear them,—
>   Ding, dong, bell.

is compared by Charles Lamb to a song of Webster's:

> Call for the robin redbreast and the wren,
> Since o'er shady groves they hover,

[1] *A Vision*, by W. B. Yeats, Introduction by Owen Aherne, page xxiii.

> And with leaves and flowers do cover
> The friendless bodies of unburied men;
> Call unto his funeral dole
> The ant, the field-mouse, and the mole
> To rear him hillocks that shall keep him warm
> And (when gay tombs are robb'd) sustain no harm;
> But keep the wolf far thence, that's foe to men,
> For with his nails he'll dig them up again.

Lamb says of them,

> As that is of the water, watery; so this is of the earth,
> earthy.   Both have that intenseness of feeling, which
> seems to resolve itself into the element it contemplates.

Shakespeare resolves himself into water, Webster into earth, Mrs. Gamp into pickled salmon, Stevenson into a dog, Buddha into a flower, Gu-tei[1] into his own finger, Bashô into a frog.

But in this kind of thing there is a great danger again, of poetry losing contact with facts, and as Mrs. Gamp herself states,

> Facts is stubborn things and can't be drove.

Poetry is not only ordinary life, it is common sense.   Georgias Leontinus, quoted by Aristotle, said,

> Humour is the only test of gravity, and gravity of
> humour.   For a subject which will not bear raillery is
> suspicious; and a jest which will not bear a serious exami-
> nation is certainly false wit.

In the same way, poetry and common sense test each other.

> Here, with green Nature all around,
>   While that fine bird the skylark sings,
> *Who now in such a passion is*
>   *He flies by it and not his wings,*

says Davies, and this is true, and the fact is poetry.

[1] 無門關、第三則。

Contrast Andrew Young's *March Hares*. This could never be countenanced by Zen, because not by common sense; it is not poetry because it is false.

> I made myself as a tree
> No withered leaf twirling on me;
> No, not a bird that stirred my boughs,
> As looking out from wizard brows
> I watched those lithe and lovely forms
> That raised the leaves in storms.[1]
>
> I was content enough,
> Watching that serious game of love,
> That happy hunting in the wood,
> Where the pursuer was the more pursued,
> To stand in breathless hush
> With no more life myself than tree or bush.

If you make yourself as a tree, you can't watch hares. You live the life of a tree, dimly aware of day and night, the passage of the seasons. If you become a tree, you must become a tree and done with it. If you say the above verses mean, "I watched the hares as a tree would watch them if it could do so," you are only talking like the natural philosopher who asked, "How much wood could a woodchuck chuck, if a woodchuck could chuck wood?" If you are going to watch hares, you must forget yourself and whether you are "content" or discontented, "breathless" or otherwise. You must forget to compare yourself to a tree, and tell people your brows are "wizard," whatever that means. You must become a hare and done with it, and the poem that comes out of that experience will be worth reading. This is just like M. Duthuit's Chinese recipe for painting bamboos:[2]

[1] Second verse omitted.
[2] Quoted in Suzuki's *Zen Buddhism and its Influence on Japanese Culture.*

Draw bamboos for ten years, become a bamboo, then forget all about bamboos when you are drawing.

When Bashô looked at an onion, he saw the onion; when he looked at the Milky Way, he portrayed the Milky Way; when he felt a deep unnameable emotion, he said so. But he did not mix them all up in a vague pantheistic stew or symbolic potpourri. In poetry, as in life itself, distinctness, the individual thing, directness is all-important.

CHAPTER IV

DIRECTNESS IS ALL

Zen is above all things direct; no intermediaries, no mediators between God and man, no symbolism. Emerson says in *Self Reliance,*

> The relations of the soul to the divine spirit are so pure that it is profane to seek to interpose helps.

Zen would not say it is profane or holy to do anything, nor would it say that the so-called helps are hindrances. All things are ends in themselves. This truth is easy to grasp, difficult to retain; a moment's inattention and we do as Prof. Suzuki does in his *Buddhist Philosophy and its Effects on the Life and Thought of the Japanese People,* where he says, explaining the meaning of a Buddhist *kuyô* in regard to a painter's worn-out brushes,

> It is no doubt a lifeless instrument constructed by human hands, and we can say that there is no "soul" in it, whatever we may mean by this term. But the fact is that the brush is an extension of the painter's own arm, as every human instrument is, and as such it is endowed with life, for with it the painter can express himself and give spirit to his works. The brush in the hands of the painter is surely possessed of life and spirit.

This is not so. The brush has its own existence; it exists for and in itself, whether used or usable or not. When worn out and thrown into the dustbin, its absolute value is unchanged. So Wordsworth, speaking of the Thames, says,

It glideth *at its own sweet will,*

apart from whether it is used to float vessels, to create electricity, as drinking water, or as the subject of Wordsworth's poem.   This was the opinion of Kant and of Goethe.

> Die Ansicht, dass jedes Geschöpf um sein selbst willen existiert, und nicht etwa der Korkbaum gewachsen ist, damit wir unsere Flaschen pfropfen können: dieses hatte Kant mit mir gemein, und ich freute mich, ihm hierin zu begegnen. (Eckermann, *Gespräche mit Goethe,* April, 1827)

Dean Inge makes precisely the same mistake but at the other end of the scale.   He says in *Personal Idealism and Mysticism,*

> It seems to me that Truth and Beauty are ideals too august to be ever regarded as means only.   Science and Art are both false to themselves if they suffer themselves to be mere handmaids of morality.

As I said above, the corpse of a bed-bug, the parings of the fingernails, are too august to be treated as means.   There are no means in this or any other world.   But from another point of view we must say that Truth and Beauty are nothing in themselves; they can never be ends.   What is the end of man? Wordsworth says, rushing in where angels fear to tread,

> Our destiny, our being's end and home
> Is with infinitude and only there.

Maybe; but also,

> Closer is He than breathing, and nearer than hands and feet,

says Tennyson; then let Wordsworth himself amend it to

> With hope it is, hope that can never die,

> Effort and expectation and desire,
> *And something evermore about to be.*

But hear what the angel said one thousand three hundred years before Wordsworth was born:

> Plucking chrysanthemums along the east fence;
> Gazing in silence at the Southern Hills;
> The birds flying home in pairs
> Through the soft mountain air of dusk—
> In these things there is a deep meaning,
> But when we are about to express it,
> We suddenly forget the words.

採 菊 東 籬 下　悠 然 見 南 山
山 氣 日 夕 佳　飛 鳥 相 與 還
此 中 有 眞 意　欲 辨 已 忘 言　(陶 淵 明)

Truth, Reality, is inexpressible in words,—and yet it is expressed in words! It is expressed, if we can hear it, in all the sounds and sights of this world. Blake says,

> The roaring of lions, the howling of wolves, the raging of the stormy sea, and the destructive sword, are portions of eternity too great for the eye of man.

It is expressed also in the simplest conversation, if only we can forget, for even a moment, the purely intellectual content of the words, and listen to the voice of eternity.

> A certain monk said to Hôgen,
> "I, E-chô, ask you, 'What is the Buddha?'"
> Hôgen answered, "You are E-chô."

> 僧 問 法 眼。慧 超 咨 和 尙 如 何 是 佛。
> 法 眼 曰。汝 是 慧 超。

The monk wanted to understand the Nature of the Universe, the Secret of Life, its Meaning Hôgen says, "All these things will be added unto you, once you know, 'Who is E-Chô? Who am I?' And I will tell you the answer at once, without beating about the bush, the answer to the whole Riddle of Existence:

You are E-Chô!"

As Engo says,

How the spiritual war-horses of past times sweated blood to attain this state!

從 前 汗 馬 無 人 識。 (碧 巖 錄、七、)

It is just this directness, this perfect sincerity, which is so difficult to attain. In order to reach this state, two things are necessary, one negative, the other positive. First, we must realise that for the understanding of the meaning of Life (which is no different from that of our own life) it is useless to rely on the intellect working alone; and that since the intellect has got into the habit of working by itself, acting like a dictator to the rest of the personality, it must, temporarily, be put into a strait waistcoat. Second, that we are to do what Confucius said in *The Great Learning,* that the superior man does,

In all things, he does his utmost.

君 子 無 所 不 用 其 極 (大 學、二、四、)

Here is an example of how the superior man plays billiards for the first and last time:

Once only do I remember seeing him play a game of billiards, and a truly remarkable performance it was. He played with all the fire and dramatic intensity that he was apt to put into things. The balls flew wildly about, on or off the table as the case might be, but seldom indeed ever threatened a pocket or got within a hand's breadth of a canon. "What a fine thing a game of billiards is," he remarked to the astonished onlookers, " — once a year or so ! "[1]

Let us take the first poem in the *Golden Treasury,* Nash's *Spring,* from *Summer's Last Will and Testament :*

Spring, the sweete spring, is the yeres pleasant King,
Then bloomes eche thing, then maydes daunce in a ring,
Cold doeth not sting, the pretty birds doe sing,
    Cuckow, jugge, jugge, puwe, towittawoo.

The Palme and May make countrey houses gay.
Lambs friske and play, the Snepherds pype all day,
And we heare aye birds tune this merry lay,
    Cuckow, jugge, jugge, puwe, towittawoo.

The fields breathe sweete, the dayzies kisse our feete,
Young lovers meete, old wives a-sunning sit :
In every streete, these tunes our ears doe greete,
Cuckow, jugge, jugge, puwe, towittawoo.
    Spring the sweete spring.

Several times, when collecting best pieces of English Poetry (the intelligent young man's substitute for a diary) I hesitated over this poem, but finally, not following my instincts, excluded it. It has no purple patches, no exquisite epithets, nothing to mark the chooser of it as a poetical highbrow. And look at the last line of each verse ! Who would dare to read such a poem aloud ? But it breathes the spirit of spring as no other poem in the English language. Let us take another on the same subject by Blake :

O thou with dewy locks, who lookest down
Thro' the clear windows of the morning, turn
Thine angel eyes upon our western isle,
Which in full choir hails thy approach, O Spring !

[1] *Life of Stevenson,* by Graham Balfour.

> The hills tell each other, and the list'ning
> Vallies hear ; all our longing eyes are turned
> Up to thy bright pavillions : issue forth,
> And let thy holy feet visit our clime.
>
> Come o'er the eastern hills, and let our winds
> Kiss thy perfumed garments ; let us taste
> Thy morn and evening breath : scatter thy pearls
> Upon our love-sick land that mourns for thee.
>
> O deck her forth with thy fair fingers ; pour
> Thy soft kisses on her bosom ; and put
> Thy golden crown upon her languished head,
> Whose modest tresses were bound up for thee !

Comparing Nash's poem with Blake's, is like comparing bread and butter with a chocolate éclair. The éclair has its virtues no doubt, but éclairs are bad for the complexion ; what is more important, they spoil the appetite ; and what is most important, they spoil the taste. Zen reminds us that " directness is all." It is with Zen as with virtue ; according to Bacon,

> It is like a rich stone,—best plain set.

Look at the end of Francis Thompson's *Ode after Easter:*

> Reintegrated are the heavens and Earth !
>   From sky to sod,
> The world's unfolded blossom smells of God.

That's the trouble. Everything is spiced up until it fairly stinks of God. They can't leave it alone, they can't just take it as it is. I dread the coming of the day when everything will smell of Zen ; tongues in trees, books in the running brooks, sermons in stones, and Zen in everything.

When we say Zen is vitally concerned with directness we must not make the mistake of supposing that Zen has any objection to such a poem as Keats' *Ode to a Nightingale,* on the ground that there is practically nothing, in eighty lines, concerning the nightingale itself. Take, for example, the second verse:

O, for a draught of vintage! that hath been
Cool'd a long age in the deep-delved earth,
Tasting of Flora and the country green,
Dance and Provençal song, and sunburnt mirth!
O for a beaker full of the warm South,
Full of the true, the blushful Hippocrene,
With beaded bubbles winking at the brim,
And purple-stained mouth;
That I might drink, and leave the world unseen,
And with thee fade away into the forest dim.

What is the subject of this verse? It is an unreal, so-called poetical world, in which life is beauty and joy everlasting. This is expressed as directly, as concretely, as Nash's *Spring,* perhaps more so. The *subjects,* then, of Nash's poem and Keats', are different; one is the Spring of this world, of England: the other is the Eternal Spring, the Eternal Nightingale ——which sings

Not a senseless trancèd thing
But divine melodious truth;
Philosophic numbers smooth,
Tales and golden histories
Of heaven and its mysteries.

The directness of Nash and Keats is undoubted, but the subject of Keats' poem is a dangerous one indeed. The road where

daisies are rose-scented,

is a road that leadeth to destruction, and that nightingale

Procuress to the Lords of Hell.

The Nightingale Ode is Keats' answer to the question, "What can Art and beauty do for the pains of life?" and concludes that beauty, that is,

> the fancy, cannot cheat so well
> As she is famed to do.

What then becomes of

> Beauty is truth, truth beauty?

In the history of Zen itself we find the cult of directness carried so far, that Tai-E in the 12th century actually burned and destroyed the great text book of Zen, the *Hekiganroku*. This may seem like the Burning of the Books by Shi-kô-tei (始皇帝) in BC. 213, but was utterly different. The Zen monks of that time were people who knew everything, they knew what life and death, God and man were,

> And why the sea is boiling hot,
> And whether pigs have wings.

They were the people of whom it is written,

> They went to sea in a sieve they did,
> In a sieve they went to sea;
> In spite of all their friends could say,

but they were anxious lest their friends should mistake the finger for the moon it was pointing at, so they cut it off. To prevent people from mistaking the expression in words of the truth, for the truth itself, they went to the same extreme as the Jews did in regard to graven images. This was in accordance with an over-literal interpretation of the Four Statements of the Zen Sect,[1]

[1] 教外別傳。　不立文字。　直指人心。　見性成佛。

1. A special transmission outside the scriptures.
2. No depending on books or words.

This is the condition of a poet. Keats writes of himself,

A poet is the most unpoetical thing in existence, — *because he has no identity*.[1]

The setting sun will always set me to rights, and if a sparrow come before my window, I take part in its existence and pick about the gravel.

His books, his body, his soul—all is gone; he so empty that he can contain anything, everything. He has got to the state of

3. Direct pointing to the soul of man.
4. Seeing into one's nature and the attainment of Buddhahood.

that is, seeing into the nature of the Sun and attainment of Sparrowhood. If you ask " What is the connection between Buddhahood and Sparrowhood? " remember Tennyson's

> Flower in the crannied wall,
> I pluck you out of the crannies;—
> Hold you here, root and all, in my hand,
> Little flower—but if I could understand
> What you are, root and all, and all in all,
> I should know what God and man is.

But a Zen master might take the flower and crush it, and ask,

[1] Compare,

> The butterfly having disappeared,
> My spirit
>   Came back to me.
> 蝶消えて魂我に返りけり   和 鳳

This of course has some echo in it of Sôshi's dreaming he was a butterfly, and, on waking, "Am I a man who dreamed of being a butterfly; or am I a butterfly dreaming myself to be a man?" (不知周之夢爲胡蝶與、胡蝶之夢爲周與。)

"*Now* do you know what God and man is?" The crushing of the flower is like the burning of the text book.

It is hardly necessary to say that Zen has nothing to do with symbolism. In fact it might be called the opposite of Zen, and this is borne out by a perusal of what Symonds says, in his *The Symbolist Movement in Literature,* of the various French symbolists. Let them speak for themselves:

Gérard de Nerval;
"I was very tired of life."
Villiers de l'Isle-Adam;
"As for living, our servants will do that."
"Moi, je vivais par politesse."
Arthur Rimbaud;
"Action is not life but a way of spoiling something."
Paul Verlaine;
"The ennui of living with people and in things."
Stéphane Mallarmé;
"A weariness, outworn by civil hopes, still clings,
To the last farewell handkerchief's last beckonings."
Huysmans;
"And art is the only clean thing on earth, except
holiness."
Symonds himself (actually included in *The Oxford Book
of Mystical Verse !*)
Where shall this self at last find happiness?
O soul, only in nothingness.
Does not the Earth suffice to its own needs?
And what am I but one of earth's weeds?

But in all these poets there is something which, disciplined by morality and Nature, appears as poetry in Wordsworth; harmonised by comprehended experience, displays itself in the plays of Shakespeare; subdued in the flesh, reappears in the spirit of Buddha and Daruma. The French Symbolists singe their wings and perish, but it is at a lamp

Which lighteneth every man that cometh into the world.

Nevertheless, they illustrate the fact that in the search for truth, aesthetic or moral, poetical or scientific, a man takes his life in his hands.[1] See, for example, Gérard de Nerval, who wrote the following:

Homme, libre penseur! te crois-tu seul pensant
Dans ce monde où la vie éclate en toute chose?
Des forces que tu tiens ta liberté dispose,
Mais de tous tes conseils l'univers est absent.
Respecte dans la bête un esprit agissant:
Chaque fleur est une âme à la Nature éclose;
Un mystère d'amour dans le métal repose;
"Tout est sensible!" Et tout sur son être est puissant.
Crains, dans le mur aveugle, un regard qui t'épie!
A la matière même un verbe est attaché. . . .
Ne la fais pas servir à quelque usage impie!
Souvent dans l'être obscur habite un pieu caché;
Et comme un oeil naissant couvert par ses paupières,
Un pur esprit s'accroît sous l'écorce des pierres!

This may not be precisely Zen, but it is good Buddhism. The Master of Zen says, "Jump into the foaming waves of the whirl-pool below!" The monk jumps, and finds himself on his feet, walking along the road that leads to his own home. With no master, no tradition, no health of mind or body, we are liable to jump and be found, like Gérard de Nerval, dead, hanging by the Queen of Sheba's garter to the bar of the window of a penny doss.

It should be noted however that Carlyle's conception of a

[1] To a man who has not eaten
        A globe-fish,
            We cannot speak of its flavour.   Taibai (d. 1842)
            ふぐくはぬ人にはいはじ鰒の味   大　梅
(Globe-fish are often very poisonous)

symbol, which Symonds quotes with approval, is very different from that of the Symbolists.

> In a Symbol, there is concealment and yet revelation: hence therefore, by Silence and by Speech acting together, comes a double significance. [this "double," no doubt means "doubly deep"]
> In the Symbol proper, what we can call a Symbol, there is ever, more or less distinctly and directly, some embodiment and revelation of the Infinite; the Infinite is made to blend itself with the Finite, to stand visible, and as it were, attainable there.

Zen does not like this talk of Finite and Infinite, visible and invisible, Symbol and Reality, but through the mesh of words we can see that Carlyle perceived, to some degree, that the symbol *is* reality and reality *is* the symbol, and that the word "symbol" is on a par with the word "unnatural," meaningless, since all things are natural. Or rather, it would be better to say, it is like the word "natural," (which is also meaningless, having no contrary) since there is nothing which is *not* a symbol, "a Symbol proper," as Carlyle calls it.

CHAPTER V

SUBJECTIVE AND OBJECTIVE

We may distinguish four kinds of poetry:

1. The object treated objectively.
2. The object treated subjectively.
3. The subject (=the Poet himself as theme) treated objectively.
4. The subject treated subjectively.

Zen of course takes the attitude of 1 and 3, ordinary people being in the state of 3 and 4, still wandering about in ignorance of the laws of their being, which govern them even while they wander in ignorance.

> Lead me O Zeus, and Thou, O Destiny,
> The way that I am bid by you to go.
> To follow I am ready. If I choose not,
> I make myself a wretch, and still must follow.

This is shown by Dante also:

> E pronti sono a trapassar lo rio,
>   Chè la divina giustizia gli sprona
>   Sì che la tema se volge in disìo.
>   (Inferno, III, 124-6)
> They are ready to cross the stream,
>   For Justice Divine so spurs them on,
>   That fear is changed to desire.

Even by opposing the will of God we do it; the very fear of death hastens its coming; dread of punishment is the punishment itself. In the same way, 'subjective and objective' is a false distinction, and we must never forget this fact as we make it.   Nevertheless, the generality of people are in the condition expressed by Emerson in,

> Things are in the saddle
> And ride mankind,

that is, though we speak of the subjective, introverted, senti-mental man as colouring the outside world, as if he were the master, in actual fact he is the slave of things.   We don't buy a new neck-tie; the neck-tie buys us.   A man who shudders at the sight of a snake or licks his lips before a pretty girl, is "ridden" by them, has no freedom or power.   To contain things we must empty ourselves:

> He who would be first among you shall be your ser-vant.

The word "subjective," is used, then, to designate the state of mind in which a man looks at the outside world, or at himself, as he would like it to be.   When Byron says,

> And Ardennes waves above them her green leaves,
> Dewy with nature's tear-drops, as they pass,
> Grieving, if aught inanimate e'er grieves,
> Over the unreturning brave,

he is speaking of Nature as it is not; Nature cares nothing for the deaths of brave men or cowards.   (Of course, Byron knew this.)   When Mrs. Gummidge in *David Copperfield* says of her-self,

> "I am a lone, lorn creature, and everythink goes con-trairy with me,"[1]

[1] Dickens knew what was wrong with Mrs. Gummidge and a great many other people, and he knew the remedy:
Steerforth left her *so little leisure for being miserable* that she said next day she thought she must have been bewitched.

she mistakenly supposes herself an object worthy of pity.

Here I give examples of each of these four types of poetry, from (*a*) The Bible (*b*) the literature of Zen (*c*) Japanese literature (*d*) English literature. Actually, in Zen, I and III are of course undifferentiated.

I THE OBJECT TREATED OBJECTIVELY

(*a*) For, lo! the winter is past, the rain is over and gone; the flowers appear on the earth; the time of the singing of birds is come, and the voice of the turtle is heard in the land.   *Song of Solomon,* ii, 11, 12.

(*b*) When Fu-ketsu was asked by a monk how to free oneself from relativity, from the absolute, he answered,

I often think of Kô-Nan in the month of March;
The partridge chirps among the scented flowers.

長 憶 江 南 三 月 裏、 鷓 鴣 啼 處 百 花 香
(無 門 關 第 二 十 四 則)

(*c*) By the roadside,
        A Rose of Sharon;
            The horse has eaten it.

道 ば た の む く げ は 馬 に く は れ け り   芭 蕉

(There is colour, there is movement; the horse's strange, rubber-like nose nuzzling the flower; no poet anywhere to be seen.)

        The peony has fallen;
            A few scattered petals
                Lie one on another.

牡 丹 散 つ て 打 ち か さ な り ぬ 二 三 片   蕪 村

Fleas, lice,
    The horse pissing close by,—
        A lodging for the night.

蚤虱馬の尿する枕元　　　　　芭　蕉

(The lotus does not hate the mud from which it arises and to which it returns.)

> A summer shower;
>> The rain beats upon
>>> The heads of the carp.

夕立にうたるる鯉のあたまかな　　子　規

(d) In English poetry, almost all of Chaucer; Shakespeare's songs ("When icicles hang by the wall," is the greatest masterpiece of this kind); Keats' *Ode to Autumn;* much of John Clare, whose *Young Lambs* follows:

The spring is coming by a many signs;
    The trays[1] are up, the hedges broken down,
That fenced the haystack, and the remnant shines
    Like some old antique fragment weathered brown.
And where suns peep, in every sheltered place,
    The little early buttercups unfold
A glittering star or two—till many trace
    The edges of the blackthorn clumps in gold.
And then a little lamb bolts up behind
    The hill and wags his tail to meet the yoe,
And then another, sheltered from the wind,
    Lies all his length as dead—and lets me go
Close bye and never stirs but baking lies,
    With legs stretched out as though he could not rise.

II THE OBJECT TREATED SUBJECTIVELY

(a) Be sober, be vigilant, because your adversary the Devil, as a roaring lion, walketh about seeking whom he may devour.　　　　　　　　　　　　1 *Peter* V 8.

(b) Hyaku-jô called his monks together and said, "He

1 Hurdles.

who can answer my question best shall be head of the temple of I-san." He brought a water-bottle and set it in the midst of them. "Do not call this a water-bottle; what will you call it?" Ka-rin, the head monk, said, "It can't be called the stump of a tree."

對衆下語、出格者可往、百丈遂拈淨瓶置地上、設問云、不得喚作淨瓶、汝喚作甚麼、首座及云、不可喚作木橛也。　　　　　（無門關、四十）

Karin forgot or did not understand what Rôshi (Laotse) had told him a thousand years before:

The name that can be named is not an eternal name.[1]

名可名非常名

He was thinking, "If I can't colour it with the name of 'bottle,' what name shall I colour it with? 'Tree-stump' seems a worse colour than 'bottle.' In what relation *to myself* can I express this wretched water-bottle?"

(c)　The morning glory too
Can never be
My friend.

朝顔やこれもまた我友ならず　　　芭　蕉

(Living in poverty at the end of an alley.
裏屋のつきあたりに住居して)

The cool breeze—
Crooked and meandering
It comes to me.

凉風の曲りくねつて來りけり　　　一　茶

(It goes without saying that it was Issa's heart that was crooked.)

---

[1] Compare Eckehart:
So wenig man für Gott einen eigentlichen Namen finden mag, so wenig kann man der Seele eigentlichen Namen finden.

How beautiful
The usually hateful crow,[1]
This snowy morning!

日頃にくき烏も雪のあしたかな   芭　蕉

In the spider's web
Hang butterflies dead—
A grievous sight!

蜘蛛の巣に胡蝶のからのあはれかな   子　規

(How about the dead fish and dead animals in his own larder?)

(d) In the following lines from the beginning of Act IV Sc. 1 of *King Henry the Sixth,* Part II, we see the *conscious* use of the pathetic fallacy:

The gaudy, blabbing, and remorseful day
Is crept into the bosom of the sea;
And now loud-howling wolves arouse the jades
That drag the tragic melancholy night;
Who, with their drowsy, slow, and flagging wings,
Clip dead men's graves, and from their misty jaws
Breathe foul contagious darkness in the air.

Contrast this with the following, supposed to be written about Buddha; he is all "dolled up," painted and powdered with the writer's pretended emotions:

Lord Buddha, on thy lotus throne,
With praying eyes and hands elate,
What mystic raptures dost thou own,
Immutable and ultimate?
What peace, unravished of our ken,
Annihilate from the world of men?

It is this kind of thing that makes English people fight shy

[1] Of course, this may be interpreted as, "hated by most people," excluding the poet himself

of Buddhism. It may be thought that much of Hardy's poetry belongs to this class, but not so, for in Hardy the colouring of the mind is conscious, and artistically controlled. In fact, we can say that this colouring of the mind, *treated as an object,* is the real theme of many of his poems. In *The Garden Seat,*

> Its former green is blue and thin,
> And its once firm legs sink in and in:
> Soon it will break down unaware,
> Soon it will break down unaware.
>
> At night when reddest flowers are black,
> Those who once sat thereon come back;
> Quite a row of them sitting there,
> Quite a row of them sitting there.
>
> With them the seat does not break down,
> Nor winter freeze them, nor floods drown,
> For they are as light as upper air,
> They are as light as upper air!

the separation of the object (the seat) and the colouring of the mind (the ghosts) is here complete, and *both* are treated objectively. Compare Bashô's,

> They say the pheasant
>   Eats the snake;
>   How fearful now, its voice!

蛇くふと聞けばおそろし雉子の聲　　芭　蕉

III THE SUBJECT TREATED OBJECTIVELY

(*a*) Did not our hearts burn within us while he talked with us?   *Luke,* XXIV, 32.

I have fought the good fight, I have finished my course, I have kept the faith.   2 *Timothy,* IV, 7.

This objective 'I' rises into a transcendent 'I' in

> I am the light of the world,

and in the next example:

(b) A certain monk asked Hyakujô, "What is Truth?"
Hyakujô said, "Here I sit on Daiyū Peak!"

僧問百丈、如何是奇特事、丈云獨坐大雄峰

（碧巖錄、第二十六）

(c) The cob ambles slowly
> Across the summer moor;
>> I find myself in a picture.[1]

馬ほくほく我を繪に見る夏野哉   芭 蕉

Now let's be off!
> Let's go snow-viewing till
>> We tumble down!

いざ行かん雪見にころぶ所まで   芭 蕉

Leaves of the willow tree fall;
> The master and I stand listening
>> To the sound of the bell.

ちる柳あるじも我も鐘をきく   芭 蕉

(The ear full of sound; the heart full of silence; the communion of saints.)

(d) Shakespeare's sonnets; Wordsworth anywhere; Donne.
Here is an example from George Herbert, *Life*.

> I made a posie, while the day ran by:
> Here will I smell my remnant out, and tie
>> My life within this band,

[1] Compare,

> I gazed to my heart's content at the scenery of Shôshô,
> Painting even my own boat into the picture.
> 看盡瀟湘景和舟入畫圖 （禪林句集）

But time did beckon to the flowers, and they
By noon most cunningly did steal away
    And wither'd in my hand.

My hand was next to them, and then my heart:
I took, without more thinking, in good part,
    Time's gentle admonition:
Who did so sweetly death's sad taste convey,
Making my minde to smell my fatall day,
    Yet sugring the suspicion.

Farewell, deare flowers, sweetly your time ye spent,
Fit, while ye liv'd, for smell or ornament,
    And after death for cures.
I follow straight without complaints or grief,
Since, if my scent be good, I care not if
    It be as short as yours.

IV THE SUBJECT TREATED SUBJECTIVELY

(a) And Jesus answered and said, "O faithless and perverse generation, how long shall I be with you? How long shall I bear with you?" *Matthew,* xvii, 17. (To box their ears all round, or call them names — that would have been all right.)

(b) The Emperor Bu of the Ryô dynasty asked Daruma, when he first saw him, "I have erected temples, enrolled monks: what will my merit be?"

達磨初見武帝、帝問、朕起寺度僧有何功德。
（碧巖錄、一、評唱）

(c) The morning-glory
    Clings to the well bucket—
        I get water elsewhere.

朝顔に釣瓶とられて貰ひ水　　　千代女

The action itself was all right, but we must say of the poem what Chôkei said to Hofuku, when the latter said, pointing at the mountains, "Is not this Reality?"

"It is, but it's a pity to say so."

福以手指曰、只這裏便是妙峰頂。
慶曰、是則是、可惜許。　　（碧巖錄、二十三）

Contrast this with Robert Frost's poem, *The Tuft of Flowers:*

> A leaping tongue of bloom the scythe had spared,
> Beside a reedy brook the scythe had bared.
>
> The mower in the dew had loved them thus,
> By leaving them to flourish, not for us,
>
> *Nor yet to draw one thought of ours to him,*
> But from sheer morning gladness at the brim.

Other examples, similar to that of Chiyo:

> I sat in the shadows,
>   And bequeathed the chamber
>   To the bright full moon.

陰に居て月に座敷をゆづりけり　　成　美

> Behind me
>   I cast all my cares—
>   The summer moon!

うさくさをうしろに捨てて夏の月　　子　規

Contrast this with

> Hanging a lantern on
>   A blossoming bough—
>   What pains I took!

工夫して花にランプを吊し鳧　　子　規

which has the true objectivity.

(*d*) This is a Chamber of Horrors. The larger part of Byron, a great deal of Shelley and Keats, nearly all Mrs. Brow-

ning, and all that she encouraged in her husband. Arnold is
not free from it, though he is always talking of the classics:

> And I, I know not if to pray
> Still to be what I am, or yield and be
> Like all the other men I see.

To this happy band of pilgrims belongs Landor with his,

> I strove with none, for none was worth my strife,

but the pièce de résistance is Yeats'

> Had I the heaven's embroidered cloths,
> Inwrought with golden and silver light,
> The blue and the dim and the dark cloths
> Of night and the light and the half light,
> I would spread the cloths under your feet;
> But I being poor have only my dreams;
> I have spread my dreams under your feet;
> Tread softly because you tread on my dreams.

The first line is magnificent and the second little inferior, but
the jazz rhythm of the next two lines leads to the sentimentality
of the rest, from the confusion of which emerges the quavering
saxophone solo of the last line.   There is nothing to equal this
in English Literature; but in case you have missed it, I quote
the following, from Milne's *Not that it Matters, The Diary
Habit:*

Monday. — "Rose at nine and came down to find a
letter from Mary. How little we know our true friends!
Beneath the mask of outward affection may lurk unknown
to us the serpent's tooth of jealousy.   Mary writes that
she can make nothing for my stall at the bazaar as she has
her own stall to provide for.   Ate my breakfast mechani-
cally, my thoughts being far away.   What, after all, is
life?   Meditated deeply on the inner cosmos till lunch-
time.   Afterwards I lay down for an hour and composed

my mind.   I was angry this morning with Mary.   Ah,
how petty! Shall I never be free from the bonds of my
own nature?   Is the better self within me never to rise to
the sublime heights of selflessness of which it is capable?
Rose at four and wrote to Mary, forgiving her.   This has
been a wonderful day for the spirit."

Note, by the way, that the use of the 1st person is no sign
of subjectivity, nor the use of the 3rd person a sign of objectivity.   Chaucer's

> Of alle the floures in the mede
> Than love I most these floures whyte and rede,
> Swiche as men callen daysies in our toun.
> To hem I have so great affection
> As I seyde erst, whan comen is the May,
> That in my bed ther daweth me no day
> That I nam up, and walking in the mede
> To seen these floures agein the Sonne sprede,
> Whan hit upryseth erly by the morwe;
> That blisful sighte softneth al my sorwe

is as objective as

> April, April,
> Laugh thy girlish laughter;
> Then the moment after,
> Weep thy girlish tears!

is subjective and sentimental.

The relation of Zen to Poetry concerns also the question
whether the poet finds, or creates the values which we know
by such names as Beauty, God, Truth, Reality.   Let us ask
the poets themselves what they think of the question.

Coleridge, as one would expect of a poet-philosopher, is
all for the idealist position.   In *Dejection* he says,

> O Lady!   We receive but what we give,
> And in our life alone does Nature live.

Browning seems to agree with him:

> To know
> Rather consists in opening out a way
> Whence the imprisoned splendour may escape,
> Than in effecting entry for a light
> Supposed to be without.

Wordsworth is at one with many modern philosophers in speaking of

> all the mighty world
> Of eye and ear,—both what they half-create
> And what perceive.

Shakespeare characteristically gives us both and lets us take our choice; in *Hamlet,*

> There is nothing either good or bad but thinking makes it so,

and in *Antony and Cleopatra,*

> I see men's judgements are
> A parcel of their fortunes; and things outward
> Do draw the inward quality after them
> To suffer all alike.

Shelley, in *Adonais,* gives a profounder answer than the others:

> He is a portion of the loveliness
> Which once he made more lovely.

Herbert's

> I got me flowers to straw Thy way,
> I got me boughs off many a tree;
> But Thou wast up by break of day,
> And brought'st Thy sweets along with Thee,

is the most beautiful but needs Emerson's words from *Compensation,*

> Everything in Nature contains all the powers of
> Nature.   Everything is made of one hidden stuff

to resolve the dualism. In actual fact the dilemma of 'creation
or discovery' is, as hinted by Shelley, a purely verbal one, and
arises from the fact that the intellect can survey only the intellectual data.   The passion, the willing of the creating-dis-
covering which takes place, cannot be understood by the reason
working alone. This is why Buddha would never answer such
questions as, "Is the soul mortal or immortal? Is the universe
finite or infinite?"   And notice that this attitude has no connection whatever with that of the man who says, "Yes, there is
truth in everything: the truth lies between the two extremes,"

> And finds, with keen discriminating sight,
> Black's not so black, nor white so *very* white.

Truth lies *beyond* the extremes, not in the middle; is beyond
good and evil, not partly both.   Or, to express this in another
way, suggested to me by Prof. Suzuki, in connection with
"seeing into our own nature," 見性, poetry is the *something*
that we *see,* but the *seeing* and the *something* are one; without
the *seeing* there is no *something,* no *something,* no *seeing.* There
is neither discovery nor creation: only the perfect, indivisible
experience.

CHAPTER VI

CONCRETE AND ABSTRACT

Zen is not philosophy and has no philosophy. If you say Zen is the Hegelian Absolute, the totality of all existence and of all thought, it will say, "Thank you." If you say it is Pragmatism, truth is utility, a true belief is one that works, it will say, "Why not?" If you call it Materialism, yes, there is nothing of Supernaturalism[1] in Zen. If you call it Idealism, yes again, everything depends on the mind. Determinism? Buddhism is nothing if not deterministic. Free Will? The will is everything in Zen. Zen is pluralistic? It is *bagiri-jigiri,* that is, acting according to the circumstances, at that moment, in that place, for the world is a collection of a number of things. Zen is monistic; but

Do not become attached to the One.

一 亦 莫 守 （信 心 銘）

The question of Concrete and Abstract, then, is not a problem of metaphysics, but a practical matter. In the life of action, the question does not arise; we deal only with concrete things, with men and women. But slaves to some definition of it, men die for Freedom, kill themselves for Honour, slaughter millions in the name of Democracy or Communism. Zen denies nothing, has nothing negative in it, but it says, "Beware of Abstractions!"

[1] But, "Thy will be done on Earth as it is in Heaven," is the heart of Zen.

> I could not love thee, Dear, so much,
> Loved I not Honour more

is a lofty, but dangerous, Pecksniffian doctrine.

> Charity begins at home,

is a safer and better one.   The danger is, of course, self-deception.   Johnson says,

> Patriotism is the last refuge of a scoundrel

but it is also the first refuge of a great many good citizens. Johnson is for the moment in strange company; Blake supports him, in

> He who would do good to another must do it in Minute Particulars.   General Good is the plea of the scoundrel, hypocrite, and flatterer.

We must not forget that, as Hobbes says,

> Words are wise men's counters,—they do but reckon by them; but they are the money of fools.

If words are so, much more are abstractions mere conveniences of thought.   But let us take some examples from English poetry, first, the conclusion of Shelley's *Prometheus Unbound:*

> To suffer woes which Hope thinks infinite;
> To forgive wrongs darker than death or night;
>   To defy Power, which seems omnipotent;
> To love and bear; to hope till Hope creates
> From its own wreck the thing it contemplates;
>   Neither to change, nor falter, nor repent;
> This like thy glory, Titan, is to be
> Good, great and joyous, beautiful and free;
> This is alone Life, Joy, Empire, and Victory.

Charles Lamb, in a letter (August, 1824) to Bernard Barton, says of Shelley's "nostrums," that they are

> ringing with their own emptiness. Hazlitt said well of 'em— Many are the wiser and better for reading Shakespeare,

(and one might add, Wordsworth and Chaucer,)

> but nobody was ever wiser or better for reading Shelley.

Keats' advice,

> Load every rift with ore,

and Lamb's criticism in the same letter,

> His poetry is " thin sown with profit or delight,"

point to the same fatal defect as Arnold's

> beautiful and ineffectual angel beating in the void his luminous wings in vain,

in the essay on Byron and quoted from himself at the end of the essay on Shelley.

We can stand a certain amount of abstraction; but not too much. In Wordsworth's *Ode to Duty,* the beginning,

> Stern Daughter of the Voice of God !

is vague and vast, but the ending,

> The spirit of Self-sacrifice;
> The confidence of reason give :
> And in the light of truth thy Bondman
> let me live !

trite and feeble. What remains in our memory is not the abstraction Duty, but the particular *things,* Wordsworth himself,

> Me this uncharter'd freedom tires;
> I feel the weight of chance-desires;
> My hopes must no more change their name,
> I long for a repose that ever is the same.

and

> Flowers laugh before thee on their beds,
> And fragrance in thy footing treads;
> Thou dost preserve the stars from wrong;
> And the most ancient heavens, through Thee, are
>   fresh and strong.

It is this principle of the sparing use of abstractions that distinguishes Pope and Milton. Pope says,

> Here blushing Flora paints the enamelled ground,

Milton, in *Lycidas*,

> Throw hither all your quaint enamell'd eyes
> That on the green turf suck the honied showers,

and there is not much to choose between them; but Milton continues,

> Bring the rathe primrose that forsaken dies,
> The tufted crow-toe, and pale jessamine,
> The white pink, and the pansy freakt with jet,
> The glowing violet,
> The musk-rose, and the well-attir'd woodbine,
> With cowslips wan that hang the pensive head.

Compare this to Pope when he also is writing about particular things:

> In the worst inn's worst room, with mat half-hung,
> The floors of plaister, and the walls of dung,
> On once a flock-bed, but repaired with straw,
> With tape-tied curtains, never meant to draw,
> The George and Garter dangling from that bed

> Where tawdry yellow strove with dirty red,
> Great Villiers lies.

Christ is the greatest poet who ever lived and his concreteness is alarming. A man is not a hypocrite, he is a "whited sepulchre," Herod is "a hyena"; as for a deceiver,

> It were better that a millstone were hanged about his neck and he cast into the sea.

When he has finished speaking, his speech full of salt, bread, lilies, pearls, towers, the wind, he says,

> Gather up the fragments that remain, that nothing be lost.

If we are going to have a God at all, let us have "Our Father which art in Heaven." Look at Matthew Arnold with his

> stream of tendency, by which all things seek to fulfil the law of their being.

In some way or other the abstract exists, no doubt, but the point is that the mind does not desire the abstract, it desires the thing. So in the *Summa Theologica*, Aquinas says,

> He who is drawn to something desirable does not desire to have it as a thought but as a thing.

If we want God, we want him as a Father, not as a stream of tendency, and this is the secret of the power of Christianity. Its so-called anthropomorphism is nothing less than the nature of the mind which cannot be satisfied with anything but whole things. Even the expression "stream of tendency," is better than mere "tendency," for we feel that the concrete word "stream," though only a metaphor, gives more peace to the mind than the abstract word. In Zen this fact was early per-

ceived, and nothing more distinguishes Zen from the other
Buddhist sects than its emphasis on the concrete.   Yet when
Daruma was asked by the Emperor Bu,

"What is the essence, the first principle, of the Holy
Teaching (of Buddhism)?"

梁 武 帝、 問 達 磨 大 師、 如 何 是 聖 諦 第 一 義。

Daruma replied,

"It is a vast emptiness, with nothing holy about it."

磨 曰、 廓 然 無 聖。

The first part, "a vast emptiness," seems a very un-Zen-like
answer, but we must remember the circumstances under which
it was made.   It is the old distinction of faith and works,
Martha and Mary.   The Emperor supposed that religion was
a set of doctrines which one believed and that, faith without
works being dead, his putting on the Buddhist surplice, ex-
pounding the *Hannyaparamita Hridaya Sutra,* promulgation
of edicts, building of temples and registration of monks, were
all a proper expression in action of his religious feelings.   Daruma tries to correct this double fallacy, tries to cut off the two
heads of the dragon.   "All this talking of religion, reading the
scriptures, setting up of temples, has nothing to do with true
religion; 'the holy doctrine,' as you call it, has nothing holy
about it, no, nor anything not-holy.   Give up your notions of
merit and demerit, gain and loss, for-Buddhism, and against-
Buddhism, I and the doctrine, Reality and phenomena; these
are all *abstracted* from life.   And in the degree that they are
abstract, in that degree also they are unreal, non-existent,
hallucinations."

Later in the history of Zen, the answer to "What is Buddhism?" became more and more concrete, from the tree in the

garden, pounds of flax, toilet paper, to the most concrete of all, kicks and blows. Such things, that are so round and perfect that the intellect cannot get its teeth into them, were found, in practice, to " clear the mind of cant."

I give you the end of a golden string.

That is enough, just simply that; but then *you* must do something,

Only wind it into a ball;
It will lead you in at Heaven's gate
Built in Jerusalem's wall.

What is the meaning of life, of all life, my life, your life? The moment the question is asked, it has no meaning and of course, no answer; no possible, no conceivable meaning. (In the same way, the object of morality, as has been often noted before, is simply self-destruction, that is to say, the removal of the opportunities to help and to do good to others.) Philosophers wish to understand the universe; and when they have done this, what then? A blank. By some, this questioning as to the meaning of life is called instinctive. It may be so, but it is an unhealthy instinct, in the sense that when the soul is in health and not morbid, it does not concern itself at all with such problems. Emerson says somewhere that we should live in this world like healthy schoolboys who do not wonder where their next meal is coming from, taking no thought for the morrow.[1] The "meaning" of life is a question of cause and effect, that is to say, it is a question of time, of yesterday, and today and tomorrow. It is unhealthy because it is a turning of energy into improper channels, into negativity and doubt.

[1] Ah, evening swallow!
My heart is full of
Fears for the morrow.
夕燕我には翌日のあてもなし   一 茶

> If the sun and moon should doubt,
> They'd immediately go out,

and when we say, "What is the meaning of my life?" the spiritual life, spontaneously generated up to that moment, is extinguished, the world is a darkness that can be felt.   However, the question has been asked; the man is sick, it is too late to recapitulate the laws of health, he needs medicine.   There are many answers to the question; I give some of them below.

There is (1) the optimistic: Browning's

> The year's at the spring,
>   And day's at the morn;
>   Morning's at seven;
>   The hill-side's dew-pearled;
> The lark's on the wing;
>   The snail's on the thorn;
>   God's in his heaven—
>   All's right with the world!

(2) the pessimistic: Macbeth's

> Tomorrow, and tomorrow, and tomorrow,
> Creeps in this petty pace from day to day
> To the last syllable of recorded time,
> And all our yesterdays have lighted fools
> The way to dusty death.   Out, out, brief candle!
> Life's but a walking shadow, a poor player
> That struts and frets his hour upon the stage
> And then is heard no more: it is a tale
> Told by an idiot, full of sound and fury,
> Signifying nothing.

(Expressed so well, it seems not so bad after all.)

(3) the sentimental false: from Coleridge's letter to Charles Lamb on the occasion of his sister's killing, while insane, her own mother.   (Lamb asked for "as religious a letter as possible.")

Your mother is in heaven. It is sweet to be roused from a frightful dream by the song of birds and the gladsome rays of the morning. Ah, how infinitely more sweet to be awakened from the blackness and amazement of a sudden horror by the glories of God manifest and the hallelujahs of angels.

(4) the heroic: Henley's *Invictus,*

> Out of the night that covers me,
>   Black as the pit from pole to pole,
> I thank whatever gods may be
>   For my unconquerable soul.
>
> In the fell clutch of circumstance
>   I have not winced nor cried aloud.
> Under the bludgeonings of chance
>   My head is bloody, but unbow'd.
>
> Beyond this place of wrath and tears
>   Looms but the Horror of the shade,
> And yet the menace of the years
>   Finds and shall find me unafraid.
>
> It matters not how strait the gate,
>   How charged with punishments the scroll,
> I am the master of my fate:
>   I am the captain of my soul.

(Notice, in connection with what was said about subjective and objective, that this poem would be intolerable in the 3rd person.)

(5) the jocular :

> Nothing to do but work,
> Nothing to eat but food,
> Nothing to wear but clothes,
> To keep from going nude.

(6) the despairing-hopeful of *In Memoriam:*

> Oh yet we trust that somehow good
> Will be the final goal of ill.

> But what am I?
> An infant crying in the night:
> An infant crying for the light,
> And with no language but a cry.

(7) the resigned: Matthew Arnold's,

> the mute turf we tread
> The solemn hills around us spread,
> This stream which falls incessantly,
> The strange-scrawl'd rocks, the lonely sky,
> If I might lend their life a voice,
> Seem to bear rather than rejoice.

(8) the desperate: Thomas Huxley thought so badly of the whole business that

> if some great Power would agree to make me always think what is true and do what is right, on condition of being turned into a sort of clock, and wound up every morning before I got out of bed, I should instantly close with the offer.

One point must be noticed, before we go on to consider how the solution of the problem may be arrived at, and that is the fact that, as Voltaire says in *Candide,* ironically but truly,

> Tout est pour le mieux dans le meilleur des mondes
> possibles.

It is all very well to say,

> Ah, Love! could thou and I with Fate conspire
> To grasp this sorry Scheme of Things entire,
>   Would we not shatter it to bits—and then
> Re-mould it nearer to the Heart's Desire!

or like Alphonso the Wise, about Ptolemy's astronomy,

> Had I been present at the creation, I would have given
> some useful hints for the better ordering of the universe,

but how, in actual fact, would you improve it? Do away with
pain and distress? Bernard Shaw says,

> A lifetime of happiness! No man alive could bear it:
> it would be hell on earth.

Do away with death? No Christianity, no Buddhism, no
Hamlet, no *Divine Comedy,* no *Paradise Lost,* no Beethoven, no
Bach — what should we be living for? As to whether the
agonies of life are worth all these works of art—that is another problem. Now the question simply is, how would you
personally make the world better, in any one single respect, remembering that the slightest change in one part has far-reaching repercussions in every other. The problem of the meaning
of life is perhaps an external, or at least, externalised one;
there are many good and clever people who "do not worry
their heads about such things." For all, however, except that
very small class,

> There are who ask not if thine eye
> Be on them; who, in love and truth,
> Where no misgiving is, rely
> Upon the genial sense of youth:
> Glad hearts! without reproach or blot;
> Who do thy work and know it not,

there is the problem of conduct: how to get through the petty
annoyances of life and undergo the major operations of marriage and death. How can we establish a harmony between ourselves and the outside world full of misunderstandings, deceit,
violence, and the suffering and death of those we love, when
all the while we ourselves are full of that same stupidity, insincerity, cruelty and sloth?

CHAPTER VII

THE UNREGARDED RIVER OF OUR LIFE

Matthew Arnold, in *Empedocles on Etna,* describes the desperate struggle we make for freedom and harmony:

> We would have inward peace,
> Yet will not look within;
> We would have misery cease,
> Yet will not cease from sin;
> We want all pleasant ends, but will use no harsh means.

> Once read thy own breast right
> And thou hast done with fears;
> Man gets no other light
> Search he a thousand years:
> Sink in thyself! there ask what ails thee, at that shrine!

Since we know ourselves most intimately, most directly, is it not inside, that the solution must be sought? And is it not possible that if we could attain unity and order in the mikrokosmos that the problem of the makrokosmos might somehow or other solve itself? No, says Arnold,

> Yet, even when man forsakes
> All sin,—is just, is pure,
> Abandons all which makes
> His welfare insecure,—
> Other existences there are, that clash with ours,

forgetting what Shakespeare said, that nothing clashes or agrees with us, but thinking makes it so. What is this mind, so overlaid with the rubbish of passion and the entanglements of thought, yet out of which come the airs and floating echoes

that we call music, art, religion? Notice one thing before we
go on to speak of the search for mind. Ignorance, in Buddhist
terminology, Sin, Evil, in the Christian, that is, the state in
which

> We do not what we ought,
> What we ought not, we do,

may change, must change, will change the Adam and Eve
state of Original Enlightment of animals,

> There is a power whose care
> Teaches thy way along that pathless coast,—
> The desert and illimitable air,—
> Lone wandering but not lost,[1]

of children,

> Dear Child! dear Girl! that walkest with me here,
> If thou appear untouched by solemn thought,
> Thy nature is not less divine,

of idiots,

> But when the pony moved his legs,
> Oh! then for the poor Idiot Boy!
> For joy he cannot hold the bridle,
> For joy his head and heels are idle,
> He's idle all for very joy,

into the state of Enriched Enlightenment which Buddha attained to. And this is both a hint at the solution of the problem of evil, and an exposition of the Zen doctrine that, (transcending the category of time) the ordinary man *is* the Buddha,
that this passional rubbish and entangling intellect *is* the Mind.

From the 16th century, the thought of the importance of

[1] Bryant: *To a waterfowl.* Compare Dôgen's poem, page 1.

the mind enters into English Literature. We must be careful by the way, to distinguish, both in life and in art, *talking* about Zen, and Zen itself. So in the following examples, Zen is being alluded to, hinted at, dimly descried. (If we want to find Zen itself, we may begin at *Beowulf* and speak of his *Bushidô.*) In the anonymous 16th century poem *As ye came from the Land,* in the lines,

> His desire is a dureless content
>   And a trustless joy:
> He is won with a world of despair,
>   And is lost with a toy,

false love, or the (superficial) mind is described; and in the last verse, true Love, or the Mind:

> But true love is a durable fire
>   In the mind ever burning,
> Never sick, never dead, never cold,
>   From itself never turning.

Dyer says,

> My mind to me a kingdom is.

(Puzzle: find the king.)

Milton, typifying the best (and worst) of Puritanism, speaks of

> A mind not to be changed by place or time.
> The mind is its own place, and in itself
> Can make a heaven of hell, a hell of heaven

—so near the truth, yet with a suggestion of the impervious water-tight self, unchanging, indestructible even by God himself; so far from the fluidity and self-lessness of love, that it gives us a feeling of death rather than of life, the same cold feeling as in,

> Know then thyself, presume not God to scan;
> The proper study of mankind is man.

We are taken much deeper by Shakespeare, when Jessica says,

> Must I hold a candle to my shames?

going further and further down to

> the insane root
> That takes the reason prisoner,

until Macbeth asks,

> Canst thou not minister to a mind diseas'd,
> Pluck from the memory a rooted sorrow,
> Raze out the written troubles of the brain,
> And with some sweet oblivious antidote
> Cleanse the stuff'd bosom of that perilous stuff
> Which weighs upon the heart?

Not even God[1] can do this.   The doctor answers,

> Therein the patient must minister
> to himself.

For years the 2nd Patriarch, E-ka, had been in the same condition, his bosom stuffed with doubts, his heart weighed upon
with sins of omission and commission.   When he came to the
doctor, Daruma, he was told the same thing "This is not to be
sought through another." (諸佛法印匪從人得。)[2] He then asked
that his mind should be set at rest, and when Daruma asked
him to bring his soul to have it set at peace, he was forced to
say, with Arnold,

[1] Using the word in the unmystical, Father Christmas sense.   In
actual fact, the Christian doctrine of Grace is identical with the Zen
principle of "Direct pointing to the Soul of Man," (直指人心) and when
St. Juliana of Norwich says, in *Revelation of Divine Love*, "To seek God
without already having him, is of all things the most impossible," she is
explaining the conversion of E-ka, given here.

[2] 傳燈錄、卷三、quoted in 冠註無門關、第四十一則。

> And long we try in vain to speak and act
> Our hidden Self, and what we say and do
> Is eloquent, is well, but 'tis not true.

In his own words,

> "I have sought it but could not find it."

> 覓 心 了 不 可 得。

Now was the question,

> To see if we will poise our life at last,
> To see if we will now at last be true
> To our own true, deep-buried selves,
> Being one with which we are one with the whole world;
> Or whether we will once more fall away
> Into some bondage of the flesh or mind,
> Some slough of sense, or some fantastic maze
> Forg'd by the imperious lonely thinking power.

But when Daruma said,

> "There! I have set your soul at rest for you!"

> 我 與 汝 安 心 竟。

E-ka felt that transformation described as,

> A bolt is shot back somewhere in our breast,
> And what we mean, we say, and what we would, we know.

Everything depends on what Byron calls, in the *Corsair,*

> The power of thought,—the magic of the mind.

Just open the door, and there you are. Emerson says, in *Self Reliance,*

> Nothing can bring you peace but yourself.

From such a point of view, how profound the words of Coventry Patmore become:

> Resolve to be thyself, and know that he
> Who finds himself, loses his misery.

The man who finds himself, that is, Himself, loses both his misery and his joy, but finds his Joy.   And those words of Polonius; heard for the first time merely sententious, then hackneyed out of all meaning, now, most profound:

> This above all: to thine own self be true,
> And it must follow, as the night the day,
> Thou canst not then be false to any man.

To the Self be true: how can you then be false to anything? How can you be one

> Who needlessly sets foot upon a worm,

or feels contempt or hatred of the man who does so?

Before we go on to speak of the Mind, it is as well to refer to the Buddhist doctrine that we are only apparently a unity, a stream of innumerable selves following one another like a series of cinematographic pictures, so quickly that they seem one continuous whole (the Buddhist simile is a whirling rope burning at one end, which thus seems to be a ring of fire). This idea of many selves, which by the way, has no connection with what is called multiple personality, is very touchingly expressed in *Dombey and Son*.   The captain thinks Walter has been drowned at sea.

"He warn't my flesh and blood," said the Captain, looking at the fire—"I an't got none—but somewhat of what a father feels when he loses a son, I feel in losing Wal'r. For why?" said the Captain.   "Because it an't one loss, but a round dozen. Where's that there young school-boy with the rosy face and curly hair, that used to be as merry in this here parlour, come round every week, as a piece of music? Gone down with Wal'r.   Where's that

there fresh lad, that nothing couldn't tire nor put out, and
that sparkled up and blushed so when we joked him about
Hearts Delight, that he was beautiful to look at?   Gone
down with Wal'r.   Where's that there man's spirit, all
afire, that wouldn't see the old man hove down for a
minute, and cared nothing for itself?   Gone down with
Wal'r.   It an't one Wal'r.   There was a dozen Wal'r that
I know'd and loved, all holding round his neck when he
went down, and they're a-holding round mine now!"[1]

Look now at this poem by Henry Vaughan, *The Search.*

> Leave, leave, thy gadding thoughts;
>   Who Pores
>   and spies
> Still out of Doores,
>   descries
> Within them nought.
>
> The skinne, and shell of things
>   Though faire,
>   are not
> Thy wish, nor pray'r,
>   but got
> By meer Despair
>   of wings.
>
> To rack old Elements,
>   or Dust
>   and say
> Sure here he must
>   needs stay,
> Is not the way,
>   nor just.
> Search well another world; who studies this
> Travels in Clouds, seeks Manna, where none is.

[1] Compare also Wordsworth in *The Prelude,* II, 31, thinking of himself in past days:

> Musing on them, often do I seem
> Two consciousnesses, conscious of myself
> And of some other Being.

The beautiful but irregular rhyme-scheme makes the thought rather vague and wayward, but "out of doors," is this external world, it is "the skinne, and shell of things;" "another world," is indoors, one's real self.   Put simply, what Vaughan means is, "Enquire within. Examine your present and past experiences."   I remember when I was young, like many another boy, while travelling by train I used to turn one of the nobs in the compartment when the train started or stopped, pretending it was I who was the cause of it all.   The true Christian or Buddhist life is just this.   When it rains, it is God's will, and God's will is my will, God's rain is my rain. Thus it is my rain that rains, it is my own specially ordered rain that wets me to the skin and chills me to the marrow, gives me consumption and kills me.   It is my sun that shines, it is my time that silvers my hair by my request, loosens my teeth at my command.   This is the faith, the love, that moves the sun and the other stars,

> L'amor che move il sole e l'altre stelle,

and the mountains as well :

> If ye have faith as a grain of mustard seed, ye shall say unto this mountain, Remove hence to yonder place, and it shall remove, and nothing shall be impossible unto you.

In Zen Kôans such as " Stop that vessel, sailing across the bay," the same principle is involved, that of complete self-abandonment, and self-identification with the "suchness" of things.   If you will all possible things, what is impossible? Nothing, for

> With God all things are possible.

Hokushi, one of the ten disciples of Basho, has the following poem:

> I kept hanging the moon
>> On the pine-tree and taking it off,
>>> Gazing at it the while.

月 を 松 に 懸 け た り 外 し て も 見 た り　　　北 枝

Issa also expresses this vast thought, which includes all religion, all poetry, all the meaning of life, in seventeen syllables:

> I take a nap,
>> Making the mountain water
>>> Pound the rice.

山 水 に 米 を 搗 か せ て 晝 寢 か な

Here we have the identification of man with Nature; Man =Nature. Issa-in-the-water turns the mill-wheel that pounds the rice, while Issa-by-the-water slumbers,—yet there is only one Issa.[1]

Thoreau tells us that it is Nature that does the best part of the work of a carpenter, Nature that does the best part of the work of an artist, a poet. This is the identification of Nature with man; Nature=Man. That is to say, Nature-in-the-water drives the water-wheel; Nature-in-Issa sleeps, — yet there is only one Nature. Combining the two, Issa pounds the rice while asleep; Nature sleeps while pounding the rice.

Now perhaps you can see the Zen in the following familiar lines, remembering that "Thee" is Autumn, Nature, Man.

> Who hath not seen Thee oft amid thy store?
> Sometimes whoever seeks abroad may find
> Thee sitting careless on a granary floor,
> Thy hair soft-lifted by the winnowing wind;

[1] Bertrand Russell, in *What I believe*, Chapter one, kindly gives us confirmation of this:

Metaphysicians have advanced innumerable arguments to prove that the soul *must* be immortal. There is one simple test by which all these arguments can be demolished. They all prove equally that *the soul must pervade all space.*

Or on a half-reap'd furrow sound asleep,
Drowsed with the fume of poppies, while thy hook
Spares the next swath and all its twinèd flowers;
And sometimes like a gleaner thou dost keep
Steady thy laden head across a brook;
Or by a cider-press, with patient look,
Thou watchest the last oozings, hours by hours.

This same condition of mind, though attained by very different means, is described in Tolstoy's *Master and Man*.   Vassili, money-lover and self-lover, who has left his servant Nikita to die in the snow, returns, and lying on him, warms him back to life, dying himself.   The following lines describe his thoughts as he wakes, for the last time, from his frozen sleep.

Yes, he awoke — but awoke a very different man to what he had been when he fell asleep.   He tried to rise, and could not.   He tried to move his hand, and could not. He tried to move his leg, and could not.   Then he tried to turn his head, but that also he could not do.   Nikita was lying beneath him, and that Nikita was growing warm and was coming back to life.   It seemed to him that he was Nikita, and Nikita he, and that his life was no longer within himself, but within Nikita.   He strained his ears till he caught the sound of breathing—yes, the faint, deep breathing of Nikita.   "Nikita is alive!" he cried to himself in triumph, "and therefore so also am I!"

The Buddha is the tree in the garden.   Issa flows over the water-wheel.   Autumn is sitting on the floor.   Vassili, the master, is Nikita his servant.   I and my Father are one.   Do they not all say the same thing?

CHAPTER VIII

EVERYTHING DEPENDS ON THE MIND

There is an interesting story related in Bacon's essay *Of Boldness,* which is pertinent here. I do not know if it is true or not, but if true, it marks Mahomet as a leader of men.

> Mahomet made the people believe that he would call a hill to him, and from the top of it offer up his prayers for the observers of his law. The people assembled. Mahomet called the hill to come to him, again and again; and when the hill stood still, he was never a whit abashed, but said, "If the hill will not come to Mahomet, Mahomet will go to the hill."

The "never a whit abashed" is the important point here. The mountain stood still and was not abashed. Mahomet went to the mountain and was not abashed. In *Two Gentlemen of Verona,* the outlaw asks Valentine if he is content

> To make a virtue of necessity,

that is, live the life of Zen, unabashed by poverty.

Wordsworth defines the character of a Happy Warrior. He is one

> Who, doomed to go in company with Pain
> And Fear and Bloodshed—miserable train!—
> Turns his necessity to glorious gain.

In the *Paradiso,* (III, 73,) Piccarda tells Dante,

> "Si disiassimo esser più superne,
> Foran discordi li nostri disiri
> Dal voler di colui che qui ne cerne,

> Che vedrai non capere in questi giri,
>   S'essere in carità è qui *necesse,*
>   E se la sua natura ben rimiri."

"Were we to desire to be in yet a higher realm,
    Such longings were discordant
    With the will of Him who allots our places here.

For thou wilt see that for such longing, these spheres
                            can have no place,
    If Love is here *Necessity,*
    And if thou ponderest well its nature."

As she says, in the sublimest words of the *Divina Commedia,* (what is yet one more definition of Zen),

> E'n la sua voluntate è nostra pace.

Issa says the same thing but in his own inimitable way:

> O snail,
>   Climb Mt. Fuji,
>   But slowly, slowly!

> 蝸牛そろそろのぼれ富士の山

That is, act according to your nature, snail; act according to God's will, be a snail! Goethe also writes somewhere,

> The effort of religion is to adjust us to the inevitable.

When this adjustment is complete, complete, that is to say, in the will, we have the perfect life of Christ, of Buddha, of St. Francis, of Daruma, of many of the Stoic philosophers. Epictetus says,

> Dare to look up to God and say, "Make use of me for the future as Thou wilt. I am of the same mind; I am one with Thee. I refuse nothing which seems good to Thee. Lead me whither Thou wilt."

and again,

> Two rules we should always have ready,—that there is nothing good or evil save in the will; and that we are not to lead events, but to follow them.

Marcus Aurelius says,

> The controlling Intelligence understands its own nature, and what it does, and whereon it works.

Again,

> All that is harmony for thee, O Universe, is in harmony with me as well.   Nothing that comes at the right time for thee is too early or too late for me. Everything is fruit to me that thy seasons bring, O Nature.   All things come out of thee, have their being in thee, and return to thee.

It is of importance to notice here that though the Stoics above quoted were no doubt noble men, faithful to these principles in life and death, one feels a great difference between such men, and Jôshū, Baso, Isan, Obaku, Rinzai and many smaller fry. Zen has in it a kind of gusto, a kind of energy, which shines forth in the smallest thing.   Unmon raises his staff.[1]   That is all; but it has the power and force of the Niagara Falls, carrying all before it.   Jôshū says, "Wash your bowls,"[2] and these words have more significance than the periods of Burke or Demosthenes.   That is to say, there is a residuum of *unresolved necessity* in the Stoics; not all the necessity is made into virtue, into freedom.   There is something cold, lifeless, heavy, something of helplessness and resignation in them.

In the Kwannon-kyô (Avalokitesvara Sutra) there is a passage identical in meaning with the words of Christ, p. 103:

[1] 雲門有時云、乾坤大地。 殺活總在這裏。 (雲門錄)
[2] 無門關第七則。

Suppose you were on the topmost peak of Mt. Sumeru and somebody pushed you over; if you prayed in absolute faith to Kwannon, you would remain suspended in mid-air, like the sun.

或は須彌の峯にありて、人を推し墮されん
に、彼の觀音の力を念ぜば、日の如くにし
て虚空に住せん　　　　（觀音經、普門品偈頌。）

Baso says,

Drink up at one gulp all the water in the Western River and I will tell you (what is the spiritual state of the man who is independent of all things),

待汝一口吸盡西江水即向汝道．（傳燈錄、八。）

that is, the man of faith.　Here let me note one thing.　The teachers of Zen make their doctrine appear very esoteric, but they should remember that a man who understands the words of Christ can understand the words of Buddha or Baso or Jô-shū.　If a man understands

Blessed are the poor in spirit,

if he understands the music of Bach, he understands

Mu, 無。[1]

that is to say, to the same extent.　But for him to *know that he understands*—for this he needs a teacher.　Further, they must remember Emerson's words,

Men are better than their theology.

Orthodox Christian theology is really extraordinarily childish, but not always the Christians who *think* they believe it, and certainly not those who understand it in the same profound esoteric way as with, for example,

[1] *Mu* is the state of absolute spiritual poverty.

The Buddha is toilet paper.

乾屎橛。 無門關、第二十一則

Look once more at the following:

Lay not up for yourselves treasures upon the earth, where moth and rust doth consume, and where thieves break through and steal, but lay up for yourselves treasures in heaven, for where thy treasure is, there will thy heart be also.

This is not hackneyed, though it has been the text of thousands of sermons; the words of Christ have something in them of an elemental quality like air or water, of which we can never grow tired. The first part of Christ's words is quite clear, but "lay up for yourselves treasures in Heaven" may be taken in several ways. It may be taken as an injunction to accumulate merits in the Buddhist sense; such an interpretation seems too materialistic, too calculating. It may be taken as meaning "live a spiritual life." This is too nebulous, too vague, makes hypocrisy (to oneself) difficult to avoid, above all makes a distinction between eating your dinner and reading poetry, between the real and the ideal, a distinction which is the root of all evil. We must remember that Heaven is here and now, just asking to be lived in; Hell also. "For where thy treasure is, there will thy heart be also." Finding the heart, finding the mind, that is, finding the Mind, is no easy task; Christ tells us to look where our treasure is, it is in the same place.

It is a cold winter night. The bed is just nicely warmed through; you are in that delightful realm between waking and sleeping, when the cat begins to mew outside the front door, asking to be let in. (At this moment, where is your treasure? It is partly in the warm bed, partly in the cat outside.) After lying there for some time telling yourself that the cat has a warm fur and doesn't feel the cold, that it isn't very cold anyway, that the cat should stop outside to teach it a lesson to come back earlier, that it may be some other cat, that you are jolly well going to sleep, cat or no cat,—you get up and let the cat in.

It is a cold winter night; the bed is nicely warmed through, you are nearly asleep when the cat begins to mew outside to be let in. You bounce out of bed, thinking, "I'd like to wring that blasted cat's neck," and let him in, giving him a little kick as he enters joyfully with quivering tail. Where was your treasure? You had no treasure, no warm bed, no mewing cat; you simply got up and let the cat in. Where was your heart? It was where your treasure was. When Baso was asked, "What is the Buddha?" he replied "I have no mind, no Buddha."[1] 馬祖。因僧問、如何是佛。曰、非心非佛。(無門關、第三十三則) That is, I have no bed, no cat. The bed is warm, the cat is a nuisance, but life is running freely in me, unhindered by bed or cat.

> As the bee collects nectar and departs without injuring the flower, or its colour or its scent, so let a sage dwell in the village.   Dhammapada

> 花の色香をそこなはで、ただ蜜をのみとりて行く
> 蜂の如くぞあらまほし、聖りの里にすまんにも
> (法句經 49.)

There is no friction between the bee and the flower. All things work together for good, that is, for Good; all Gain, no gain and no loss. Stevenson, in a letter to his father, 1879, writes:

[1] Solange ihr den Willen habt, den Willen Gottes zu erfüllen und irgend ein Begehren habt—auch nach der Ewigkeit, auch nach Gott—solange seid ihr nicht wirklich arm! Eckehart: *Von der Armut am Geiste.*

The wisdom of this world consists in making oneself very little, in order to avoid many knocks: in preferring others, in order that, even when we lose, we shall find some pleasure in the event, in *putting our desires outside of ourselves, in another ship, so to speak, so that, when the worst happens, there will be something left.*

Our desires belong to the self. All our wants and wishes, likes and dislikes, judgements of good and bad, belong to the self, but not to the Self. If we realise that these desires are outside the Self, in another ship, when the worst happens, that is, when everything goes against our desires and wants and judgements, something, the Self, is left. Gissing, in *By the Ionian Sea* describes a case of this self-less Self. He is speaking of a festival day in Catanzaro:

Though crowds wandered through the streets, there sounded no tumult; voices never rose above an ordinary pitch of conversation; the general bearing was dignified, and tended to gravity. One woman in particular held my attention, not because of any exceptional beauty, for, indeed, she had a hard, stern face, but owing to her demeanour. Unlike most of the peasant folk, she was bent on business; carrying upon her head a heavy pile of some ornamented fabric — shawls or something of the kind — she entered shops, and paused at house doors, in the endeavour to find purchasers. I watched her for a long time, hoping she might make a sale, but ever she was unsuccessful; for all that, she bore herself with a dignity not easily surpassed. Each offer of her wares was made as if she conferred a graceful favour, and after each rejection she withdrew unabashed, outwardly unperturbed, seeming to take stately leave. Only her persistence showed how anxious she was to earn money; neither on her features nor in her voice appeared the least sign of peddling solicitude. I shall always remember that tall, hard-visaged woman, as she passed with firm step and nobly balanced figure about the streets of Catanzaro. To pity her would

have been an insult. The glimpse I caught of her labori-
ous life revealed to me something worthy of admiration;
never had I seen a harassing form of discouragement so
silently and strongly borne.

This is what Wordsworth calls, in a late sonnet,

> The Mind's internal heaven,

but it must not be mistaken for happiness. The woman was
in heaven, but she was not happy, nor unhappy; Happy, if you
like. Another example, from Dickens' *Hard Times,* where
Sissy visits Mr. Harthouse, one of the villains of the piece.

> Her face was innocent and youthful, and its expression
> remarkably pleasant. She was not afraid of him, or in
> any way disconcerted; she seemed to have her mind en-
> tirely preoccupied with the occasion of her visit, and to
> have substituted that consideration for herself.

In the following sonnet of Wordsworth composed before 1807,
the subject is ostensibly the sonnet itself but can be taken as
equal to our own individual restricted life. To get this interpretation firmly into our minds it is better to read first of all
the last verse of Lovelace's *To Althea from Prison.*

> Stone walls do not a prison make
>   Nor iron bars a cage;
> Minds innocent and quiet take
>   That for a hermitage:
> If I have freedom in my love
>   And in my soul am free,
> Angels alone, that soar above,
>   Enjoy such liberty.

"Freedom in my love" reminds us of Mr. Pecksniff who
took a memorable advantage of this freedom on saying good-
bye to John Westlock, whom he had robbed and cheated.

"As to your forgiveness, Mr. Pecksniff," said the youth, "I'll not have it upon such terms. I won't be forgiven."

"Won't you, John?" retorted Mr. Pecksniff with a smile. "You must. You can't help it. Forgiveness is a high quality; an exalted virtue; far above *your* control or influence, John. I *will* forgive you."

And now for Wordsworth:

Nuns fret not at their convent's narrow room;
And hermits are contented with their cells;
And students with their pensive citadels;
Maids at the wheel, the weaver at his loom,
Sit blithe and happy; bees that soar for bloom,
High as the highest Peak of Furness-fells,
Will murmur by the hour in fox-glove bells;
In truth, the prison, unto which we doom
Ourselves, no prison is: and hence for me,
In sundry moods, 'twas pastime to be bound
Within the Sonnet's scanty plot of ground;
Pleased if some Souls (for such there needs must be)
Who have felt the weight of too much liberty,
Should find brief solace there, as I have found.

Here we may note the pantheistic doctrine, denied by Eckehart, that God is to be found equally anywhere. "The prison, unto which we doom ourselves, no prison is," because one thing is as good as another. The infinite is not to be seen in Heaven but "in the palm of your hand." Here once more we see that the finite *is* the infinite, the mind *is* the Mind, the ordinary man *is* Buddha. These apparently preposterous, not to say crazy notions are found to be true in experience. What experience? Wordsworth tells us, in the experience of nuns, hermits, students, maids, weavers, bees: last, but not least, in the experience of Wordsworth himself, who found, in his practice of the sonnet, that the infinite meanings of Nature and Art could be expressed only through the restrictions of the material itself.

In *Resolution and Independence* we find the solitary line

By our own spirits are we deified,

and we think immediately of the monk who wished to be free, and the counter-question by the master, Sekito (石頭),

"Who put you under restraint?"

The answer is given by Blake in the last line of the second verse of *London*.

I wander thro' each charter'd street,
Near where the charter'd Thames does flow,
And mark in every face I meet,
Marks of weakness, marks of woe.

In every cry of every Man,
In every Infant's cry of fear,
In every voice, in every ban,
The mind-forg'd manacles I hear.

There is the same thought in *The Sisters,* where Tennyson says,

My God, I would not live,
Save that I think this gross, hard-seeming world
Is our misshaping vision of the Powers
Behind the world, that makes our griefs our gains.

This self-betrayal, self-imprisonment of the mind, caused by its misshaping vision, is expressed in some famous lines from the IIIrd Act of *The Borderers:*

Action is transitory—a step, a blow,
The motion of a muscle—this way or that—
'Tis done, and in the after-vacancy
We wonder at ourselves like men betrayed.

Wordsworth states the problem, but his wording of it shows that he does not understand it properly. A better word than transitory would be instantaneous; there is no gap between the mind and the action. But afterwards when there is a separation between the mind and the Mind, there is a sense of separation, of betrayal,—not only in the after-vacancy but in the pre-vacancy also. This is what Unmon means when he says to his monks,

If you walk, just walk. If you sit, just sit; but don't wabble, whatever you do.

行但行。 坐但坐。 總不得動著。

But we need not go to China for anything. Our own experience will tell us what we want to know if only we have the genius to recognize it. Listen to Dickens in *Bleak House*. It is a humorous passage where Mrs. Badger, married for the third time, is speaking of her second, naval spouse, and quoting him in reference to Richard Carstone who, like Beowulf in his youth, was " slack."

"It was a maxim of Captain Swosser's," said Mrs. Badger, " speaking in his figurative naval manner, that when you make pitch hot, you cannot make it too hot; and that if you only have to swab a plank you should swab it as if Davy Jones were after you."

The problem is how to make this instantaneous state of non-separation between mind and Mind, a continuous one. The state of pre-and after-vacancy is a grievous one. It is Hell, for Hell is alienation from God, the Mind. An example of the pre-vacancy is the killing of the kitten by Nansen, given in a later chapter.

Another beautiful example is that of Kashin and his friend.[1]

[1] *Essays in Zen Buddhism*, No I, p. 295.

When his friend picked up a piece of tile, and putting it on a flat rock, asked him to say a word of Zen at that moment, Kashin only wabbled. The stream of life was dammed up by a small piece of tile. Just a little piece of tile and he was dead, poor fellow.

Wordsworth continues:

> Suffering is permanent, obscure, and dark,
> And shares the nature of infinity.

Suffering is living. Life is suffering. Not, there is suffering *in* life but life = suffering; this is how suffering shares the nature of infinity, of infinite life, and like life, is obscure and dark. It is permanent because the wider and deeper our life, the more the suffering. Christ himself was

> A man of sorrows and acquainted with grief.

Buddha did not cease to suffer when he arose from under the Bodhi-tree. Sweet was sweet, and sour was sour, pain was pain, and pleasure was pleasure, just the same. The meddling intellect mangles experience so badly, as Wordsworth says, that when we look at the membra disjecta, pain, pleasure, joy, grief, man, God, good, they seem as if they never have had, and never will have any connection among them. It is only when we remember the Mind, that our intellectual puzzles are solved, or rather, dissolved. You ask, "Is not good, good, and bad, bad?" The answer is that good is Good and bad is Good; or as Shinran Shônin might have said, "Even the good is Good, how much more so the bad." Never forget,

> There is nothing either good or bad, but thinking
> makes it so.

Everything, that is God, that is Good, is both good and bad, according as we look at it. Is there no Bad? Shakespeare again:

> There is some soul of goodness in things evil,
> Would men observingly distil it out.

Not that things are partly good and partly bad, but that in moments of insight, of inspiration, of anger, of extreme fear or pain, we see the absolute value, the No-value, the Goodness of things evil.

Bad, Pain, Wrong, Evil, do not exist, though bad, pain, wrong, evil certainly do. It is true that as Juliana of Norwich said,

> "To me was shown no harder hell than sin."

That is why Daruma sat nine years wall-gazing, why E-ka cut his own arm off, and died a martyr, why E-nô wandered fifteen years with the hunters. But mere self-reproach and resistance of temptation is not enough. Chômei, in the *Hôjôki,* says

> In the three worlds, everything depends on the mind. If the mind is not at rest, what are palaces and mansions? Horses and cattle, the Seven Treasures—of what avail are they?

> それ三界はただ心一つなり。心もし安からずば
> 牛馬七珍もよしなく、宮殿樓閣ものぞみなし
> (方丈記)

By "the three worlds" is meant here not the past, present and future, but 色界, the material world, 欲界, the world of sensuous desire, and 無色界, the formless, immaterial, spiritual world. Chômei is here quoting from the *Kegonkyô.* The whole passage is:

> 三界唯一心。　心外無別法。　心佛及衆生。
> 是三無差別。

> The triple world is but one Mind.   Outside the Mind there is no other reality; Mind, Buddha, all Sentient Creatures,—these three are not different things.

Christ says exactly the same thing but in very different language.

> There is nothing from without a man that going into him can defile him: but those things which proceed out of the man are those that defile the man.

The Mind cannot be defiled by its actions.   God, the Universe, cannot suffer loss or gain, defilement or purification.   If we realise that the mind is the Mind, all our actions are pure, for

> To the pure, all things are pure.

This must be understood, to the Pure, all things are Pure. Christ does not mean that to a pure-minded man the distinction between purity and impurity disappears.   Far from it; it is rather stronger than for ordinary people.   This is the answer to those who suggest that there is something dangerous about this doctrine.   It is dangerous in so far as all truth is dangerous, but to say that vicious people will make such a doctrine an excuse for viciousness—this may be so, but such people are like the wolf in Æsop's fable of the Wolf and the Lamb, they will find any excuse for wickedness, and if there is none they will do it without one.   Christ has the following parable concerning sin, emphasising the need for repentance:

> Two men went up to the temple to pray; the one a Pharisee, and the other a publican.   The Pharisee stood and prayed thus with himself, God, I thank thee, that I am not as other men are, extortioners, unjust, adulterers, or even as this publican.   I fast twice a week, I give tithes of all that I possess.

And the publican, standing afar off, would not lift up so much as his eyes unto heaven, but smote upon his breast, saying, God be merciful to me a sinner.

The word 'repentance' is not in the vocabulary of the 6th Patriarch, who says instead,

> Our pure mind is in the depraved one.

淨 心 在 妄 中。

and, in the last words he uttered, describes the enlightened man:

> Calm and lofty, he works no righteousness;
> Noble and dispassionate, he works no evil;
> Peacefully, quietly, he hears and sees nought;
> Poised and balanced, his mind abides nowhere.

兀 兀 不 修 善　　騰 騰 不 造 惡
寂 寂 斷 見 聞　　蕩 蕩 心 無 著

Stevenson agrees with him in a short fable:

The Penitent.

A man met a lad weeping. " What do you weep for ? " he asked.

"I am weeping for my sins," said the lad.

"You must have little to do," said the man.

The next day they met again. Once more the lad was weeping. "Why do you weep now ? " asked the man.

"I am weeping because I have nothing to eat," said the lad.

"I thought it would come to that," said the man.

The idea of sin, of defilement, like that of the permanence of things, rests upon the poorness of our perceptions. We say. " My hands are dirty," but they are not. The dirt is outside the hands. We might as well lay our hands on the earth itself and say, "My hands are dirty." Even if the dirt is injected into the blood, it is still separate from the blood itself; the blood is not dirty. Can you have a dirty atom, a dirty electron? So it is with the Mind. The Mind cannot be defiled by its actions. I cut off someone's leg. The action itself is neither good nor bad. I may be a doctor cutting off a leg to save a life. I may be a soldier cutting off an enemy's leg, to save, as I believe, my country. I may be a sadist, causing pain and suffering for my own pleasure. The action itself is indifferent. Everything depends on the mind, that is, whether the mind is the Mind or not. An odd definition of dirt is "Matter in the wrong place." In the same way, sin is energy in the wrong place. When the energy is in the mind, all our actions, good or bad, are sin. When it is in the Mind, when there is no separation between mind and Mind, there is no sin. "Energy in the wrong place" implies, like "matter in the wrong place," that the ordering, organising power is absent. This power is the Mind. There is nothing from without a man that can defile him. God cannot defile him. The soldiers who crucified Christ did not sin. They obeyed their orders. Christ could not forgive them. He was obeying his orders. When he said,

Father, forgive them, for they know not what they do,

this is what he meant. "They know not what they do." None of us know what we are doing, none of us can forsee the multifarious results of our actions. We must simply *act* as the soldiers acted and as Christ acted, accepting the results of the actions as they inevitably arise. This is the thought expressed in

Work out your own salvation with fear and trembling, for it is God which worketh in you both to will and to work, for his good pleasure.

In the three worlds, everything is the Mind.

But be careful, or rather, be good. When a Christian says, "I overcame the temptation with God's help," don't try to deny it; it's not necessary to explain that it's not really some separate being who did it but the Mind. Remember you are only a couple of clumsy animals making uncouth sounds to represent your inexpressible and incommunicable experiences.[1] If you feel that the experience is the same or similar, it is not necessary to force the other person to adopt your terminology. In so doing you may throw the baby out together with the bath water. Further, "we are all members one of another," and thwarting his best impulses, "causing one of these little ones which believe on me to stumble," because you dislike his vocabulary, is simply a cosmic case of cutting of the nose to spite the face. The Bible itself does not recognise this verbal distinction of *jiriki* and *tariki,* (自力、他力) self-power and other power. It says both in one breath, in the above-quoted:

Work out your own salvation with fear and trembling, for it is God which worketh in you both to will and to work, for his good pleasure.

What Zen calls the Mind, distinguishing it from the individual mind, St. Paul calls the "new man" as opposed to the "old man," and in his letter to the Colossians, he says

Ye have put off the old man with his doings, and have put on the new man, which is being renewed unto knowledge after the image of him that created him,

and, showing the absence of relativity for the "new man," continues,

[1] Weisheit ist nicht mitteilbar.
         (*Siddhartha,* Hermann Hesse)

Where there cannot be Greek and Jew, circumcision and uncircumcision, barbarian, Scythian, bondman, freeman; but Christ is all, and in all.

That is, the "new man" is Christ, just as the Mind is Buddha.

CHAPTER IX

THE MIND OF MAN

Both in Buddhism and in Christianity, when the Mind is reached, this unity is felt most strongly in regard to persons, to Christ, to Buddha, to Daruma, to the Virgin Mary, to Kwannon, to one's teacher. Zarathustra, the founder of Parsiism, doomed his religion as a world faith, by suppressing his own personality so much that we cannot realise or idealise him. The closer we are to the Mind, the closer we are to persons. Goethe's weakness lies here, Shakespeare's strength. Wordsworth tells us it is not Nature but Man that he primarily wishes to know,

> The mind of Man,
> My haunt, and the main region of my song. (*Recluse,* 793)

In memorable words Christ declares the same thing:

> And he said unto them, "The Sabbath was made for man, and not man for the Sabbath."

And not only the Sabbath exists for man but all things, Christ, God himself, were made for man, not man for them. This truth is expressed more philosophically though not more strikingly, by the 6th Patriarch in the 2nd chapter of the *Rokusodankyô*:

> Should there be no human beings, there would be no Dharmas; and hence we know that all Dharmas are made for men.

若し世人なくば、一切の萬法本自ら有ならず、
故に知らんぬ萬法は本人に自つて興ること を。
(六祖壇經)

"Dharma" is one of those very convenient words which can mean almost any thing you like. Here we may understand by Dharmas, Real Things, Reality. "Without man, there is no Reality," that is, value. It is evident that man gives value to things, value which is non-existent or at best latent in the things themselves.

The importance and unimportance of the self cannot be exaggerated.[1]

The paradox seems to disappear if we write the importance of the Self and the unimportance of the self, but this is purely a trick of words, since the self is the Self. Though arrayed or not arrayed in capital letters the paradox remains in all its glory. Buddha himself, though repudiating the idea of a separate, individual, eternal self, as being the origin of all pain and suffering, strongly emphasised the importance of self.

By self the evil is done, by self one suffers; by self evil is left undone, by self one is purified. Purity and impurity belong to the self; no one can purify another.

[1] Conversion (*satori* 悟) exemplifies this contradiction. See *The Psychology of Religion*, by E. D. Starbuck, in which a great number of cases are collected and grouped. The new life consists partly in an exalted selfhood. "God was *my* Father and Heaven *my* home." "The truths of the Bible seemed meant for me." "I began to reflect on the Bible and to perform acts of self-denial. All these things were now a part of me." This exaltation of self has in it at the same time, a self-forgetfulness, a sympathetic out-going, a process of unselfing. "I began to work for others; immediately I was anxious that all should experience the same." "I had a special feeling of reverence toward nature." The author concludes from a great number of such examples: —

In conversion, the element that is most fundamental from the standpoint of priority is the awakening of self-consciousness, while the essential factor from the standpoint of development is the process of unselfing.

我曲れるに我濁り、我正しきに我は清む、清む
も濁るも我に由る、誰かは我に代るべき。
(法句經, 165)

But though this self is so important, it is only by the oblitera-
tion of self that anything can be known, that anything can be
truly done.　As Byron, with his customary sense, remarks in
Don Juan,

> There's naught, no doubt, so much the spirit calms
> As rum and true religion.

We find the connection between rum and poetry (remember,
religion=poetry) in the poets, especially the Chinese poets.
Most of the poems praising it are of poor quality, as are poems
praising Zen, but the rum itself has a releasing power by which
the self is no longer the master: it is the servant of the Self.
It brings about the state described in the *Flaming Heart:*

> Leave nothing of my Self in me;
> Let me so read thy life, that I
> Unto all life of mine may dy.

George Herbert tries to express this God-drunken state but
fails in the attempt.

> Lord, I am Thine, and Thou art mine;
> So mine thou art that something more
> I may presume Thee mine than Thine,
> For Thou didst suffer to restore
> Not Thee, but me, and to be mine:
> And with advantage mine the more
> Since thou in death wast more of Thine,
> Yet then as mine didst me restore.
>   O, be mine still; still make me Thine;
>   Or rather make no Thine and Mine.

In spite of the belated last line, the "mine" and "Thine" are reiterated so many times that the religion disappears with the poetry.   Unity cannot be attained nor expressed by such a means.   Zen would prefer

> East is East and West is West,
> And never the twain shall meet!

Let us take one more example of what the selfless self can perceive, the first a passage from the Gospel of John, the second from a Sutra.

> There cometh a woman of Samaria to draw water from the well: Jesus saith unto her: "Give me to drink."   The Samaritan woman saith unto him therefore, "How is it that thou, being a Jew, asketh drink of me which am a Samaritan woman?" (for Jews have no dealings with Samaritans) Jesus answered and said unto her, "Every one that drinketh of this water shall thirst again, but whosoever drinketh of the water that I shall give him shall never thirst."

(Notice the relative water, of thirst and repletion, dirty and clean; and the absolute water, to which thirst and repletion have no meaning.)

> Ananda, the favourite disciple of Buddha, having been sent by the Lord on a mission, passed by a well near a village, and seeing a girl of the Matanga caste, he asked her for water to drink.   She said, "O Brahman, do not ask service of me, lest your holiness be contaminated, for I am of low caste."   Ananda replied, "I ask not for caste but for water."[1]

He asked for water, but gave her in return an eternal truth — that *water is water,* water that quenches our thirst, water that drowns us in lonely mid-ocean, the water of our tears, the

[1] Quoted in Carus, *The Gospel of Buddha*, from Burnouf, *Introduction à l'histoire du Bouddhisme Indien*, Paris, 1844; from what Sutra?

water we receive from our friends, from our enemies,—it is all water. The charming young lady next door is 60% water. To see water always simply as water, not as beneficent or malefi-cent, not as your water or my water, not as holy water or pro-fane water, "whosoever drinketh of *this* water that I shall give him, shall never thirst, but the water that I shall give him shall become in him a well of water springing up unto eternal life." This water is the elixir of life which the Chinese Emperors and the European alchemists tried to find. It was right under their noses, like Poe's Purloined Letter. But when you see a man drinking water it is not so easy, at first sight, to see whether he is drinking water or Water.

Let us ask once more, "What is the meaning, the object of Life?" Here is the answer. Remembering what Spinoza said, that

> Whoso loveth God truly must not expect to be loved
> by him in return,

and that Religion=Poetry="Comely Grace," and Science=Law="Constant Heart," read the following anonymous poem of the 17th century. It is from a young woman to a young man; but *suppose* that it is an address by Reality *to you,* as the answer to your question, "What is my relation to You, the Reality of the Universe?"

> Love not me for comely grace,
> For my pleasing eye or face,
> Nor for any outward part,
> No, nor for my constant heart,—
>   For those may fail, or turn to ill,
>   So thou and I shall sever:
> Keep therefore a true woman's eye,
> And love me still, but know not why—
>   So hast thou the same reason still
>   To doat upon me ever.

In the following short story by T. F. Powys,[1] the Mind, the mind of Mr. Cronch, is called the Oddity. This story is an example of "living by Zen" (禪に生くる) the life of perfection. Mr. Cronch is morally reprehensible, but morality, though it may be, as Arnold said, three-fourths of life, is not life itself. We must not imitate Mr. Cronch; we must not imitate Christ, or Buddha, *except in their imitating no one.* All true life is inimitable, unique, astonishing. But as Chesterton is always pointing out, we are not astonished at the right things.

Lie Thee Down, Oddity!

Though the sun shone with summer heat, the damp August warmth, giving the rather faded countryside a new glow in her cheeks — for there had been a good all-night's rain—yet Mr. Cronch wore his black felt hat, of the cut that used to be worn by evangelical clergymen in the last century.

The Honourable George Bullman, who employed Mr. Cronch as head-gardener, had spoken to him some years before about this hat of his, which was the only thing about Mr. Cronch that gave a hint of peculiarities. 'Your Methodist hat will be the ruin of you one day, Cronch,' Mr. Bullman had observed, while discussing with his gardener about the making of a new lawn.

Mr. Cronch was mowing the lawn; he had bid the under-gardener work elsewhere. To please and humour Cronch, Mr. Bullman used no motor mowing-machine. Cronch did not like them. But the under-gardener had hardly looked at the old-fashioned mower before he complained that such labour was beyond his power. To push all day such an awkward instrument 'that might,' the young man said, 'have been used by Adam,' was out of the question for anyone who understood the arts and fancies of oil-driven machinery.

Mr. Cronch did the work himself. 'One has, you know, to pay for one's oddities,' he told his wife, Jane.

[1] Reprinted from *The Listener*, 19 Sept. 1934.

At Green Gate House the grounds were always in the best order; there was never a weed in the kitchen-garden or a plantain on the lawn, but at one place, bordering the lawn, there were railings, and over these railings there was the heath.

A different world, that looked with contempt upon the soft pelt of a smooth lawn, which was indeed like the skin of a tamed beast that did nothing else but lie and bask in the sun while its sleek hide was being curry-combed by Mr. Cronch. The heath was a different matter from the garden. All was nature there, and she is a wild, fierce, untutored mother. Flowers and weeds, unnoticed, lived there, fighting the battle of their lives, careless of man, but living as they were commanded to live at the first moving of the waters. The raven and the falcon nested in the tall trees beyond a desolate swamp, and only a solitary heath-cutter might sometimes be seen with his load, taking a long track towards the waste land. Who, indeed, would view such barrenness when there was the Honourable George Bullman's garden to admire?

Mr. Bullman could afford a good gardener. The head-gardener's cottage, where Mr. Cronch and his wife lived, had every comfort of a modern well-built house. No servant of Mr. Bullman had anything to complain of. No one would leave such service, could they avoid doing so.

Over the heath, even the winds blew differently from the gentle garden ones. Out there the blasts could roar and bellow, wrench the boughs from the trees, and rush along madly, but in the summer-time garden all winds were soft.

Mr. Cronch stopped. He took the box from the mower and tipped the cut grass into the wheelbarrow. The wheelbarrow was full of sweet-smelling grass. Mr. Cronch then whistled softly, and Robert, the under-gardener, left his weeding and trundled the barrow to the cucumber-frames. He returned with the empty barrow at a slow, even pace — the gait of a well-paid gardener, as learned from Mr. Cronch.

Mr. Cronch began to mow again. He came near to

the railings beyond which was the heath. Then he stopped. He took off his hat and looked into it. He looked at the lawn. Nowhere in the world, out of England, could any lawn have been smoother or more green. There was not the smallest clover leaf there that was not consecrated to the fine taste of a proper gentleman and ready to be pressed by the elegant foot of a real lady. The smooth banks, the beds of flowers nearby, might have been a modern picture in colours; they were so unlike nature. There was nothing rude or untidy there, and every cabbage in the kitchen-garden wore a coronet.

Mr. Cronch had not changed, as the garden was changed when it became the heath. He was the same Mr. Cronch who had, at one o'clock, cut the finest cucumber in the garden for Mr. Bullman's lunch. He waited for another moment or two and then softly put on his hat. After doing so, he spoke aloud, 'Lie thee down, Oddity!' said Mr. Cronch.

Then Mr. Cronch shook his head, as much as to say that if the Oddity would not lie down, it was no fault of his. For such a being it was impossible to control. Had the Oddity lain down, then Mr. Cronch would have gone on with his work, as a wise man should who earns four pounds a week, with a good house and garden, and with leave to sell whatever he likes from his master's.

But Mr. Cronch did not start work again. It was no good; whatever happened to him the Oddity must be obeyed. The Oddity knew best. Mr. Cronch left the machine where it was, near to the railings. He walked, with the same slow gardener's walk — that showed, as much as any walk could, a hatred of all untidiness and disorder—and came to the potting-shed. There he put on his coat.

The hour was three in the afternoon. Mr. Cronch learned that from his watch. Then he listened. What he expected, happened; the church clock that was just across the way struck three.

Mr. Cronch's watch was always right.

It was no use mentioning that to the Oddity. He

would not lie down the more because Mr. Cronch's gold watch — a gift of Mr. Bullman's — went with the Church time.

Mr. Cronch shut the potting-shed door and went home. He remarked, when he saw his wife, as though he said nothing of particular interest that he had given up work at Green Gate House.   He told her to begin to pack, for they were leaving the gardener's cottage as soon as possible.

Jane thought him mad, and when the under-gardener, Robert, heard of it, he blamed the mowing-machine.   ' To have to push anything like that would drive any man away,' he said to Mr. Bullman.

The Honourable George Bullman was anxious that Mr. Cronch should still remain in the gardener's cottage. He would give him a pension, he said, for he did not want to lose so good a neighbour, whose advice he valued so highly.   Mr. Bullman, of course, blamed the hat for the trouble.

Jane wished to stay, but as the Oddity would not lie down, Mr. Cronch said they must go.

About two miles away from Green Gate House, upon the heath, there was a wretched cottage that had once been inhabited by a rabbit-catcher.   Mr. Cronch chose this hut as a residence.   About an acre of land went with it.   Mr. Cronch repaired the cottage with his own hands, and put up new railings round the garden.   In order to do this neatly, he spent most of the money he had saved in service. Then he began to reclaim the garden, that was fallen out of cultivation and was become heath again.

The wild spirit of the waste land struggled against him.   But here the poverty of the soil met its match. Nature is no respecter of persons ; she gives alike to the good and to the evil.   The potato-blight will ruin a good man's crop as well as a naughty one's.   The heath was not a curry-combed creature, tamed with milk and wine. It was a savage animal, now friendly and kind, now cruel and vindictive, then mild.   One day smiling like a pretty maid, and the next biting at you with ugly-shaped teeth.

There was no pleasant shelter there, no glass-houses, no high walls, no trimmed box-hedges. The winds of heaven had free passage, a snake could roam at large and find only its natural enemies to attack it. The wild birds had rest. Mr. Cronch bowed his head and laboured. It needed a better man than nature to cast him down. With the Oddity asleep, he could go on with his work. There was no need for him to rest, he was an obedient servant. He required no telling what to do in the way of work; even the Honourable George Bullman had put himself under Mr. Cronch's guidance. While he had hands and tools he could compel the most sour-tempered soil to serve his needs. His broad shoulders were ever bent over the ground as he turned the earthen clod.

It was not long before Mr. Cronch compelled the heath to pay him tribute, and soon a pleasant cottage and a large well-cultivated garden arose in the wilderness. There were many who respected Mr. Cronch for leaving so much good at Mr. Bullman's to do battle with nature upon the heath, but others said he only left his master out of pride. Mr. Cronch smiled when he heard that. 'Here was a fine matter, indeed,' he thought, 'that a mortal man should have pride—a nice folly to call a leaf proud that is driven willy-nilly before a November gale. A fine pride that leaf must have when, at the last, it is buried in a dung-hill!'

But if Mr. Cronch was proud, as some thought, it was only because be had the knowledge that, within him, something slept. . . .

Mr. Cronch was resting contentedly one Sunday, reading a country paper. Even that morning he had been busy in his garden, and was glad now to rest while Jane prepared the dinner.

Mr. Cronch sat there, a simple respectable working-class man—in years too—wearing spectacles, and reading his paper.

He found something to read that interested him, for he read the same paragraph three times.

This was a police case. An old woman, who was employed on Saturdays by the Stonebridge town clerk to scrub his floors, had found upon the dining-room floor a blank cheque. This cheque she had filled in herself, and because she was a simple woman, without pride, she had written the town clerk's name instead of her own.

For thirty years Mrs. Tibby had kept herself and her husband, John—who spent all his time in leaning over the town bridge to watch the water flow under—and now his one wish was to go to London to see the king. His wife wished to give him this treat; ''E do need a holiday,' she said.

When a charwoman picks up money she has a right to it. Mrs. Tibby thought the cheque money. Money, after a card-party, which there had been at the clerk's, is often left on the floor for the sweeper — that is the custom of the country.

Mrs. Tibby was not greedy: she only wrote 'four pounds' upon the cheque. She supposed that sum to be enough to take her husband to see the king. If the clerk were annoyed, she knew she could work the money out in scrubbing the floors.

When she was taken up, she could get no bail, so she went to prison.

Mr. Cronch carefully folded the paper.

The month was November. Over the heath, dark sweeping clouds, like great besoms, were driving. The two ravens, who nested in the high fir tree, enjoyed the wind. The mist from the sea brought memories to their minds; they remembered stories told of men hanged in chains on Blacknoll Mound, whose bones could be pecked clean. The ravens flew off and looked for a lamb to kill.

Mr. Cronch laid the paper on the table, beside a smoking dish of fried beef and onions – there were other vegetables to come—and a rice pudding.

Mr. Cronch rose slowly and sniffed.

But the Oddity would not lie down. So Mr. Cronch told his wife he was going out. The distance to Stonebridge was twelve miles. Mr. Cronch put on his overcoat; he went to a drawer and took out twenty-five pounds. He put on his large black hat, opened the cottage-door and went out—the rain greeted him with a lively shower of water-drops. Jane let him go. She supposed him to be in one of his mad fits, that the Giant Despair in the Pilgrim's Progress used to have.

Mr. Cronch walked along, with his usual slow steady step—the gait of a careful gardener. When he reached Stonebridge he was not admitted into the jail, and so he took a lodging for the night.

In the morning he visited Mrs. Tibby. 'I wish to be your bail,' he said, cheerfully.

Mrs. Tibby was in a maze. She did not know what she had done wrong. She was happy where she was, she was allowed to gossip with the prison charwoman, who was an old friend of hers. She begged Mr. Cronch, if he wished to be good to her, to allow her to stay with her friend, and to take her husband to London to see the king. Mrs. Tibby liked the prison, 'Everyone is so kind,' she said, 'and when I complained to the doctor about my headaches, he ordered me gin. I have never been so happy before.'

Mr. Cronch found Mr. Tibby smoking his pipe and leaning over the town bridge. He told him he was going to take him to see the king, and Mr. Tibby agreed to go, but first he knocked his pipe out on the stone coping of the bridge.

When they reached London, the king was out of town. He was soon to return, and Mr. Tibby spent the time happily, smoking his pipe and leaning over Waterloo Bridge, although the fog was so dense he could not see the river. When the king came, Mr. Cronch took Mr. Tibby into the crowd to see the king go by. Mr. Tibby sang 'God Save the King,' and shouted 'Hurrah!' The king bowed.

'Now I shall die happy,' said Mr. Tibby, 'but how shall I get home?'

Mr. Cronch paid his fare to Stonebridge, and saw him off at the station.

The weather had improved; a brisk wind from the south-west had driven off the fog. Mr. Cronch, to please

himself, walked into the city. He had fifteen pounds in
his pocket, and he looked into the shop-windows. He still
wore his large black hat, and the beggars avoided him.
They thought him a Jewish money-lender, or else a Baptist
minister. Beggars are shrewd judges of character. They
have to decide quickly. Their income depends upon it.
To beg from the wrong man means loss of time – perhaps
prison.

Mr. Cronch went down a narrow street where some
offices were. One of these was the office of a money-lender.
A gentleman, who looked worn out by sickness and trouble,
came out of that door. A woman, his wife, who carried a
baby in her arms, waited for him in the street. The gentleman shook his head. Evidently the security that he had
to offer was not good enough.

Then there arose a little conversation between them.

'I could go to mother's,' the woman said.

'If I had money, I could go with you,' the man observed, 'the change would do me good, and I might get
work in Bristol.'

'Baby will be easier to manage in a few months,' the
woman said. 'Mother will not mind taking us, but you
will have to stay here.'

'I can't let you go,' said the man.

He made a curious sound in his throat.

Mr. Cronch stood near on the pavement. Who would
have noticed Mr. Cronch? The couple paid no heed to
him. But presently they turned to where he stood, for
Mr. Cronch spoke.

'Lie thee down, Oddity!' he said, aloud.

The gentleman smiled, he could do nothing else. The
baby held out her arms to Mr. Cronch; she wanted his
hat. Mr. Cronch took two five pound notes from his wallet
and gave them to the woman. Then he walked away.

For his own pleasure, he walked out of the city into
the poor parts of the town. He walked along slowly and
looked at the vegetables in the greengrocers' shops. He
wondered that people could buy such old stuff. If he offered anything like that at the Weyminster market, he

would never find a purchaser. He remembered the lordly
freedom of the wild heath. There, nature might be cruel,
but life and death joined hands in the dance. The sun
could shine, and when darkness came it was the darkness
of God. The town was different.

Mr. Cronch went down a dingy court. Clothes were
hung from house to house, and barefooted children played
in the gutter. The air was heavy with human odours and
factory stench. Then Mr. Cronch came upon something
worse than misery.

A man sat leaning against a wall, with half his face
eaten away. His eyes were gone; he cried out to everyone whose footstep he heard, to lead him to the river.
When Mr. Cronch came by, he cried out the more. Mr.
Cronch stopped.

'Lie thee down, Oddity!' he said, angrily.

'Lead me to the river,' the man begged.

'Come,' said Mr. Cronch, and led the man to the river.
A policeman who knew the man's wish, followed them.
At the brink of the river, the man said, 'I am afraid; only
give me one little push, and I shall die.'

'Certainly,' said Mr. Cronch, and pushed him into the
river. The man sank like a stone.

The police officer came up to demand Mr. Cronch's
name and address; he had made a note of what had happened.

'You will appear at court, charged with murder,' he
said. 'But now you may go!'

Mr. Cronch walked out of the great city. He had
enough money to take him home by train, but he liked
walking. As he went along he decided to plant a part of
his garden with spinach. He had seen a good deal of this
green stuff in the London shops, and he thought he could
sell it at home.

He walked ten miles out of town, and then took a
lodging for the night. Since the Oddity had risen last,
Mr. Cronch had behaved just as a sober gardener would
when out for a holiday. When he came to an allotment,
he would look into it to see what was grown. He found

the ground good. But he believed that more glass might be used, and the city dung, he thought, too heating for the soil. He was especially interested in the window-flowers that he saw, but wondered that no hyacinths were seen, the bulbs having been all planted too late to bloom at that season.

Starting his walk again the next morning, Mr. Cronch came upon a large crowd watching a high factory chimney. This immense chimney, as high as the clouds and weighing many thousands of tons, was being brought down. The workmen were busy at its base, and the crowd watched from a safe distance.

All was ready for the fall; the masons and engineers left the chimney. But one of the men remained to give the final stroke that would cause the huge structure to sway and fall. This mason completed his task, and began to walk to safety.

When he was a few yards off the chimney, he trod upon a wet plank, hidden in the mud, and fell heavily. The spectators expected him to jump up and run off. But he did not do so.

An official held his watch in his hand, 'One, two, three,' he counted. When he reached sixty seconds the chimney would fall.

Its direction was known. It would fall directly upon the man. He tried to rise, but his leg was broken. He tried to crawl, but the pain prevented him. He raised himself up, and looked at the huge mass above him; he knew what was coming. None of the onlookers moved. It was too late to save the man; to go to him would mean certain death.

The chimney began to totter, to rock.

Then Mr. Cronch said softly, 'Lie thee down, Oddity!' but the Oddity would not listen to him. Mr. Cronch spoke in so low a tone that perhaps the Oddity never even heard what he said.

Mr. Cronch walked, with his slow gardener's step, to the man.

'What are you afraid of?' he asked him.

'Of the chimney,' cried the man, 'it's falling.'

'What if it does fall,' observed Mr. Cronch, looking up as though he thought the huge mass above him was a small pear-tree.

'It's coming,' cried the man.

Mr. Cronch took off his hat. The man smiled.

CHAPTER X

WORDS, WORDS, WORDS

This was Hamlet's answer to Polonius'

"What do you read, my Lord?"

This "words, words, words" has a deeply tragic meaning in the play. It is, in fact, the secret of Hamlet's character, the cause of the tragedy. Hamlet is the Zen-less man, whose energy, like a mouse in a wheel, goes round and round inside him and issues, not in action, but in talking. When he *does* act, as in the killing of Polonius, boarding of the pirate ship, fighting with Laertes in the grave, the final duel and killing of the king, he acts well, but it is spasmodic, it has no guiding principle in it, leads to nothing, adds difficulties instead of solving them as action should. This the king describes:

> O limèd soul, that, struggling to be free,
> Art more engaged.

From this fact comes our deep sympathy with Hamlet. Our father has not been murdered, no ghosts appear to us, no duty of revenge is laid upon us, our sweetheart does not go mad and die of grief, we do not kill our foster-father and rival in love. But we are all Hamlet in the profound sense that in our circumscribed and restricted lives, we live, that is, act truly, in fits and starts, we are dragged willy-nilly across the stage of life by circumstances. Our true life should be that of the Mind, or that of God as expressed by the King:

But 'tis not so above; *there* is no shuffling,—there the action lies in his true nature.

Let me quote Unmon once more:

If you walk, just walk.   If you sit, just sit; but whatever you do, don't wabble.

Compare this to the King's words, which apply to himself, to Hamlet, and to all of us:

And, like a man to double business bound,
I stand in pause where I shall first begin,
And both neglect.

In Oriental literature the classical example of the doctrine of silence is that of Rôshi (Laotse):

He who knows, speaks not; he who speaks knows not.

知者不言、言者不知。

Hakukyo-i (Hakurakuten) makes fun of him in the following short poem:

READING RÔSHI

The speaker knows not;
The knower speaks not;
So says Rôshi.
If Rôshi is a knower,
Why did he write 5,000 words?

讀 老 子

言者不知知者默
此語吾聞於老君
若道老君是知者
緣何自著五千文

One would have to use another five thousand words to justify

Rôshi. A better way would be to attack the enemy with another paradox: that Shakespeare was one of those who knew but did not speak. There is a famous passage in the New Testament which is pertinent here:

> Now when Herod saw Jesus, he was exceedingly glad, for he was of a long time desirous to see him because he had heard concerning him and he hoped to see some miracle done by him.
> And he questioned him in many words, but he answered him nothing.

We over-eat and hope some miracle will happen. It does not happen. We are bilious or have stomach-ache, and our health suffers afterwards. We sin and expect Christ to perform some miracle. It does not happen. We suffer for our sins, instantaneously as well as in the future. This truth is recognised even by Dante. When, in the XIVth Canto of the Inferno, Campaneus defies God to subdue him by the most dreadful punishments, Virgil retorts,

> "O Capaneo, in ciò che non s'ammorza
> La tua superbia, se' tu più punito:
>   Nullo martirio, fuor che la tua rabbia,
>   Sarebbe al tuo furor dolor compito."

> "O Capaneus, in that thy pride is yet unquenched,
> Art thou the more chastised!
>   No torment other than thy rage
>   Would be sufficient pain for this thy fury!

The wages of sin is death. No miracle will intervene, for 'sin' and 'death' are two names of one thing.

> "Can you pluck the heart out of my mystery?"

by asking questions, the meaning of which you yourself do not understand? Suppose Christ had answered Herod. Suppose he had said, "Blessed are the poor in spirit." This is "all ye know on earth and all ye need to know," but Herod could not have understood because *he didn't know what the words meant.*

Take the word "dog." To one, it means a dirty flea-incubator, to another, something to kill and eat, to another, a lovely, living creature, to another hardly anything at all, and so on, and so on. A "good" dog: in price? fierce? gentle? honest? pretty? "My" dog: as many meanings as there are "I"s in the world. So with every word in the dictionary, from aardvark to zymosis, and so with all the permutations and combinations of words that make speech. The wonder is that we understand one another at all. "Blessed are the poor in spirit." "Blessed" and "happy" look similar in meaning, but they are Heaven and Hell apart. "The poor in spirit"—how Nietzsche pitied them, that is, his connotation of the words. Confucius rightly said,

> Without knowing the force of words, it is impossible
>   to know men.

不 知 言、 無 以 知 人 也、 (論 語 二 十、 三)

But the attitude of Zen to words is, of course, not quite the same as this. It does not object to words simply because they are *clumsy* tools, but because they are *tools;* means, not ends. Or rather, it is because they are used instead of actions, because "actions speak louder than words," because we are all of us only too ready to do the Samaritan, without the oil and twopence. Montaigne reminds us of this in the following:

Zeuxidamus répondit à un qui luy demanda pourquoy les Lacédémoniens ne rédigeaient par écrit les ordonnances de la prouesse, et ne les donnaient à lire à leurs jeunes gens: que c'était parce qu'ils les voulaient accoutumer aux faits, non pas aux paroles.

On the other hand, some people speak of Zen as if it were synonymous with action. This is misleading. As Hegel said,

Das Denken ist auch Gottesdienst.

Zen is not action. Zen is the activity of the mind-body as a total entity (total here meaning universal). Zen is mind-less activity, that is, Mind-ful activity, and it may often be advisable to emphasize the mind, and say, "Take care of the thoughts and the actions will take care of themselves."

An example of this insistence on mind and of the spiritual dangers of words, both heard and spoken, is given in *Dumbness,* a poem of the 17th Century poet Thomas Traherne. The only speaking he will allow is from the Mind to the mind, and from things to the mind. Section by section, I give a paraphrase, together with quotations from Zen writings, followed by the original.

DUMBNESS

The object of our lives is to look at, listen to, touch, taste things. Without them,—these sticks, stones, feathers, shells,—there is no Deity.

> How joyful to sit by the window alone,
> Watching the leaves fall, the flowers bloom in their
>   season.

爭如獨坐虛窓下
葉落花開自有時 （碧巖錄、八十八）

The knowledge of these things is Life (not the life of life and death) and Love (not the opposite of hate).

> *Sure Man was born to meditate on things,*
> *And to contemplate the eternal springs*
> *Of God and Nature, glory, bliss, and pleasure;*
> *That life and love might be his eternal treasure.*

Man is born dumb; this typifies the fact that his real life is an inner one, not concerned with the outside world:—

> Bodhi is within our own mind:
> You will seek in vain for a solution of the
> mystery in the outside world.

菩 提 只 向 心 覓、 何 勞 向 外 求 玄。 (六祖壇經、三)

As he grows older, the speaking intellect will soon contrive the pairs of contraries by which it apprehends the outside world; then he will need an understanding of the fundamental Oneness of things to restore him to his original state of purity.

> *And therefore speechless made at first, that He*
> *Might in himself profoundly busied be:*
> *And not vent out, before he hath ta'en in*
> *Those antidotes that guard his soul from sin.*

Man is born deaf, that is, not understanding the speech of others, so that he may follow his instincts and not be confused by words.

A monk came to Unmon for enlightenment. Unmon said, "Make your bows." The monk did so and sat up. Unmon then gave him a poke with his staff and the monk retreated a little. Unmon said "You aren't blind then," and told him to come nearer; the monk did so. Unmon said, "You aren't deaf then," and added, "You understand?" The monk replied "No." Unmon said "Aha! You're not dumb, I see!" The monk realised the meaning.

僧請益雲門。 雲門云、汝禮拜着。 僧禮拜起。 雲門
以柱杖挃。 僧退後、門云、汝不是患盲。 復喚近前
來。 僧近前。 門曰、汝不是患聾、 門乃曰、還會麼。
僧曰、不會。 門云、汝不是患啞。 僧於此有省。

(碧巖錄、八十八)

Wise Nature made him deaf, too, that he might
Not be disturbed, while he doth take delight
In inward things, nor be depraved with tongues
Nor injured by the errors and the wrongs
That mortal words convey.   For sin and death
Are most infused by accursed breath,
That flowing from corrupted entrails, bear
Those hidden plagues which souls may justly fear.

(Compare this to Dai-Ô Kokushi's

Wishing to entice the blind,
The Buddha playfully let words escape his golden mouth;
Heaven and earth are ever since filled with entangling
   briars.)[1]

I was once like this: I existed in perfect Happiness, with
mountains, rivers and skies, houses, men and all creatures,
until I began to speak—and then the spell was broken!

If the fish moves, the water becomes turbid; if the bird
flies, it drops a feather.

魚 行 水 濁。   鳥 飛 毛 落。 (碧 巖 錄、十 七)

This, my dear friends, this was my blessed case;
For nothing spoke to me but the fair face
Of Heaven and Earth, before myself could speak,
I then my Bliss did, when my silence, break.[2]

Before words, that is, other people's false way of thinking,
false values, had spoiled my spontaneous intuitions, I knew
my mind only, there being no means of communication with
other minds.

[1] Quoted in Suzuki's *Manual of Zen Buddhism*, p. 175.
[2] This line is italicised in the original.   Compare Bashô's
      When I speak,
            My lips feel cold —
                  The autumn wind!
      物 い へ ば く ち び る 寒 し 秋 の 風

If we return to the root, we understand the meaning of life.
Many words, much thinking—the farther from the truth.

歸 根 得 旨　　多 言 多 慮　　轉 不 相 應 　(信 心 銘)

My non-intelligence of human words
Ten thousand pleasures unto me affords:
For while I knew not what they to me said,
Before their souls were into mine conveyed,
Before that living vehicle of wind
Could breathe into me their infected mind,
Before my thoughts were leavened with theirs, before
These any mixture was; the Holy Door,
Or gate of souls, was close, and mine being one
Within itself to me alone was known.

At that time, I lived in the Mind, not in the world of particulars. I by myself perceived Truth. My eye was single, one function alone occupied my mind—that was, to see all things as spiritual beings, above all, myself as such.

Then did I live within a world of light
Distinct and separate from all men's sight
Where I did feel strange thoughts, and such things see
That were, or seemed, only revealed to me.
There I saw all the world enjoyed by one;
There I was in the world myself alone;
No business serious seemed but one; no work
But one was found; and that did in me lurk.
D'ye ask me what? It was with clearer eye
To see all creatures full of Deities;
Especially one's self:

(The worms in the wine-butt, beetles and other small creatures,—each one sends out rays of Infinite Light, each one is an independent, self-sufficient, all-sufficing peak of life.)

醯 雞 蚊 蠓　　蠢 動 含 靈　　一 々 放 大 光 明 一 々 壁 立 萬 仞
(碧 巖 錄、 十、 垂 示)

Further, every wish based on Reality is gratified, all is Good, all is to be Enjoyed, all things are at their best; all emotions in me united in one pure, all-including ecstasy.

This is Wordsworth's

> all that we behold
> Is full of blessings.[1]

> *And to admire*
> *The satisfaction of all true desire:*
> *'Twas to be pleased with all that God hath done;*
> *'Twas to enjoy even all beneath the sun:*
> *'Twas with a steady and immediate sense*
> *To feel and measure all the excellence*
> *Of things;*

This "steady and immediate" is the hall-mark of Zen, as it is of all art, all religion.   It is the immediateness of Bashô's

> The firefly:
> > As it dropped from a leaf
> > It suddenly flew away.

草 の 葉 を 落 る よ り 飛 螢 哉

and Davies'

> Butterflies will make side-leaps,
> As though escaped from Nature's hand
> Ere perfect quite.

This steadiness, in the centre of movement, is seen in the following poem of Hakurakuten:

> The insects chirp and then are silent;
> The candle sinks, and flares up again;
> The broad leaves of the *bashô* outside the window
> Are the first to speak of the rain that begins to fall.

[1] Quoted by Suzuki in 禪の第一義, page 41; I did not notice it until then.

早 蛬 啼 復 歇   殘 燈 滅 又 明
隔 牕 知 夜 雨   芭 蕉 先 有 聲

I lived the true, Divine life.

> *'twas to inherit endless treasure,*
> *And to be filled with everlasting pleasure:*
> *To reign in silence, and to sing alone,*
> *To see, love, covet, have, enjoy, and praise in one:*
> *To prize and be ravished; to be true,*
> *Sincere and single in a blessed view*
> *Of all His gifts.*

While deaf and dumb I was infallible and unassailable; as soon as I spoke and heard, I was undone.   Before then, my mind learned from the Mind.

> *Thus I was pent within*
> *A fort, impregnable to any sin:*
> *Until the avenues being open laid,*
> *Whole legions entered, and the forts betrayed:*
> *Before which time a pulpit in my mind,*
> *A temple and a teacher I did find,*
> *With a large text to comment on.*

All existing things were divine, and spoke of Deity.

One speck of dust contains the whole earth; when one flower opens, the whole world comes into being.

一 塵 舉 大 地 收   一 花 開 世 界 起
(碧 巖 錄、 十 九、 垂 示)

> *No ear,*
> *But eyes themselves were all the hearers there,*

(Compare Bashô's

> Over the darkening waves,
>   The wild ducks' cries
>   Are dim and white.)

海くれて鴨の聲ほのかにしろし　　芭　蕉

And every stone and every star a tongue,
And every gale of wind a curious song.
The Heavens were an oracle, and spake
Divinity: the Earth did undertake
The office of a priest; and I being dumb
(Nothing besides was dumb) all things did come
With voices and instructions;

But as soon as I began to express myself, to explain, to
compare, illusions arose, things which have no basis in Reality.
The voice of the Mind became inaudible; the passional rubbish
and intellectual subtleties, all the more pernicious because intangible, destroyed my peace.

But when I
Had gained a tongue, their power began to die.
Mine ears let other noises in, not theirs,

(Compare

All relativity is the result of intellection;
Why grasp so earnestly after hallucinations and
flowers of air?)

一切二邊　妄自斟配
夢幻空華　何勞把提　(信心銘)

A noise disturbing all my songs and prayers.
My foes pulled down the temple to the ground;
They my adoring soul did deeply wound,
And casting that into a swoon, destroyed
The Oracle, and all I there enjoyed:
And having once inspired me with a sense
Of foreign vanities, they march out hence
In troops that cover and despoil my coasts,
Being the invisible, most hurtful hosts.

These "foreign vanities" are described by Daitô Kokushi as

Reading the Scriptures, reciting prayers, sitting in contemplation for hours at a stretch, sleeping little, eating only once a day, observing the religious festivals, spending all the hours of the day in religious practices.

誦 經 諷 呪　長 坐 不 臥　一 食 卯 齋　六 時 行 道

Such things have nothing essentially religious in them.

Yet the first instincts and intuitions were so deep as to be ineffaceable.　Above all the tumult of this world I still can hear, when I will, that still, small voice.

> *Yet the first words mine infancy did hear,*
> *The things which in my dumbness did appear,*
> *Preventing all the rest, got such a root*
> *Within my heart, and stick so close unto 't.*
> *It may be trampled on, but still will grow*
> *And nutriment to soil itself will owe.*
> *The first Impressions are Immortal all,*[1]
> *And let my enemies hoop, cry, roar, or call,*
> *Yet these will whisper if I will but hear,*
> *And penetrate the heart, if not the ear.*

So with regard to the Buddha holding up a flower before the congregation of monks and Mahakasyapa smiling as he understood the meaning,

> Buddha was silent, but explained everything;
> Kashô heard nothing, but apprehended all.

世 尊 不 說 說　迦 葉 不 聞 聞　(禪 林 句 集)

---

[1] This line is italicised in the original.

CHAPTER XI

FIGURES OF SPEECH

Like Emerson, who, since he was a boy, wished to write a discourse on Compensation, I have always wished to write one on the figures of speech, for it seemed to me that on this subject life was ahead of rhetoric, and the poets knew more than the grammarians taught. The text-books tell us that "a figure of speech is a deviation from the plain and ordinary way of speaking, for the sake of effect." This is not so. Byron says,

> I am as a weed
> Flung from the rock, on ocean's foam, to sail
> Where'er the surge may sweep, the tempests' death prevail.

Wordsworth,

> It is a beauteous evening, calm and free:
> The holy time is quiet as a Nun,
> Breathless with adoration.

Tennyson, speaking of a woman staring hopelessly out of a window,

> Fixed like a beacon tower above the waves
> Of tempest, when the crimson-rolling eye
> Glares ruin, and the wild birds on the light
> Dash themselves dead.

The above three similes are not deviations from the ordinary way of *saying* things; the things are *seen and felt* so differently so strongly, that the expressions of them necessarily have a different form, a different figure, of speech. But this figure of

speech, is a figure of apprehension, a form of enlightened perception; it is, that is to say, a soul state in which the barriers
between soul and soul, soul and Soul become lower (simile,
metonymy, synechdoche,) or entirely disappear (metaphor).
Figures of speech are therefore in no sense of the word orna-
ments of language or embellishments of literature, any more
than child-birth could be termed "a deviation from the ordinary way of living, for the sake of effect." A vast number of
figures of speech, it is true, originally living and vigorous, are
now mere fossils of language without power to move themselves or us, but philological passion can imagine them as
once they were,

> Voyaging through strange seas of thought, alone.

Yet others were from the beginning only intellectual conceits,
or imitations, or actual conscious deviations from the ordinary
way of speaking for the sake of variety or to bolster up a
feeble thought. But here we wish to speak not of the figures
of speech which have built up our language and ways of
thought, which are in our blood, so to speak, nor of the flashy
imitations or spiritless counterfeits of poetasters and dilettantes,
but of the discoveries and revelations of the poets in their most
inspired moments. The proverb says, "Great wits jump," and
figures of speech are jumps, jumps out of appearance into reality, a return to the unity of things, to the ever-blessed One.
The simile says, "That looks like your long-lost brother!" the
metaphor says, "It *is* your brother!" All things are Buddha.
I am Buddha. The flower is Buddha. I am the flower. These
statements are not syllogistic, not deducible one from another,
neither are they disconnected. When Heine says,

> Du bist wie eine Blume,

or Burns,

> O my Luve's like a red, red rose
> That's newly sprung in June:

from the point of view of Zen they are far from speaking extravagantly or fancifully, — rather they are understating a matter of fact. It is amusing to see how difficult the textbooks find it to explain the difference between simile and metaphor, for, if they are both merely comparisons, what fundamental difference can it make whether the word 'like' or 'as' is omitted or not? When we see that the simile is an approach towards and the metaphor a consummation of identity, the difference between the two and the degree of passion and intensity becomes understandable. It is the difference between "I and the Father are one," and "I and the Father are two." Nevertheless it cannot be laid down as a rule that the simile is always weaker emotionally than the metaphor; as evidence, the three similes quoted at the beginning of this chapter, and

> pity, like a naked new-born babe
> Striding the blast.

However, the simile is usually more decorative in its nature and has less identity in it than the corresponding metaphors. Compare the simile in *King John,*

> Life is as tedious as a twice-told tale
> Vexing the dull ear of a drowsy man,

with the metaphor in *Macbeth,*

> It is a tale
> Told by an idiot, full of sound and fury,
> Signifying nothing.

In the latter example, God is the idiot; human beings are the voice of God, raving and boasting, just meaningless gibble-gabble. From the intellectual standpoint, nothing less and nothing more can be said of the meaning of life in this world, than is expressed in this metaphor. Take another example, from Shelley:

> Like a star of heaven
> In the broad day light,
> Thou art unseen, but yet I hear thy shrill delight.

The simile of the first part is charming and no more: it takes us nowhere; but "I hear thy shrill delight" is much more profound even than the simile of the previous verse:

> Like an unbodied joy whose race is just begun.

To hear the actual skylark, that is difficult enough, but to go beyond even that, and hear "joy," hear "delight," to hear, not one's own joy reflected from elsewhere, but the joy of the skylark, the joy of nature, the joy of the 9th Symphony, — to hear Joy, is indeed a wonderful experience. This is a very different thing from the

> Joy, whose hand is ever on his lips
> Bidding adieu;

Keats is speaking here of the relative joy, opposed to melancholy and says, rightly enough, that the two are inseparable, they go together. The other Joy of Shelley's *Skylark,* appears in the *Ode to Autumn* and the *Ode on a Grecian Urn,* but unnamed.

Another example from the *Skylark* is

> All the earth and air,
> With thy voice is loud,

that is, not only the skylark is singing but the trees and stones and rivers, the clouds, winds and air,—all is singing, singing with the voice of the skylark. If we explain it "The Skylark is singing and the voice is echoed everywhere," we have allowed the intellect to destroy the poetry and reduce the vision to a decoration.

The intellect is like armour, it guards us from mistakes, but it cannot warm us, cannot give us the life it protects. If once we sink down from the absolute to the relative, from Joy to joy, from the voice of Nature to the voice of the individual bird, it is difficult to reattain these lofty regions; we feel like poor Susan in Wordsworth's poem:

She looks, and her heart is in heaven: but they fade,
The mist and the river, the hill and the shade:
The stream will not flow, and the hill will not rise,
And the colours have all pass'd away from her eyes!

Another metaphor, or rather, personification, which takes our heart into heaven, is Herrick's *Daffodils*.

Fair Daffodils, we weep to see
    You haste away so soon;
As yet the early-rising sun
    Has not attain'd his noon.
        Stay, stay
    Until the hasting day
        Has run
    But to the evensong;
And, having pray'd together, we
    Will go with you along.

Is to speak of the daffodils praying only a "figure of speech"? Did not a greater poet than Herrick say, "Consider the daffodils how they pray; they toil not, neither do they spin, like Martha, but only sit at the feet of God, like Mary. Yet even Solomon's father David, the greatest man of prayer in the history of the Jews, for all his eloquence, could not pray as well as one of these daffodils." Did he not also say, when his disciples were rebuked for allowing the people to shout "Hosannah,"

"I tell you that if these should hold their peace, the stones would immediately cry out!"

If a man can pray with the daffodils he need never enter a church. This is the mood in which the well-off Kikaku saw a beggar one fine day:

> The beggar wears
> Heaven and earth
> As his summer clothes.

夏衣天地を著たる乞食かな   其 角

In the example already quoted,

> It is a beauteous evening, calm and free,
> The holy time is quiet as a Nun
> Breathless with adoration.

If we take this as a formal simile we shall be compelled to ask the question, "Whom does the evening adore?" But such is not the point here: the real thought is not a comparison between the evening and a nun. Wordsworth felt that that particular moment was holy. True enough, all moments are holy, equally holy, but we cannot feel them so. And just as Shelley heard Joy, so Wordsworth felt Adoration, not his own adoration of nature or a nun's adoration of the Godhead, but simple Adoration as such, to which the adjectives "calm and free," are to be applied. There is passion in Nature, but it is calm. There is religion in Nature ("Natural piety") but it is free. Man is the only religious animal in the sense that he is the only animal who finds it necessary to assert the fact, who indulges in the imperfect offices of prayer and praise, the only animal which needs figures of speech. The white hot nebulae, the blazing suns of the galaxy separated by unthinkable myriads of miles of empty space—they are the daffodils of the sky,

> stretched in never-ending line
> Along the margin of a bay.

Metaphors and similes have the double power — A is like B, then B is like A.   A is B, then B is A.

> Am not I
> A fly like thee?

sings Blake in a rather simple-simon way, but immediately afterwards we get the lines

> Or art not thou
> A man like me?

which changes the whole matter.   This is what Issa means when he says in his poem of the Fly,

> See how it wrings
>   Its hands, its feet!
>   O, kill it not!

やれうつな蝿が手をすり足をする　　一　茶

Keats says,

> I who still saw the universal sun
> Heave his broad shoulder o'er the edge of the world.

Dr. Bain, author of *English Rhetoric and Composition,* says of this:

> The similitude of "heaving the shoulder" is not fitted to elevate the subject, nor is it suited to give the pleasure of fanciful comparison. It is wanting in dignity, as applied to the sun, and may even suggest ludicrous associations.

This criticism is not to be taken as typical of the attitude of rhetoriticians but rather as a *reductio ad absurdum* of their principles. We do not wish to elevate or degrade any subject, nor to give pleasure by fanciful comparison. To speak of dignity in regard to the sun or a squib, the Pacific Ocean or the drip on the end of someone's nose, is equally meaningless. There is no need to be afraid of associations. Ludicrous associations are rather to be sought for, as showing a thing shorn of false ornament and in the state of nature. James Legge, translator of the Chinese classics, after giving details of Confucius' life and manners, way of eating, sleeping, and so on, says,

"Somehow he is less a sage to me after I have seen him at his table, in his undress, in his bed, and in his carriage."

What would the reverend gentleman say of Johnson with his dislike of clean linen, and table manners of a hog, of Ryôkan with his lice and Issa full of fleas? But from the point of view of Zen the "broad shoulder" of the sun is important because the sun has a broad shoulder and therefore my shoulder is the sun's. If I lift my shoulder the sun rises; if I lower it, it sinks. If you only *think* about this kind of statement it seems crazy beyond all endurance, but then so does that of Blake when he declares that to him the sun is not a golden disk the size of a shilling, but an infinite company of holy angels singing hallelujah. To see the sun as a shoulder, that is not so difficult, but to see a shoulder as the sun, that needs poetry, inspiration, religion, Zen.

The mixing of metaphors so severely castigated in the text books and held up to derision by schoolmasters, that feeble tribe, far from being a vice, is the highest of virtues, *if you can do it properly,* for, as its name implies, it is God seen not merely as a Trinity but as an even higher multiple of real things.

In Addison's well known lines,

> I bridle in my struggling muse with pain
> That longs to launch into a bolder strain,

what is wrong is not the mixing of metaphors but the separate
metaphors themselves, which are feeble and hackneyed and in
no sense forms of the apprehension of reality, but disguises of
platitudes.   In Shelley's

>   O thou,
> Who chariotest to their dark wintry bed
> The wingèd seeds, where they lie cold and low,
> Each like a corpse within its grave,

far from feeling any incongruity among "chariotest," "bed,"
"winged," "corpse," the immobility of the flying seeds, the
immateriality of all vehicles, the identity of sleep and death —
all these truths are spontaneously and simultaneously perceived.
Another example, from Part VI of *The Ancient Mariner*:

> The moonlight steeped in silentness
> The steady weathercock.

Moonlight is neither silent nor noisy.   To understand the connection between the moonlight, the silence and the steadiness
of the weather-cock we must first re-read a passage from the
Rokusôdangyô.   After staying in *Shi-e* with a party of hunters
for fifteen years, the 6th Patriarch, who had taught them as
befitted their understanding, began to think it was time for
him to go out into the world again, so he left for Hôshôji in
Canton.

> In those days Inshū was preaching on the Maha
> Parinirvana Sutra (Nehankyô.) At a certain time a flag
> was blowing about in the wind. One monk said, "The
> wind is moving"; another said, "The flag is moving," and

the quarrelling was endless. Enô (the 6th patriarch) said, "The wind is not moving, the flag is not moving; what is moving is your minds." The assembled monks were thunderstruck at this.

遂 出 至 廣 州 法 性 寺、 值 印 宗 法 師 講 涅 槃 經、 時 有 風 吹 旛 動、 一 僧 曰 風 動、 一 僧 曰 旛 動、 議 論 不 已、 慧 能 進 曰、 不 是 風 動、 不 是 旛 動、 仁 者 心 動、 一 衆 駭 然。

"The moonlight steeped in silentness the steady weather-cock." It was the mind of the Ancient Mariner, the mind of Coleridge that was steeped in silentness, that was moonlit, that was steady. "The darkness steeps in turbulence the whirling weather-cock." It is our minds that are dark and turbulent and whirling.

There's not the smallest orb which, thou behold'st
But in his motion like an angel sings,
Still quiring to the young-eyed cherubins.

But Shakespeare tells us where this music of the spheres has its origin:

Such harmony is in immortal souls,

and why the moonlight seems silent and the stars of night without voice:

But whilst this muddy vesture of decay
Doth grossly close it in we cannot hear it.

The Parables of Christ, especially the apparently irrational and perverse ones, are full of Zen, for the parable with its meta-phorical form is a chance to circumvent the intellect and its pedestrian logic. The parable of Dives and Lazarus is a good example. This is not to show that rich men will go to Hell and poor men will go to Heaven, however much we would like to believe it sometimes. It is to show that the apparent values of persons and of their actions, has no connection whatever with their real ones. It teaches the *irrationality* of the universe, as judged by our ordinary relative, intellectual standards. There is the same irrationality in the parable of the Lost Sheep where there is so much joy over the one sinner that repents. Again in the parable of the Prodigal Son, where vice is rewarded, not virtue. ("A fool who *persists* in his folly will become wise": the importance is the persistence, not the goodness or badness; following your instincts to the bitter end, not behaving like a virtuous machine). Christians find great difficulty in explaining away the parable of the Unjust Steward. (Luke 16.) Christ shows us that the world is a place where cleverness is as important as goodness. Othello ruined himself and others because he was a fool: stupidity is not virtue. The parable of the Importunate Friend, (Luke 11), is likewise in praise of energy, importunity.

Ask, and it shall be given you, seek, and ye shall find; knock, and it shall be opened unto you.

"Knock," of course, means run your head against the door like a battering ram. While you stand wondering what is the meaning of life, it has no meaning.

The parable of the Great Supper, with the phrase "compel them to come in," used to justify persecution of heretics during the Middle Ages, expresses Christ's intense feeling of the spiritual determinism of the Universe, a "stream of tendency" by which all men, all sentient creatures, shall become Buddha, willingly, if they wish, and willy-nilly, if they do not. When, again, we interpret the parable of the Sower according to Zen, it gains greatly in depth. The Universe is the great Sower. The seeds are sown everywhere, indiscriminately, impartially.

Everything shouts the truth in our ears, brandishes the truth in our faces, but seeing, we see not, hearing, we hear not. What is this seed of truth that we will not receive into our hearts? It is what the Roman Centurion understood so well as to be praised by Christ above all the Jews he had ever known. The universe says "Come!" and we come, "Go!" and we go, "Be angry!" and we are angry, "Be sad!" and we are sad. While we look for truth or look for pleasure, all is dark and mysterious but when we simply obey orders,

> Safely through the world we go.

Synechdoche, the naming of a thing by its part is a figure of speech illustrating the ability of the mind to perceive the whole in the part, or as Confucius says, "Seeing one we know the other three" 舉一明三 .

> How beautiful upon the mountains are the feet of him
> that bringeth good tidings, that publisheth peace.
> (*Isaiah* 52, 7.)

In general, feet are seen as things devoid of poetry, but suddenly, as the feet of the messenger of peace, they are things of power and beauty, never again merely the dirty, dusty, smelly things they were before. Just as the style is the man, so the feet are the man.

Metonymy, the naming of a thing by some accompaniment, shows our innate capacity to perceive the weakness and instability of the divisions the mind invents between one thing and another.

> O for a beaker full of the warm South.

The blue sea, the hot sun, the brown peasants, the vines, the grapes, the wine, the ecstacy of feeling — all are one in this line, and this all-one is the essence of poetry, of art, of religion. It is Zen.

> Lycidas, your sorrow, is not dead.

The man himself, the grief we feel at his death, these are separated by the mind, by language, by speech into these two different things. But in our experience these two are one, and in the figure of speech, "Lycidas, your sorrow," they are seen as they really are, two names for a single reality. "Is not dead" refers only to Lycidas; just for an instant, while the eye moves across the three words "Lycidas, your sorrow," this unity of Subject, predicate, object, (I sorrow for Lycidas, I= sorrow=Lycidas) is perceived in a flash of enlightenment, then all is dark again,—but with a difference.

The transferred epithet is another interesting example of the interchangeability of subject and object. The adjective qualifying the subject is transferred to the object and *vice versa*. So, "I lay my head on the weary pillow." (When this unity of subject and object is not properly understood, we get the pathetic fallacy. That is to say, the head and the pillow are conceived as two entirely separate objects and the weariness is ascribed to the pillow only. Once we understand that weariness may be predicated of the head or the pillow equally, the pathetic fallacy becomes impossible). The opposite case we get in

> Annihilating all that's made
> To a green thought in a green shade,

where the greenness of the object is ascribed to the subject. Another very beautiful example occurs in one of Hardy's novels, *The Woodlanders,* I think. A man with a great love of trees and special ability in tree-planting, is said to have "the green hand."

> The little fields made green
> By husbandry of many thrifty years.

What a history of millions of mankind, dead and living, in those two words "thrifty years"; and how different from "years of thrift." In "thrifty years" we feel the deep connection between man and the passing of time, and

> "In the sweat of thy face shalt thou eat bread."

It is like seeing for the first time the picture of Millais' *The Man with the Hoe.*

> Where the rude axe with heavèd stroke
> Was never heard the nymphs to daunt.

of Milton's *Il Penseroso,* does not go so deep, it is more charming, but it is a good example of the moment of heaving the axe when we forget ourselves and the axe and the tree, and the epithets themselves become interchanged. One more example from Gray's *The Bard:*

> With haggard eyes the Poet stood
> (Loose his beard and hoary hair
> Streamed like a meteor to the troubled air)
> And with a master's hand and prophet's fire
> Struck the deep sorrows of his lyre.

Anyone who plays a musical instrument can testify to this identification. We play, not with our fingers but through our fingers. We play with our characters. The bard plucks the strings of the lyre. He strikes the lyre, a part of his own body. He strikes his own breast, arouses and expresses his passions, his sorrows. So he strikes, not the material lyre, but the sorrows themselves which reverberate in the strings of the lyre. So we say, "I play Bach, I play Handel," not "the music of

Bach and Handel" or "the piano works of Bach and Handel."
The mind, the body, its instruments; the musician, his hands,
the music; the player and what is played,—

> Draw, if thou canst, the mystic line
> Severing rightly his from thine,
> Which is human, which divine.

This chapter is rather scrappy and rambling, but the point
to be grasped is that in some ways language is wiser than the
men who use it; that we often say more than we mean, especially the poets; that we speak more truly than we know.
Further, that figures of speech, when passion-inspired, reveal
the identity of what is separated by the logical intellect.   And
last, that we should constantly strive, in our reading of literature, to recreate with the writer, that mood in which we are
able, if only for a moment, to apprehend things in their unity,
their oneness of nature, their absoluteness.

CHAPTER XII

THE PALE CAST OF THOUGHT

The intellect has suffered a good deal of abuse at the hands of writers of all kinds. Hamlet, as befits a poet, speaks slightingly of the pure intellect:

There are more things in Heaven and Earth, Horatio,
Than are dreamt of in your philosophy.

Fitzgerald has his famous lines:

Myself when young did eagerly frequent
Doctor and Saint, and heard great Argument
About it and about: but evermore
Came out by the same door as in I went,

which many no doubt have tested and approved in experience. Even Bacon says in his essay *Of Goodness,*

The desire of power in excess caused the angels to fall: the desire of knowledge in excess caused man to fall.

Both Keats and Wordsworth agree that science is the arch-enemy of poetry. In *Lamia,* Keats says,

There was an awful rainbow once in heaven;
We know her woof, her texture; she is given
In the dull catalogue of common things.
Philosophy will clip an angel's wings.

Wordsworth, in *A Poet's Epitaph,*

Physician art thou?—one, all eyes,
Philosopher!—a fingering slave,

> One that would peep and botanize
> Upon his mother's grave?

and in *The Tables Turned,*

> Our meddling intellect
> Mis-shapes the beauteous forms of things:—
> We murder to dissect.
>
> Enough of Science and Art;
> Close up those barren leaves;
> Come forth, and bring with you a heart
> That watches and receives,

berates the intellect soundly.   Newman in *The Dream of Gerontius* goes so far as to say

> It is the very energy of thought
> Which keeps thee from thy God;

but no one has equalled Blake in his denunciations of Reason! His vocabulary is very peculiar and misleading, but if we read the following passages from *Jerusalem,* we can understand his use of "intellect" meaning the poetic imagination:

I know of no other Christianity and of no other Gospel than the liberty both of body and mind to exercise the Divine Arts of Imagination.
What is the Divine Spirit?   Is the Holy Ghost any other than an Intellectual Fountain?
What are all the gifts of the Gospel?   Are they not all mental gifts?
What is the life of Man but Art and Science?

I care not whether a man is Good or Evil, all that I care Is whether he is a Wise man or a Fool.   Go! put off Holiness,
And put on Intellect.

For a Tear is an Intellectual thing.
But the Spectre, like a hoar frost and a mildew, rose over

Albion,
Saying: I am God, O Sons of Men! I am your Rational
Power!
Am I not Bacon and Newton and Locke, who teach Humility, to Man,
Who teach Doubt and Experiment?

He can never be a friend to the Human Race who is the
preacher of Natural Morality or Natural Religion.

I will not Reason and Compare: my business is to Create.

This is the Spectre of Man, the Holy Reasoning Power.

This Reasoning Power is "a murderer of every Divine
Member," in that it takes the life from every object by abstracting the Relative qualities in which every object exists,
and makes a dead thing of it.

The Zen expression for intellection is "grasses" 草 or
"briars and wistarias" 葛藤. Blake's expression is similiar:

Reasonings like vast Serpents
Enfold around my limbs, bruising my minute articulations. . . .
I turn my eyes to the Schools and Universities of Europe,
And there behold the Loom of Locke whose Woof rages dire,
Washed by the Water-wheels of Newton: cruel Works
Of many Wheels I view, wheel without wheel, with cogs
tyrannic,
Moving by compulsion each other.

The Reason, or Spectre of man, is the state of the ordinary
man bound hand and foot by the contraries under which we
perceive the world; the Mind, Blake calls Humanity, in the
following, descriptive of the moment when a man becomes free
of life-death, gain-loss, here-there.

Each Man is in his Spectre's power
Until the arrival of that hour,
When his Humanity awake
And cast his Spectre into the Lake.

All this begins to make one think there must be something good about the rational power, if it can stir up such indignation. It is hard for a rich man to enter into the Kingdom of Heaven, but it is also hard for a fool. Is it a coincidence that Christ and Buddha had extremely powerful and subtle intellects? Christ could quibble with the best of the Jewish Sophists, when necessary. And when we consider the case of Blake himself, is it not a fact, that, despite his mysticism and poetry and painting, his chief defect was, not being a genius or mad, but that he was a bit of a fool? To paint pictures which every one can understand, and write poems which nobody can make head or tail of without an answer book, argues lack of ordinary foresight. We do not find people like Inge or Shaw despising the reasoning faculty, because they have it. The essence of it is, of course, the power of comparison and the power of self-criticism. It is the scissors and pruning hook of the mind, without which no work of art, in its symmetric perfection, can be produced. Blake himself illustrates this in, for example, the composition of such a poem as the *Tiger,* (see the Oxford *Blake,* pages 85-88) with all the different drafts and alternatives. This is a parable of our own lives, and the relation of the intellect to Zen. Just as

The law was our schoolmaster to bring us unto Christ,

so the intellect leads us to Zen.

We are not extortioners, unjust, adulterers, even as other men. We fast twice a week, give tithes of all we possess. We read the sacred books, pray to God, repent of our sins. Yet something annoying happens, some trifling danger arises, and we find, *on thinking it over afterwards,* that however qualified we may be for playing golden harps before God Almighty, we do not know how to deal with importunate beggars, impudent servants, insolent officials, the haggling vegetable man, being pushed in and out of tram-cars, all the hundred and one trivialities of life *in this world.* The intellect it is which compares our real and ideal actions, which tells us we are not happy when we suppose we are, which reminds us that our past painful experiences are our most valuable possessions, if only we know how to use them.

> A comfort seemed to touch
> A heart that had not been disconsolate:
> Strength came where weakness was not known to be.
> (*Prelude,* IV, 153.)

To be ungrateful to your own intellect is just as bad as ingratitude to a benefactor. The only thing is, the intellect must not be divided from the energy of the personality and work in vacuo, or as a substitute for the activity of the person as a whole. *But it is the intellect which reminds us of this.* The intellect is sometimes spoken of as raising problems. It does nothing of the sort. Life raises the problems; disease, accident, violence without, greed, laziness, cruelty within, give us our daily, hourly examination. We fail; and it is the intellect which tells us so, which points to the problems, sorts and arranges them, ticks off those we have successfully solved.

After giving the intellect its due we can now define its limitations. There are three ways in which the intellect over-reaches itself.

1. It usurps the function of religion, in supposing it can understand life. The intellect can understand intellectual things; life can understand living things. But they cannot understand each other, so long as they are apart. Ikkyû says we cannot find out how the flowers grow by cutting open a tree:

> Tear open the tree!
>   And can you see
> The cherry flowers that yearly
>   Bloom on Yoshino?

> とし毎に咲くや吉野のさくら花
>   樹をりてみよ花のありかを

Emerson has a similar thought in *Each and All:*

> I wiped away the weeds and foam,
> I fetched my sea-born treasures home;
> But the poor, unsightly, noisome things
> Had left their beauty on the shore,
> With the sun and the sand and the wild uproar.

We see the necessity for that immediacy which Zen insists on, and which is not the characteristic of the intellect. The intellect is a collector.

2. It usurps the function of poetry when it replaces the imagination, the compassion, of the poet. It is particularly detestable in, for example, Tennyson's

> Faith hears the lark within the songless egg.

One would like to read some lines on a maiden asleep on a pillow stuffed with the feathers of the lark which would have come out of the egg only someone ate it. This is not poetry at all. It is a kind of proleptic vivisection. We get the same thing in the last two lines of the first verse of *The Palm Willow* of Robert Bridges.

> See whirling snow sprinkles the starved field,
>   The birds have stayed to sing;
> No covert yet their fairy harbour yields.
>   When cometh Spring?
> Ah! in their tiny throats what songs unborn
>   Are quenched each morn.

A similar case, in the human world, is Davies'

> Sweet Poesy, why thou art dumb!
>   I fear thy singing days are done;
> The poet in my soul is dying
>   And every charm in life is gone.

When a poet begins to talk like this, he is finished, done for, dead. Intellection, as in the later Wordsworth, replaces imagination, and imagination which is the becoming one with the thing contemplated, has no connection with the mere desire to write verses.

Two examples from early haiku follow:

> A fallen flower
>   Flew back to its branch!
>   No, it was a butterfly.

落 花 枝 に 歸 る と 見 れ ば 胡 蝶 か な　　　守　武

> Their skeletons wrapt
>   In silk and satin,
>   They view the cherry blossoms.

骸 骨 の 上 を 裝 う て 花 見 か な　　　鬼　貫

Of the first we may say that poetry should deal with facts, not mistakes or optical illusions; whether the things concerned are beautiful or not does not affect the question. And of the second, human beings are only skeletons, it is true, and silk and satin only rags, but cherry blossoms are only little flat pieces of coloured pulp.

3. Last, the intellect is guilty of constructing dogmas, systems of philosophy, which imprison the mind, until it mopes like a monkey in a cage. In *Empedocles on Etna,* Arnold speaks of the two enemies of life, of Zen:

> Some bondage of the flesh or mind,
> Some slough of sense, or *some fantastic maze*
> *Forged by the imperious lonely thinking power.*

"Maze" is the right word for the history of philosophy. "Fantastic" is justly applied to what leaves out of account life itself. "Forged" shows its mechanical nature; "imperious," the dreadful intensity of the destructive analysis. "Lonely" is interesting. Emotion may be communicated in a variety of ways, it is infectious. Thought is peculiarly individual, communicable only in words, and establishing barriers between the fool and the sage where emotions unite. Nothing divides men so much as thought.

It is true, in a way, to say that Zen may belong to the warrior, to the priest, to the pimp, to the Christian, to the atheist, to the fanatic, to the animal, to the saint; yet from another point of view it is not so, for, though Zen leaves a man free to believe in any doctrines, to perform any actions, in its relation to our beliefs it demands that we distinguish the essential from the unessential. What is the essential? Zen is the only essential. What is unessential? All the rest, especially the emotional and intellectual rubbish that hinders our freedom. Just as

> Perfect love casteth out fear,

so true Zen casts out every kind of bondage, which includes fear.

Freedom is perfect, pure freedom, but Milton said of liberty,

> For who loves that must first be wise and good.

Freedom means freedom from error and superstition, freedom to be good. The more freedom the more truth; the more truth the more freedom,—this is a natural law everywhere demonstrated in the history of human thought. Thus the construction of dogmatic beliefs by the highest intellect reduces man to the same state of mental slavery as the crudest and most infantile superstition.   The philosopher and the savage are just as distant from the truth. Nevertheless, as pointed out above, while there's intellect, there's hope. False and unfounded notions, impossible romantic illusions may be destroyed with the help of the very intellect which helped to create them.

If the intellect then is simply a vacuum-cleaner, there is nothing to do but rely upon instinct. Emerson accepts this alternative, saying, in *Nature*,

> If the single man plant himself indomitably on his instincts, and there abide, the huge world will come round to him.

Zen also says we are to act self-lessly, thought-lessly, instinctively, taking no thought, not only for the morrow, but for to-day, for the present as well. So be it, but what instinct are we to follow? Shall we follow them all as they arise in their wild confusion? And if we distinguish between them, the resulting action can no longer be called instinctive. The Mind is not what William James, in criticism of Hegel's Absolute, called 'block Reality.' It is alive, and in the temporal process of becoming vegetable, animal, conscious, self-conscious, many instincts have arisen and fixed themselves almost incurably on the human mind. What Zen wishes to do is to take us back to the most primitive condition of all, to lead us to become, not only children, but foetuses, amoebae. Santayana is therefore quite correct when he writes (contemptuously) of Mysticism in the last chapter of the *Life of Reason:*

Mysticism is the most primitive of feelings and only visits formed minds in moments of intellectual arrest and dissolution. It can exist in a child, very likely in an animal; indeed, to parody a phrase of Hegel's, the only pure mystics are brutes.

Wordsworth says the same thing, only complimentarily:

> Fallings from us, vanishings,
> Blank misgivings of a creature
> Moving about in worlds not realised,
> High instincts before which our mortal nature
> Did tremble like a guilty thing surprised.

What is this fundamental instinct, this ground of being which Zen wishes us to reach? Freud tells us it is sex, and Zen will not wish to dispute this. Satori is a spiritual orgasm. The sexual orgasm is a physical reunion, the primitive instinct arising from the separation of cell from cell, of the animal from its young. It is temporary, recurrent, causing immediate relief and absence of desire, leading to self-reliance and self-realisation.

The spiritual orgasm is a spiritual reunion of Man and God. It has no reaction, is not under control, coming and going like the wind; it leads to self-lessness. It causes a far more fundamental change of attitude to the outside world. In Coventry Patmore, the two are combined in a most surprising and beautiful manner. I give an interpretation of part of the *Sponsa Dei*.

Who is this woman whom you are flattering enough to love so madly, the poor best you can find for union with your soul?

> *Who is this only happy She,*
> *Whom, by a frantic flight of courtesy,*
> *Born of despair*
> *Of better lodging for his Spirit fair,*
> *He adores as Margaret, Maude, or Cecily?*

What is this emotion with which all human beings desire the unspeakable, timeless union of Matter with Spirit?

> *And what this sigh,*
> *That each one heaves for Earth's last lowlihead*
> *And the Heaven high*
> *Ineffably lock'd in dateless bridal-bed?*

Is all this human love mere physical excitement? Has it not some symbolical meaning? It is written, "Already we are children of the Deity, but the true meaning of this state is not yet realised."

> *Are all, then, mad, or is it prophecy?*
> *'Sons now we are of God,' as we have heard,*
> *'But what we shall be hath not yet appear'd.'*

Never forget, Man is God, and nothing else; God is Man.

> *O, Heart, remember thee,*
> *That Man is none,*
> *Save One.*

This woman you love, is your own Self. You who love, are God.

> *What if this Lady be thy Soul, and He*
> *Who claims to enjoy her sacred beauty be,*
> *Not thou, but God;*

Your emotion is simply self-love, or rather, Self-love. It comes from the Self, who loves the self. Eye hath not seen, nor hath it entered into the heart of man to conceive of the Joy (not joy) of that union (of self and Self, man and God)

> *and thy sick fire*
>
> *A female vanity,*
> *Such as a Bride, viewing her mirror'd charms,*
> *Feels when she sighs, 'All these are for his arms!'*

A reflex heat
Flash'd on thy cheek from His immense desire,
Which waits to crown, beyond thy brain's conceit,
Thy nameless, secret, hopeless longing sweet,
Not by and by, but now,
Unless deny Him thou!

Another figure under which this instinct is portrayed is that of death and resurrection, since it involves the renunciation of everything.   So Christ says, emphasising the primitive, aboriginal nature of this instinct,

Verily I say unto you, Except a corn of wheat fall into the ground and die, it abideth alone: but if it die, it bringeth forth much fruit.

In Zen this is called Taishi Ichiban, the Great Death (大死一番). Notice the "it abideth alone." Hell, the ordinary man's ordinary life, is alienation from God, abiding alone. We cannot dare, then, to follow our instincts unless we have first entered into that state of death of all the other instincts. Then we can follow our Instinct. We can be like flowing water, like the changing moon.

The water flows, but back into the ocean;
The moon sinks, but is ever in Heaven.
水 流 元 入 海、 月 落 不 離 天。

CHAPTER XIII

PARADOX

Usually I hate to speak of what I really feel, to that extent that when I find myself cornered, I have a tendency
to say the reverse.   (Stevenson, in a letter to his father.)

If somebody asks you a question, expecting 'Yes' for
an answer, answer 'No,' and *vice versa*. If he asks you
about an ordinary man, answer as if he asked about a
saint, and *vice versa*.   By this use of Relatives, teach him
the Doctrine of the Mean. Answer all his questions in this
fashion and you will not fall into error.

From Enô, the 6th Patriarch's final
instructions to his monks.

若 有 人 問 汝 義 問 有 將 無 對 問 無 將 有 對 問 凡 以
聖 對 問 聖 以 二 道 相 因 生 中 道 義 如 一 問 一 對 餘
問 一 依 此 作 即 不 失 理 也   (六祖壇經、十)

I once said to a lady of great philosophical attainments, "I
remember reading the following problem in some magazine:—
Which of the following pictures most truly represents Peace?

1. A fire-side scene, the kettle singing on the hob, a cat
   contentedly sitting there.
2. A small bird perched on a slender branch over a roaring cataract.
3. A skull and some bones in the desert.

Which of them would you choose?" (Of course you are supposed to choose No. 2.)

She answered "A picture of two drunken louts having a
fight.")

One definition of Zen, given me by a man who had done zazen for eight years, is worth recording. "Zen is a trick of words." How true it is! And poetry too is nothing more and nothing less. Here are some examples from the New Testament:

He that findeth his life shall lose it: and he that loseth his life for my sake shall find it.   (Matthew, x 39)

And whosoever will be chief among you, let him be your servant.   (Matthew, xx 27)

For whosoever hath, to him shall be given, and he shall have more abundance: but whosoever hath not, from him shall be taken away even that which he hath.

     (Matthew, xiii 12)

Compare this last to the 44th Case of the *Mumonkan*:

Bashô said to the assembled monks, "If you have a stick, I will give you one. If you have not a stick, I will take it away from you."

芭蕉和尚示衆云儞有拄杖子我與儞拄杖子儞
無拄杖子我奪儞拄杖子。   (無門關、第四十四)

For Zen the most important thing in these lofty ethical pronouncements is the paradox itself. A paradox is not a kind of pun, to be resolved by explaining the double meaning of the word. It does not spring from a desire to mystify the hearers or oneself. It arises from the inability of language to say two things at once. A doctor cuts off a leg causing pain and loss, which is evil, but saves a life, which is good. If we speak of the good-bad action, the mind unavoidably interprets this as partly good and partly bad. In this way music is greater than language. We can say two things at once, and the two separate melodies become one single indivisible harmony. Pater says, "All art aspires towards the condition of music." Action does the same, and when it reaches it, it is the activity of Zen.

Take for example Bach's Organ Passacaglia (Joh. Seb. Bachs Werke für Orgel, Band VI, Breitkopf and Härtel). On the pedal is given out the ever-recurring

This is the Absolute, the Voice of God, the Wheel of the Law, Nature. Then, hesitantly, in syncopation, begins the Relative; in grief and pain, from the end of bar 16, dying away to bar 24 where the soul reaches its lowest point, the same C as in the basso ostinato. From there, the resurrection, new life and hope; but the bass continues the same as ever. "There is no resurrection," it says, "there was no death;" only, "I am that I am." "Before Abraham was, I am":

> "Nature, with equal mind,
> Sees all her sons at play."

Yet the Absolute plus the Relative equals something else, which breaks through all language. Because

> Eternity is in love with the productions of time,

the unchanging bass of the pedal and the ever-changing melodies of the two manuals *together* express Something which is hinted at in the 2nd Case of the *Hekiganroku:*

Once you speak and use words, there is relativity
  or absoluteness.
But I Jôshu am not to be found in this region of Absoluteness.[1]

纔 有 語 言 是 揀 擇 是 明 白。　老 僧 不 在 明 白 裏。
（碧 巖 錄、第 二 則）

[1] Robert Bridges, in *Nightingales*, expresses his desire for the absolute:
"O might I wander there,
Among the flowers, which in that heavenly air
Bloom the year long!"

But Nature, Life, is not in the Absolute:

"Our song is the voice of desire, that haunts our dreams,
A throe of the heart."

This is Wordsworth's "Something ever more about to be," and Herbert's,
"A quickness which my God hath kissed."

Jôshū had reached the realm where the paradox of theme and variation, absolute and relative, divine and human, law and freedom, was resolved.

The Paradox must of course be a living, not a manufactured one; it must spring spontaneously out of experience and the inner life. This is only within the habitual reach of a spiritual master, but at times it comes to us all. The paradox is itself an example of what it teaches. The meaning escapes the words. Very well then, instead of further and further explanations, floundering farther and farther from Realty, let us scorn truth, turn our backs on logic, defy consistency,—and behold, the intangible is grasped, the unsayable is said.

Just as Bach thought in fugues, Hood in puns, so to Donne paradox was his natural element. The well-known sonnet, "Batter my heart, three person'd God" ends typically,

> Except you enthrall mee, never shall be free,
> Nor ever chast, except you ravish mee.

Especially worthy of praise is the violence of thought in this last line. Violence of passion is not so uncommon but such mental fire, such intellectual vehemence has few parallels. It is strong meat indeed. A gentler form is found in *The Crosse,* introduced by a very beautiful simile, expressing the identity of Buddha and man.

> Then are you to yourselfe a Crucifixe,
> As perchance, Carvers do not faces make,
> But that away, which hid them there, do take;
> Let Crosses, soe, take what hid Christ in thee,
> And be his image, or not his, but hee.

In some poets, for example, Wordsworth, the paradox is so gentle as to be almost unconscious of itself, as in *The Poet's Epitaph,* written in 1798.

> He is retired as noontide dew,
> Or fountain in a noon-day grove;
> *And you must love him, ere to you*
> *He will seem worthy of your love.*

Sometimes the truth slides so gently into our minds that we are hardly aware of it.   There seems nothing enigmatic or intellectually shocking in the last two lines of this verse, but in them Wordsworth has said something just as remarkable as Goso in the 36th Case of the *Mumonkan*:

> When you meet a master in the street, do not speak,
>   do not be silent.
> Then how will you greet him?

五祖曰路逢達道人不將語默對且道將甚麼對。
(無門關、第三十六)

You must see the invisible, do the impossible, love the unlovable, swim on the dry land and walk on the water.   But fine words butter no parsnips.   The question is, what are we to do in this continual, continuous dilemma which we call human life?   The answer is given in one of Stevenson's fables.   The Gordian knot must be cut.

THE SICK MAN AND THE FIREMAN

There was once a sick man in a burning house, to whom there entered a fireman.

"Do not save me," said the sick man.   "Save those who are strong."

"Will you kindly tell me why?" inquired the fireman, for he was a civil fellow.

"Nothing could possibly be fairer," said the sick man. "The strong should be preferred in all cases, because they are of more service in the world."

The fireman pondered a while, for he was a man of

some philosophy. "Granted," said he at last, as a part of the roof fell in; "but for the sake of conversation, what would you lay down as the proper service of the strong?"

"Nothing can possibly be easier," returned the sick man; "the proper service of the strong is to help the weak."

Again the fireman reflected, for there was nothing hasty about this excellent creature. "I could forgive you being sick," he said at last, as a portion of the wall fell out, "but I cannot bear your being such a fool." And with that he heaved up his fireman's axe, for he was eminently just, and clove the sick man to the bed.

Most of our talk about duty, religion, patriotism, Zen, is of this useless, circular character. In Buddhism, the body is called "a burning house" (火宅). We talk and talk while our life burns away. Johnson, the great example of the vice the Middle Ages called "Accidie," says in *Rasselas*,

While you are making your choice of life, do not neglect to live.

This is a little weak. Better it would be to think of the words of Tennyson in *The Charge of the Light Brigade*, words that express what many think to be an old-fashioned, out of date sentiment, but which actually cannot be withered by age or staled by custom:

Theirs not to reason why,
Theirs but to do and die.

Let us consider,

And whosoever would be first among you, shall be your servant.

How will orthodox Christians explain this in regard to God? Remember, what Christ says here is a universal law, that is, it applies to every existing thing in the universe. Who is, after all, first? God is first. Then he is my servant, will uncomplainingly, unwearyingly do my bidding, fulfil all my unspoken wishes, minister to every want, unknown though it be to myself. And is it not so? How all things support me, praise me, punish me, work together for my good! Careless of my appraisal or condemnation, they cherish and reprove me, admonish and uplift, in ceaseless change they are my Heaven or Hell according to my own sweet will. The keenness of the knife, the softness of the butter, the cat after the mouse, the moving shadows on the wall,—all for me, all my servants.

Sodô (1641-1716) says

> In my hut this spring
>   There is nothing—
>   There is everything.

宿 の 春 何 も な き こ そ 何 も あ れ　　　素 堂

If you try to explain this, as praise of poverty and contempt of worldly riches, the meaning completely disappears. You must swallow the hut and the nothing and the everything in one gulp, like Yamei's pheasant,

> In one shrill cry
>   The pheasant has swallowed
>   The broad field.

廣 き 野 を た だ 一 の み や 雉 子 の 聲　　　野 明

This instantaneous swallowing by the mind of intellectually discordant material in a paradox, is the same faculty by which we appreciate such passages as

> And pity, like a naked new-born babe,
> Striding the blast, or heaven's cherubim, horsed
> Upon the sightless couriers of the air,

or   daffodils
That come before the swallow dares, and take
The winds of March with beauty; violets dim,
But sweeter than the lids of Juno's eyes
Or Cytherea's breath.

Another example is Basho's extraordinary poem on the death
of Isshô, a young poet.

Shake, O tomb!
My wailing voice
Is the autumn wind.

塚 も 動 け 我 泣 聲 は 秋 の 風   芭 蕉

and one more of Bashô, in which the images of Buddha smell
of chrysanthemums and the chrysanthemums become en-
throned Buddhas, but the experience is of *one* thing.

AT NARA

The countless images
Of Buddha and the fragrance
Of chrysanthemums!

菊 の 香 や 奈 良 に は 古 き 佛 達   芭 蕉

The perception of the real meaning of a paradox may take
several forms, which we call humour, or poetry, or religion. In
any case, some vivacity of energy is required lest the intellect
should arrive and split hairs. The poetical or religious meaning
can never be explained any more than a joke can be explained.

Let me give some examples, mixed, and see if you can distinguish, *at a glance,* the humour, religion, or poetry in them,

From the nose
Of the Great Buddha flew out
A swallow.

大 佛 の 鼻 か ら 出 た る 燕 か な

"All things return to the One.   Where does the One return?"
"The dog laps the boiling water in the pot."

萬 法 歸 一、 一 歸 何 處。   狗 舐 熱 油 鐺。

A butterfly
>   Asleep, perched upon
>   The temple bell.

釣 鐘 に 止 り て 眠 る 胡 蝶 か な   蕪   村

His travelling-companions were two strangers, two silent
ladies, middle-aged.   The train stopped at Nuneaton.   The
two ladies exchanged a glance.   One of them sighed and
said, "Poor Eliza! She had reason to remember Nuneaton!"
(Max Beerbohm in *The Humour of the Public,* from
Yet Again.)

A sudden summer shower;
>   The ducks run round the house,
>   Quacking.

夕 だ ち や 家 を め ぐ り て 啼 く 家 鴨   其   角

In all these, at bottom there is a paradox, something inexpressible otherwise than in this form.   Hazlitt, in his *Essay
on Shakespeare*, praises his imagination for just this quality.

It glances from heaven to earth, from earth to heaven.
Its movement is rapid and devious.   It unites the most opposite extremes; or, as Puck says, in boasting of his own
feats, "puts a girdle round about the earth in forty
minutes."   He seems always to be hurrying from his subject, even when describing it; but the stroke, like the
lightning's, is as sure as it is sudden. . . .
He brings together images the most alike, but placed at
the greatest distance from each other; that is, found in
circumstances of the greatest dissimilitude.   From the re-
moteness of his combinations, and the celerity with which
they are effected, they coalesce the more indissolubly together. *The more the thoughts are strangers to each other,*

and the longer they have been kept asunder, the more intimate does their union become.

In ordinary people, the soul turns to God only at a time of great tension or extremity of anguish. Look at Rossetti's *The Woodspurge*:

> The wind flapped loose, the wind was still,
> Shaken out dead from tree and hill:
> I had walked on at the wind's will,—
> I sat now, for the wind was still.
>
> Between my knees my forehead was,—
> My lips, drawn in, said not Alas!
> My hair was over in the grass,
> My naked ears heard the day pass.
>
> My eyes, wide open, had the run
> Of some ten weeds to fix upon;
> Among those few, out of the sun,
> The woodspurge flowered, three cups in one.
>
> From perfect grief there need not be
> Wisdom or even memory:
> One thing then learnt remains to me,—
> The woodspurge has a cup of three.

This, like Wordsworth's *We are Seven*, afterwards to be referred to, resembles a *Mondô* in Zen, that is, a question by a master or pupil concerning the Ultimate Reality, and the answer. Put into regular form it would run:

Monk: "You are going to swat a fly; it comes and sits on the fly-swat itself: what will you do in such a case?"

(That is to say, you have lost everything, you are at a loss, at an Absolute Loss.)

Master: "The wood-spurge has a cup of three."

Man's extremity is God's opportunity.[1] If everything is lost,
you have the chance to see even the simplest thing just as it is.
But to see three as three, the flower as a flower — as Alice
Meynell says of the daisy,

> Thou little veil for so great a mystery,
> When shall I penetrate all things and thee?

> What will it be to look
> From God's side even of such a simple thing?

Zen, however, will hardly agree with the attitude of the
poetess here.   From the point of view of Zen, what is wrong
with us, what was wrong with Rosetti, is not that we don't
see truth, not that we can't know it, but that *we don't know
truth when we are looking at it,* when it is staring us in the
face. Rossetti sees the truth, he sees the woodspurge has a cup
of three, he actually writes it down in a poem, but does not
recognise the truth, just as in Hakuin's *Zazenwasan,* the drown-
ing man screams for water, the poor boy does not know he is
the son and heir of a rich man.

水 の 中 に 居 て 渇 を 叫 ぶ が ご と く な り 長 者 の 家 の
子 と な り て 貧 里 に 迷 ふ に 異 な ら ず   (坐 禪 和 讃)

This is also the meaning of Lady Macbeth's

> Yet who would have thought the old man to have had so
> much blood in him?

The quantity of blood in the old man her husband had
just killed, which she smeared on the faces of the men —
this Fact of the quantity of blood, her whole concentrated soul

[1] O'er-wearied,
   And seeking a lodging for the night—
      Ah, these wistaria flowers!   Bashô
   草 臥 れ て 宿 か る ゝ ろ や 藤 の 花

perceives in a moment of eternity. God is Fact, a Fact is God.
Rossetti's woodspurge, Allingham's three ducks, Lady Macbeth's blood, the dying Mercutio's barn-door, Bashô's wistaria,
is the Unknown God, whom we ignorantly worship.

It is noticeable how enlightenment, "satori," conversion,
illumination, which swallows the red-hot iron ball of paradox,
results in concentration on men and animals and things. At
the end of Masefield's *The Everlasting Mercy,* after "the bolted
door had broken in," all things had *each* an infinite value.
Not only the brook and the birds and animals, but

> The narrow station-wall's brick ledge,
> The wild hop withering in the hedge,

had the same meaning and just as much meaning.   Best of
all, because untainted with any ulterior significance:

> At the top of the rise the plough team stopped,
> The fore horse bent his head and cropped;
> Then the chains chack, the brasses jingle,
> The lean reins gather through the cringle,
> The figures move against the sky,
> The clay wave breaks as they go by.

Isaiah has a fine poetical paradox in which he denies the
scientific *ex nihilo nihil fit.*

Sing, O barren, thou that didst not bear; break forth into
singing, and cry aloud, thou that didst not travail with
child, for more are the children of the desolate than the
children of the married wife, saith the Lord.[1]

Out of suffering, Hamlet; out of old age, Lear; out of death,
Macbeth.   Out of unrequited love, physical infirmities, the

[1] Compare,
> The wooden horse neighs, the stone woman gives birth.
> 木 馬 嘶、 石 女 生 子。

later quartets of Beethoven; out of unattainable ideals, Anna
Karenina. Truly the children of the desolate are many. There
is a Greek proverb somewhat similar,

> The half is often greater than the whole.

This is why the piano is better, as an instrument, than the
organ. The organ says everything, the piano leaves much to
our imagination, for, being a percussion instrument, the notes
dwindle and fade away after being struck. Unfinished houses,
unfinished pictures and sculpture tell the same story. The
whole is the whole, but the half is infinite. For this reason
Lessing said that if there were held out to him in one hand
truth, and in the other the love of truth, and he might choose
freely between the two, he would prefer the latter to the former.

> "Sie haben wohl recht," sagte Goethe. "Lessing soll selbst
> einmal geaüssert haben, dass, wenn Gott ihm die Wahrheit
> geben wolle, er sich dieses Geschenk verbitten, vielmehr
> die Mühe vorziehen würde sie selber zu suchen." (Ecker-
> mann, *Gespräche mit Goethe,* 1827)

Zen is the love of truth, a very different thing from the
liking of or the preference for truth. Truth, the whole truth
is there, no doubt, but our life is *love* of truth. How can we
get into this state of love, this life? The greatest paradox in
the history of the world tells us:

> Verily, verily, I say unto you, Except a corn of wheat fall
> into the ground and die, it abideth alone: but if it die, it
> bringeth forth much fruit. He that loveth his life shall
> lose it; and he that hateth his life in this world, shall keep
> it unto life eternal.

If we try to explain this, and talk of physical life and spiritual
life, the real meaning totally disappears. If you wish to live,

die! Without thinking, abandon yourself, all your wants and wishes, not only for happiness, but for truth, for life, for goodness, for God. Then you have eternal life, the peace that passes understanding.

Paradoxes are the bright banners of the liberty of the mind. They proclaim that the mind is free to bestow or withhold values. It gives its categories to objects and decides their relations. Reason cannot deal with individual things, for the individual cannot be defined. It gives us rational, scientific knowledge of the forms of things, abstractions from the thing itself, types, rules, concepts. Reason grips life with a strangle-hold, but life says, "To win, is to lose," and as in Jûdô, uses the power of the enemy to escape from it.

So to express the freedom of the mind we have such sayings as,

> The moon is shining in the garden,
> But there is no shadow beneath the pine tree;
> Outside there is not a breath of wind,
> But the bamboos are rustling.

庭前有月松無影、檻外無風竹有聲。

There both is, and is not, a connection between the moon and the shadow. Absolutely, spiritually, poetically, there is no connection, because it is the mind, it is "thinking which makes it so" or not so. Rationally, intellectually, scientifically, there is a connection between moon and shadow because there is an objective cause and effect observable in Nature. Thus also, to divide is to reduce, but "Good, the more communicated, more abundant grows."

There is a danger here of trying to explain the dilemma by saying that the material world is governed by law and the spiritual world is free. Such is not the case. In the spiritual-material world there both is and is not, and *the resolution of this contradiction is life itself, and nothing but life can resolve it.* This is the spiritual, parabolic meaning of miracles; it is perhaps at the bottom of our enjoyment of conjuring and acrobatics. Again, there is a danger that the paradox may be taken as overstepping the mark, as exaggeration for the sake of effect, in answer to the overweening claims of the reason. Such is not the case. To repeat, there both is a shadow and is not a shadow beneath the pine tree. The paradox merely states one of these matters of fact, reason the other. The latter we can see any night; the former only when we are at a white-heat of vision. Yet even when we are at our lowest ebb, there is something in a paradox which calls to our real selves, and for a moment, before custom, heavy almost as life, closes the prison door upon us, we see

> the children sport upon the shore,
> And hear the mighty waters rolling evermore.

But the strange thing is that not only poetry and religion but reason also has its paradoxes. Parmenides, a mathematician, showed that according to reason, nothing can come into existence or go out of existence; Zeno of Elea showed that things cannot move, a moving arrow is an illusion, Achilles can never overtake the tortoise. But here again life solves the problems by living. We come into existence and go out of it, things move, things overtake other things. And life solves the greatest contradiction of all, the unchanging universe of Spinoza,

> There was something undefined yet perfect, existing before Heaven and Earth, soundless, formless, independent, changeless, all-pervading, unfailing.   Rôshi, 25.

有 物 混 成、 先 天 地 生、 寂 兮 寥 兮。　 獨 立 而 不 改、
周 行 而 不 殆。　　　　　　　　　　　（老子、二十五）

and the changing universe of Heracleitus,

> The moving water flows ceaselessly, yet the water is never the same.   (Opening sentence of the *Hôjôki* [1])

行く川の流は絶えずして、而も本の水にあらず
(方丈記)

So we have, not, "Though it changes, it is the same," which is intellectually understandable, but, "*The more* it changes, *the more* it is the same*.*"   This touch of life, of genius, of inspiration, of Zen, of something beyond logic and rationality, gives us a strange feeling of freedom and power.

> Green comes from indigo, but it is more beautiful than indigo;
> Ice comes from water, but it is colder than water.

青出於藍清於藍、氷生於水寒於水 (虚堂録)

Truth is expressible only in the form of a paradox.   What is not paradoxical, is not true; is not *living, inexpressible truth.* Denial is the only way to assert, blasphemy the only praise.

---

[1] Literally '10 feet square history,' a short book written by Kamo Chômei, at the beginning of the 13th century. The first half describes natural calamities, the second his life in retirement in a 10 feet square hut. Together with Bashô's *Oku no Hosomichi*, the best things in Japanese literature outside Haiku.

CHAPTER XIV

DON QUIXOTE

To include *Don Quixote* in English Literature is a piece of impudence, though a lesser one than the inclusion in it of a religious anthology of the Jews, collected by them during a period of a thousand years, called the Bible.   But though Don Quixote has taken his place with Hamlet, Joseph, Robinson Crusoe, Gulliver, Mr. Pecksniff, and Alice, his true character is not yet recognised either in his own country or that of his adoption.   Of the work of Cervantes more than that of any other, are Goethe's words true, that a poet has to be taught his own meaning.   The genius is hardly aware of the significance of his performance, since so much of it is the God that speaks through him as a mouthpiece.   In the case of *Don Quixote* this is further complicated by the fact that Cervantes, in the Second Part of *Don Quixote,* destroys, unconsciously, his own creation in the First Part.

Not only Don Quixote but Sancho Panza also, is utterly different in the two parts.   This is to some extent due to the fact that the Second Part was written (as an after-thought?) nine years after the first.   For the same reason, the Second Part of *Faust* is also very different from the First, but the two cases are otherwise not the same, for the important thing in *Faust* is the poetry, whereas in *Don Quixote* the importance lies entirely in the character of Don Quixote, the man himself and his ideals; and the change of character means that the two Parts are two entirely different books and are about two entirely different people of the same name. Mr. Pickwick is a very different person at the end of the book from what he is at the beginning. This also is due to the lapse of time, to the serial form. But he changes from a merely comic character to a mellow, kindly, and somewhat heroic character of a peculiarly British kind. In Don Quixote, we have the opposite, the sudden degeneration, the sudden putrefaction before our eyes of a personality.[1] The explanation of this apparent disintegration, this metamorphosis of a butterfly into a grub is that Cervantes did not himself understand clearly what he had done in the First Part, what kind of being he had created. Cervantes' conscious and unconscious intentions in writing the First Part were opposed. Cervantes tells us *ad nauseam* that the Romances of Chivalry were the cause of Quixote's madness. He seems to have approved of the burning of them by the curate and the barber, not on the ground that they made people go on crazy adventures, but because they were poor as literature, at once unrealistic and inartistic. At the end of Part II, Quixote recovers from his madness and declares,

" Ya soy enemigo de Amadís de Gaula y de toda la infinita caterva de su linaje; ya me son odiosas todas las historias profanas de la andante caballería; ya conozco mi necedad y el peligro en que me pusieron haberlas leído; ya, por misericordia de Dios, escarmentando en cabeza propia, las abomino."[2]   (Parte segunda, cap. 74.)

(I am now enemy of Amadis of Gaul and all his tribe: all the profane histories of Knight errantry are hateful to me. I now realise the danger and peril into which I fell by reading them. By the mercy of God, I learned by my own experience, and abhor them.)

[1] Compare Wordsworth, before and after 1800.
[2] Quotations from *Cervantes, Don Quixote de la Mancha, Edición y notas de Francisco Rodriguez Marin, Madrid, Ediciones de "La Lectura"* 1913.

On the other hand, as I shall show later in quotations, the Don
Quixote of the First Part is the quintessence of all the chivalry
of the Romances, all the knighthood of the Middle Ages, together with spiritual and noble qualities derived from Cervantes
himself. His madness is partly his idealism (of which we sane
people have so little) partly an overstrung imagination at the
service of this same idealism.[1] The Don Quixote of Part II is
a kind of travelling lecturer, whose senility is taken advantage
of in the most odious way by a couple of impudent, sophisticated creatures, the Duke and Duchess (cuyo titulo aun no se
sabe). He analyses himself and his illusions:

> ¿ Quién duda, señor don Diego de Miranda, que vuesa
> merced no me tenga por un hombre disparatado y loco?
> Y no sería mucho que así fuese, porque mis obras no
> pueden dar testimonio de otra cosa. Pues, con todo esto,
> quiero que vuesa merced advierta que no soy tan loco ni
> tan menguado como debo de haberle parecido.
>
> (Parte segunda, cap. 17.)

("Doubtless, Señor de Diego de Miranda, you look on me
as a crazy, mad fellow. And it may well seem so, for my
conduct testifies to this alone. Yet, for all that, let me tell
you that I am not so crazy and half-witted as you take me
for.")

and discourses on the probabilities of the veracity of the
romances of chivalry:

> Hay mucho que decir—respondió don Quixote—en razon de
> si son fingidas, ó no, las historias de los andantes caballeros.
>
> (Parte segunda, cap. 16.)

[1] Wordsworth was very fond of *Don Quixote.* In a letter of 1806 he
speaks of the "Nourishment that is contained in fairy tales, romances."
Thinking of Don Quixote, Wordsworth says, (*Prelude,* V, 151)

> In the blind and awful lair
> Of such a madness, reason did lie couched.

("There is a lot to be said," replied don Quixote, "both for
and against the truth of the romances of Knight Errantry.")

The Don Quixote of the First Part is Zen incarnate, of the
Second, a sententious buffoon. Sancho Panza also suffers a
complete change. In the First Part he is the ordinary man,
self-seeking, fond of money, fond of his belly, stupid, a coward,
yet not altogether devoid of some natural Zen and faith in his
master which lifts him, like Babbit, above the entirely material.
In the Second Part he becomes a just, benevolent, disinterested,
clever judge and faithful servant, and at times the foolish
knave of the First Part, but disbelieving his master's visions
and helping to make a fool of him. The Second Part is better
written, it is true; more cultivated, more urbane. It is a book.
The First Part is not a book, it is life itself with its medley of
gentleness and brutality, humour and pain, nobility and vulgarity, all united by the vision of Don Quixote himself, into a
meaningful whole. The words of Byron in *Don Juan,* though
devoid of poetical merit, need to be pondered over once more.

I should be very willing to redress
     Men's wrongs, and rather check than punish crimes,
Had not Cervantes, in that too true tale
Of Quixote, shown how all such efforts fail.

Of all tales 'tis the saddest—and more sad,
     Because it makes us smile: his hero's right,
And still pursues the right;—to curb the bad
     His only object, and 'gainst odds to fight
His guerdon: 'tis his virtue makes him mad!
     But his adventures form a sorry sight;—
A sorrier still is the great moral taught
By that real epic unto all who have thought.

Redressing injury, revenging wrong,
     To aid the damsel and destroy the caitiff;
Opposing singly the united strong,

From foreign yoke to free the helpless native:—
Alas! must noblest views, like an old song,
    Be for mere fancy's sport a theme creative,
A jest, a riddle, Fame through thick and thin sought!
And Socrates himself but Wisdom's Quixote?

Cervantes smiled Spain's chivalry away;
    A single laugh demolish'd the right arm
Of his own country;—seldom since that day
    Has Spain had heroes. While Romance could charm,
The world gave ground before that bright array;
    And therefore have his volumes done such harm,
That all their glory, as a composition,
Was dearly purchased by his land's perdition.

"All such efforts fail." It does not need Cervantes to tell
us that, and anyway, what does it matter? "Of all tales 'tis
the saddest." The only sad tales are those of men who re-
nounce their ideals as Don Quixote does at the end of the Second
Part. "His Virtue makes him mad." There is a profound
truth in this. It was their virtue that made Christ, St Francis,
Blake, Daruma, all mad, mad as hatters, compared to sane
people like you and me. Which is a sorrier sight, his life or
ours? Again, what is "the great moral taught," which is such
a sorry thing? "Noblest views" are not "mere fancy's sport:"
here Byron's sense of humour is defective, laughing at Quixote
is one thing, laughing with him is another. "Cervantes smiled
Spain's chivalry away." Cervantes could not do such a thing.
You might as well try to smile the pyramids away, smile death
away. Byron could not laugh religion away in *Cain* and the
Vision of Judgement. The chivalry which is made fun of in
Don Quixote was already dead. The chivalry which Don Quixote
embodied is as eternal as the faithfulness of Ôishi-Yoshio, the
leader of the 47 Rônin. As to the later decadence of Spain, if
it be ascribed to loss of Romance, that is to loss of idealism, to

the loss of power to love the better more than the good, this means the loss of power to distinguish the essential from the unessential in *Don Quixote* and this cannot be perversely blamed upon *Don Quixote* itself, except in so far as Cervantes defaces his original in the Second Part and confuses the issues.

What was wrong with Spain, what is wrong with every nation, every individual, is the lack of the true spirit of Don Quixote. Professor Suzuki, in his *Zen Buddhism and its Influence on Japanese Culture,* gives an example of Zen in a bull-fighter. No doubt it is correct in its way, though the bull would afford an equally good example, at the same level of intelligence and morality. But the man who in the history of the world exemplifies all that is best in Zen, the man who surpasses Hakuin, Rinzai, Enô, Daruma and Shakamuni himself is Don Quixote de la Mancha, Knight Errant. What is Knight Errantry?

> El andante caballero busque los rincones del mundo; éntrese en los más intricados laberintos; acometa á cada paso lo imposible; resista en los páramos despoblados los ardientes rayos del sol en la mitad del verano, y en el invierno la dura inclemencia de los vientos y de los yelos; no le asombren leones, ni le espanten vestiglos, ni atemoricen endriagos; que buscar éstos, acometer aquéllos y vencerlos á todos son sus principales y verdaderos ejercicios. (Parte segunda, cap. XVII.)

> (The Knight-errant searches all the corners of the world, enters the most complicated labyrinths, accomplishes at every step the impossible, endures the fierce rays of the sun in uninhabited deserts, the inclemency of wind and ice in winter: lions cannot daunt him nor demons affright nor dragons, for to seek, assault, and overcome such is the whole business of his life, and true office.)

But all this is not mere self-development, born of a desire to be an Arhat. The object of a Knight Errant, what he lives for, is

> para defender las doncellas, amparar las viudas y socorrer á los huérfanos y á los menesterosos. (Parte primera, cap. XI)

> (to defend maidens, protect widows, assist orphans and relieve the distressed.)

In this he is not to judge men, not to think of their goodness or badness, but only of their misfortunes:

> Sólo le toca ayudarles como à menesterosos, poniendo los ojos en sus penas, y no en sus bellaquerías
> (Parte primera, cap. XXX)

> (It is for him to succour them as being needy, looking on their distresses, not on their crimes.)

and this applies to all men and women equally; old and young, rich and poor, good and bad,

> porque de la caballería andante se puede decir lo mesmo que del amor se dice: que todas las cosas iguala.
> (Parte primera, cap. XI)

> (*for it may be said of Knight-errantry what is said of love: that it makes all things equal.*)[1]

His attitude to other people is that of the sane man to madmen. To him food, money, clothes, are nothing. Don Quixote himself quotes from an old romance:

> Mis arreos son las armas,
> Mi descanso el pelear;

[1] Compare Crabbe, in *Lady Barbara; or the Ghost:*
> Death's equalising arm
> Levels not surer than Love's stronger charm,
> That bids all inequalities begone,
> That laughs at rank, that mocks comparison.
Knight-errantry, death, love,—these have something in common, Zen.

> Mi cama las duras penas,
> Mi dormir siempre velar.
> > (Parte primera, cap. II.)

> My wants, arms alone,
> My rest is war;
> My bed the hard woes,
> My sleep an eternal vigil.

This reminds one of a passage at the beginning of *Sotoba Komachi*, (Waley's translation):

> A thousand leagues
> Is little road
> To the pilgrim's feet.
> The fields his bed,
> The hills his home,
> Till the travel's close.

千里を行くも遠からす。 野に臥し山に泊る
身のこれぞ眞の栖なるこれぞ眞の栖なる。

All things that the world counts evils are his good. As Shakespeare says,

> All places that the eye of heaven visits,
> Are to a wise man ports and happy havens.

So Don Quixote quoting with approval the old Spanish proverb

> Donde una puerta se cierra, otra se abre,
> > (Parte primera, cap. XXI)

> (Where one door shuts, another opens,)

reminds us of the Emersonian doctrine of Compensation. Even pleasant things and happy times may contain something good and profitable for the soul. This attitude to life, of willing acceptance of all that comes, or rather, all that we come to, for our attitude to life must be active and not passive, is expressed as follows, when Don Quixote first sallies forth in search of adventure, taking no thought for the morrow:

> Y prosiguió su camino, sin llevar otro que aquel que su caballo quería, creyendo que en aquello consistía la fuerza de las aventuras.   (Primera Parte, cap. II.)

> (He rode on his way, going where it pleased his horse to carry him, for he believed that in this consisted the very soul of adventures.)

The same attitude of mind is shown in Chapter 50 of the First Part: we see before us

> un gran lago de pez hirviendo á borbollones, y que andan nadando y cruzando por él muchas serpientes, culebras y lagartos, y otros muchos géneros de animales feroces y espantables, y que del medio del lago sale un voz tristísima que dice: "Tú, caballero, quienquiera que seas, que el temeroso lago estás mirando, si quieres alcanzar el bien que debajo destas negras aguas se encubre, muestra el valor de tu fuerte pecho y arrójate en mitad de su negro y encendido licor; porque si así no lo haces, no serás digno de ver las altas maravillas que en sí encierran y contienen los sietes castillos de las siete fadas que debajo desta negrura yacen." Y que apenas el caballero no ha acabado de oír la voz temerosa, quando, sin entrar más en cuentas consigo, sin ponerse á considerar el peligro á que se pone, y aun sin despojarse de la pesadumbre de sus fuertes armas, encomendándose á Dios y á su señora, se arroja en mitad del bullente lago, y cuando no se cata ni sabe dónde ha de parar, se halla entre unos floridos campos, con quien los Elíseos no tienen que ver en ninguna cosa.

(a vast lake of boiling pitch, in which a great number of snakes, serpents, crocodiles and many other ferocious and fearful creatures are wallowing about: a voice wails from the middle of the lake, "Whosoever thou art, O Knight, who surveyest this horrible mere, if thou wishest to obtain the blessing that lies beneath these gloomy waters, show the might of thy valorous breast, and throw thyself into these black, burning waves; doest thou not so, thou art not worthy to see the great wonders of the seven castles and their seven fairies, that lie beneath these lugubrous surges." No sooner have these awful words ceased than without a moment's consideration, without a thought of the danger he runs, without even taking off his massive arms, commending himself to God and to his mistress, he dashes into the middle of the boiling lake. And just when he does not know what will happen to him, he finds himself among flowery fields beautiful beyond those of Eliseum.)

This reminds one of the 5th case of the *Mumonkan,* the man hanging by his teeth over a precipice.[1] About the meaning of life or such foolish questions, whose answer disappears at the moment we ask them, he never troubled his head, nor as to the profit, the gain, from this kind of journey through life. It is chiefly a broken head and the loss of an ear,

No se gaña otra cosa que sacar rota la cabeza, ó una oreja menos   (Parte primera, cap. X.)

all of which he is to bear without complaint, like the *samurai* who picks his teeth though he has not broken his fast.

No es dado á los caballeros andantes quejarse de herida alguna, aunque se les salgan las tripas por ella.
(Parte primera, cap. VIII.)

(A knight-errant must never complain of a wound, even though his entrails are dropping out of it.)

Everything depends on the mind. It is the mind which decides whether a thing is a basin or a helmet. The mind is a conjurer, a magician, a wizard which can change one thing into another.

[1] See a later chapter.

Y así, eso que á ti te parece bacía de barbero me parece á
mí el yelmo de Mambrino, y á otro le parecerá otra cosa.
(Parte primera, cap. XXV)

(So it is that what looks to you like a barber's basin, I see
clearly to be Mambrino's helmet, and another man may
take it for something else.)

The mind can change day to night, grief to joy, hell to heaven.

Hágalo Dios – respondió don Quixote — como yo deseo y
tú, Sancho, has menester, y ruin sea quien por ruin se tiene.
(Parte primera, cap. XXI)

("Let God grant it thus," answered Don Quixote, "as I desire and you have need, and may he be a wretch who
thinks himself one.")

This freedom of the mind, freedom of the will, consists in
following one's instincts, disdaining all causes and effects, all
rationalizing, to act like life itself which lives the life of life.

Ahí está el punto – respondió don Quixote—, y ésa es la
fineza de mi negocio: que volverse loco un caballero andante con causa, ni grado ni gracias: el toque está en de-
satinar sin ocasión.   (Parte primera, cap. XXV)

("This is the point," replied Don Quixote, "this is the essence of my manner of life; for a knight errant to run
mad for some actual reason or other — there would be
nothing praiseworthy or meritorious in that! The perfection of it consists in running mad without the least con-
straint or necessity.")

But for all this talking and boasting there is nothing of
egotism in Don Quixote. He is in a state of *Muga* (無我), a
state in which he himself is nothing, he seeks nothing for himself, his personality is always dissolved in the valour and glory
of the action itself. So when Sancho says

Éstos son más de veinte, y nosotros no más de dos, y aun quizá no somos sino uno y medio—Yo valgo por ciento— replicó don Quixote,   (Parte primera, cap. XV)

("These are more than twenty, and we only two, or rather one and a half." "I am worth a hundred," replied Don Quixote,)

and we feel that this is an understatement. Don Quixote underestimates himself; he is worth more than a hundred in any combat. But all this spiritual strength does not derive from Don Quixote himself but from his ideal as embodied in Dulcinea, and so he tells the doubting Sancho Panza with great fury:

Y ¿ no sabéis vos, gañán, faquín, belitre, que si no fuese por el valor que ella infunde en mi brazo, que no le tendría yo para matar una pulga? Decid, socarrón de lengua viperina, y ¿ quién pensáis que ha ganado este reino y cortado la cabeza á este gigante, y héchoos á vos marqués (que todo esto doy ya por hecho y por cosa pasada en cosa juzgada) si no es el valor de Dulcinea, tomando á mi brazo por instrumento de sus hazañas? Ella pelea en mi y vence in mi, y yo vivo y respira en ella, y tengo vida y ser.
                         (Parte primera, cap. XXX)

("Do you not know, you vulgar rascal, you rogue, that were it not for the valour that she infuses into my arm, I would not have the strength to kill a flea? Tell me, viper-tongued villain, who has regained the kingdom, beheaded the giant, and made you marquis (for all this is to me as done and finished) but the power of Dulcinea which uses my arm as instrument of her deeds? She fights in me, she is victorious in me, and I live and breathe in her, receive life and being itself from her.")

Yet Cervantes does not commit the error of making Don Quixote superhuman. He is a man of like passions with ourselves, who feels the pangs of hunger and the smaller pains of the body. Like Christ, he is often peevish, unreasonable, ex-

pecting too much of human nature, and himself finds often that
discretion is the better part of valour.   Yet for all this he can
say of himself, as Christ also could have said, a wilful wrong

de voluntad y a sabiendas jamás le dí á nadie.
                              (Parte primera, cap. XLVII.)

(voluntarily and knowingly I never committed to anyone.)

Among many others, there is one especial point of resem-
blance between Don Quixote and Blake.   Just as in his visions
Blake saw and talked with many of the ancient worthies, so
Don Quixote describes the face, figure and character of the
persons of the Romances:

Ese es otro error—respondió don Quixote—en que han
caído muchos, que no creen que haya habido tales caballeros en el mundo; la cual verdad es tan cierta, que estoy
por decir que con mis propios ojos vi á Amadís de Gaula,
que era un hombre alto de cuerpo, blanco de rostro, bien
puesto la barba, aunque negra, de vista entre blanda y
rigurosa, corto de razones, tardo en airarse y presto en de-
poner la ira.   (Parte segunda, cap. I)

("This is another mistake," replied Don Quixote, "into
which many have fallen, not believing that such knights-
errant ever existed in this world.   The truth is as certain
that I may say I have seen Amadis of Gaul with those my
own eyes.   He was of great stature, fair of face, a well-
clipped beard, though black, his face at once fierce and
gentle, of few words, slow to anger and easily pacified.")

A small but interesting example of Sancho's Zen, quite accidental and natural, of course, but none the less the real thing,
is given in the 2nd Part of *Don Quixote,* Chapter XXVIII, after
Sancho has been soundly beaten (in the previous chapter), by
the townsmen of Reloxa.   The pain is so great that he turns
on his master and for a whole page pours out a torrent of

vituperation on his own folly for following him, with no profit and every kind of loss imaginable. Don Quixote then says (remember this is the Don Quixote of the Second Part who is here simply Cervantes himself speaking,)

> Haría yo una buena apuesta con vos, Sancho — dijo don Quixote—: que ahora que váis hablando sin que nadie os vaya á la mano, que no os duele nada en todo vuestro cuerpo.

> ("I'll wager," said Don Quixote, "that at this moment while you are going on like this at pleasure, that you don't feel a bit of pain anywhere.")

We feel pain when we think of it; while we forget it, from danger, anger,[1] or any other reason, we feel no pain whatever. So Blake says,

> The tigers of wrath are wiser than the horses of instruction.

It was the power of Zen that enabled Latimer to "receive the flame as it were embracing it, After he had stroked his face with his hands, and (as it were) bathed them a little in the fire, he soon died (as it appeared) with very little pain or none." It was the power of Zen that enabled Drake to finish his game of bowls and then defeat the Armada.

The humour of *Don Quixote,* its pathos,—in what does it consist? Lockhart says:

> He is the type of a more universal madness — he is the symbol of Imagination continually struggling and contrasted with Reality — he represents the eternal warfare between Enthusiasm and Necessity — the eternal discrepancy between the aspirations and the occupations of Man — the omnipotence and the vanity of human dreams.

[1] Contrast indignation. Nietzsche says, in *Jenseits von Gut und Böse,* Und niemand *lügt* soviel als der Entrüstete.

With such a view of life, a kind of spiritual Zoroastrianism, we can understand nothing at all. We cannot understand the spider catching the fly, the shining of the sun, the fall of snow, —not even the simplest things are comprehensible by this kind of dualism, let alone such a lofty creation as Don Quixote. Once we divide the world into ideal and real, imagination and reality, everything becomes a meaningless struggle, there is no central unity to be seen, it is simply a vast tragedy of Nature making a fool of Man. The humour of *Don Quixote* is the contrast between Reality and Unreality, between the ideals (that is to say the vision of Truth, the apprehension of Eternal values,) and the inadequate methods Don Quixote takes to put them into practice. It is a contrast between Wisdom and Folly, between Perfection of motive and Imperfection of means, between good aims and bad judgement. Notice that these opposites are not dualistic in character, though they sound so. Reality and Unreality, Wisdom and Folly, are names for the same one thing. We use them to explain the humour of Don Quixote, as lying in the contrast between Pure Truth and Impure Application, but actually these two are one. Defect of application means defect of vision. When a man sees the Truth of things, all his actions are perfect. Perfection means, not perfect actions in a perfect world, but appropriate actions in an imperfect one. Don Quixote's are inappropriate, but not, as in our case, as a result of defect of will, but of defect of judgement. He lacks the Confucian virtue of Prudence, the balance of the powers of the mind.

The pathos of *Don Quixote* derives from the same source as the humour, but with the addition that we ourselves, as we read the book, have an underlying sense of shame that our lives are directed to the acquisition of all the things Don Quixote so rightly despised. No man can read *Don Quixote* without a feeling of self-contempt. To forget this, many laugh at him that they may not weep at themselves.

The life of Don Quixote was a life of Zen; indifferent to the opinions of his fellows, without a single thought of self, of self-aggrandisement or self-expression, he *lived* twenty four hours every day, following his instincts (his ideals,) as whole-heartedly, as truly, as naturally, as the blooming of flowers in spring, as the falling of leaves in autumn.

CHAPTER XV

PANTHEISM, MYSTICISM, ZEN

PART I

Professor Suzuki appears to look upon Zen as a form of Mysticism, but is very down on Pantheism. In my opinion, Zen is neither. Before we enter the jungle of definitions, let us note that Homer,[1] Chaucer, Shakespeare, are full of Zen, but no one yet has called them mystics or pantheists. What about Wordsworth, you may say? For the moment I will simply ask you, is there any pantheism, is there any mysticism, in *Michael, The Daffodils,* the *Ode to Duty,* the *Lucy* poems, *The Solitary Reaper, The Cuckoo, Ruth?*

Now for the definitions, from which you will not, I am afraid, get much pleasure or profit.

Mysticism is an attitude of mind founded on an intuitive or experienced conviction of unity, of oneness in all things.
The Ideal is the only Real.
The methods of mental knowledge and spiritual knowledge are entirely different. C. E. Spurgeon

The consciousness that everything we experience, every fact, is an element and only an element in 'the fact,' i.e. that its being what it is, it is significant or symbolic of more. R. L. Nettleship

Mysticism is a belief in spiritual apprehension of truth beyond the understanding. E. Underhill

[1] When Arnold says of him, "Homer is rapid in his movement, Homer is plain in his words, Homer is simple in his ideas, Homer is noble in his manner," he is praising him for his Zen.

The Jews were not pantheists themselves because they never speculated on the relation in which omnipotence stood to natural forces and human acts.

Holiness for the mystic consists in universal mildness and insight, in freedom from all passion, bias and illusion; in a disembodied wisdom which accepts the world, dominates its labyrinths, and is able to guide others through it without pursuing for its own part any hope or desire.

G. Santayana

To the Pantheist, God is wholly immanent, all is God. To Mysticism, God is all.   Prof. Oman

Pantheism, even when psychic, ignores ideals.

Santayana

Panpsychism, the theory that nature is alive and even participant in soul-life throughout, though in very different degrees.   Inge

To distinguish mysticism from pantheism is no easy matter. So, for example, a great number of the poems of the *Oxford Book of English Mystical Verse* are simple pantheism. The compilers do not give a definition but only say they include such "poems as contain intimations of a consciousness wider and deeper than the normal," which means rather less than nothing at all. In general it may be said that pantheism supposes a more concrete and less sophisticated conception of the universe. It is more or less a matter of belief and opinion, and so we may call Emerson with his notorious *Brahma* a pantheist:

> I am the doubter and the doubt,
> And I the hymn the Brahmin sings.

Mystics, which are roughly of two kinds, religious and nature mystics, have the distinguishing feature of passion. In the religious mystics, God, though immanent, is also transcendent, as in the following of Richard Crashaw:

> Thy God was making hast into thy roofe,
>   Thy humble faith, and feare, keepes him aloofe:
> Hee'l be thy guest, because he may not be,
>   Hee'l come—into thy house? No, into thee.

and this from Cowper's *Task:*

> But all are under one. One spirit—His
> Who wore the platted thorns with bleeding brows—
> Rules universal nature.

Cowper says "universal nature" but he actually means

>   What he views of beautiful or grand
>   In nature.

This kind of thing only,

>   Prompts with remembrance of a present God!

The division here of God and nature is very disagreeable. Not to be able to look at the broad oak or "the green blade that twinkles in the sun" without being "prompted" to think of something else, must cause a perpetual splitting of the mind. This is what Christ warns us against, in "Judge not" and "Let not thy right hand know what thy left hand doeth."

The nature mystics, on the other hand, are forgetful of God, either leave him out altogether or put him in perfunctorily, or use the word God as a synonym for Nature or Reality. As pointed out above, passion distinguishes their attitude from pantheism, though there is often an insensible flowing from one to the other. The finest example of nature mysticism is found in Wordsworth, *The Excursion,* (I, 199.)

>   He beheld the sun
> Rise up, and bathe the world in light! He looked—
> Ocean and earth, the solid frame of earth

> And ocean's liquid mass, in gladness lay
> Beneath him:—Far and wide the clouds were touched,
> And in their silent faces could he read
> Unutterable love. Sound needed none
> Nor any voice of joy; his spirit drank
> The spectacle: sensation, soul and form
> All melted in him; they swallowed up
> His animal being; in them did he live,
> And by them did he live; they were his life.

Wordsworth then inserts two lines that might well have been omitted from the poem, since they represent an intellectual after-thought:

> In such access of mind, in such high hour
> Of visitation from the living God,

but continues, showing that there was actually no " visiting " of one person, by Another:

> Thought was not; in enjoyment it expired.
> No thanks he breathed, he proffered no request;
> Rapt in the still communion that transcends
> The imperfect offices of prayer and praise.

One more extract, from *Tintern Abbey:*

> A sense sublime
> Of something far more deeply interfused,
> Whose dwelling is the light of setting suns,
> And the round ocean and the living air
> And the blue sky, and in the mind of man—
> A motion and a spirit, that impels
> All thinking things, all objects of all thought,
> And rolls through all things.

These two passages represent the high water mark of nature mysticism in English Literature. They are full of Zen.

They portray a condition of 'satori,' of illumination. But the next point is of cardinal importance; these lines of the *Daffodils,*

> They stretch'd in never-ending line
> Along the margin of a bay:
> Ten thousand saw I at a glance
> Tossing their heads in spirightly dance,

are also full of Zen but are not mystical, still less pantheistic.

The first example, from the *Excursion,* shows us the mind of Man in its union with the universe. The second, from *Tintern Abbey,* shows us the universe as perceived by the man in union with it. The third, *Daffodils,* shows us something very different, apparently, from either. We see, not the mind of man, nor the universe, but the daffodils, and when we see them as Wordsworth also saw them, as they really are, that is sufficient. Mysticism is like Zen, in this respect, that you cannot believe or disbelieve in mysticism. You are either a mystic or nothing. But the great gulf fixed between mysticism and Zen is this. *Mysticism uses the object, the finite, as a telescope to look into the infinite. Zen looks at the telescope.*

We say, very loosely, "There is Zen in this," "This is far from Zen," but we must notice there is a great difference, both in art and life, between Zen and talking about Zen. Compare with the extract from the *Excursion,* the following poem of Bashô on a similar subject:

> A wild sea,
>   The Milky Way stretching across
>   To the isle of Sado.

荒海や佐渡によこたふ天の川　　　芭　蕉

Another of Bashô, to compare with the *Daffodils.* (Note that though both poems speak of the author's feelings, both are equally objective, since they do so to express the nature of the flower itself.)

> How they pull the heart-strings—
>> Coming along the mountain road—
>>> These violets!

山路來てなにやらゆかし菫草　　　芭　蕉

The most famous of all *haiku,* of which I give an unconventional translation, has this same quality, that is, of expressing an unsymbolical, unallegorical fact, which is nevertheless a Fact, and The Fact.

> The old pond.
>> A frog jumps in—
>>> Plop!

古池や蛙飛びこむ水の音　　　芭　蕉

Against this translation it may be urged that "plop" is an unpoetical, rather humorous word. To this I would answer, "Read it over slowly, about a dozen times, and this association will disappear largely." Further, it may be said, the expression "plop" is utterly different in sound from "mizu no oto." This is not quite correct. The English "sound of the water" is too gentle, suggesting a running stream or brook. The Japanese word "oto" has an onomatopoeic value much nearer to "plop." Other translations are wide of the mark. "Splash" sounds as if Bashô himself had fallen in. Yone Noguchi's "List the water sound," shows Bashô in a graceful pose with finger in air. "Plash," by Henderson, is also a misuse of words. Anyway, it is lucky for Bashô that he was born a Japanese, because probably not even he could have said it in English. Now we come to the meaning. An English author writes as follows:

Some scholars maintain that this *haiku* about the frog is a perfect philosophical comment on the littleness of human life in comparison with the infinite. Such poems are hints, suggestions, rather than full expressions of an idea.

No *haiku* is a philosophical comment. Human life is not little: it is not to be compared with the infinite, whatever that is. *Haiku* are not hints; they suggest nothing whatever.

One of the great merits of this poem is that it lends itself to almost any interpretation that may be put upon it. But in general these may be reduced to four:

1. It is an ordinary poem of no special merit. This modern view allows it historic importance, and marks for its objectivity.

2. It is an expression of silence and serenity, accentuated in prospect and retrospect, by the sound of the water made by the frog. This, I think we may say, is the impression made on the average reader, who has some appreciation of Bashô's way of life.

3. It is a symbolic and mystical poem. The sound of the water is the Voice of God, "old" means timeless, the pond is infinity, the plunging of the frog into the water is the baptism of the soul in death, the death of the self. (To be quite honest, I must say that I have just invented this interpretation myself.) Almost all Japanese would recoil from this instinctively. When I translated what I have just written, to my wife, she said, "It reminds me somehow of the Olympic Games," and this is the reaction of a healthy, lively mind to such a false and forced explanation. God, eternity, infinity, death, the soul, — such conceptions are possible though hardly attractive subjects for *haiku,* but as stated above, *haiku* are not hints, they do not suggest such notions to us.

4. Suzuki[1] relates the story of this *haiku* being an answer to the question "What is reality?", but this seems as apochryphal as that of Kikaku's suggesting 山吹や (The yellow rose) as the first part of the poem and Bashô's rejection of it for 古池や. Suzuki further says, "The source of life has been grasped," and this is no doubt true, and it is equally true of all poetry, all art, all music, though the grasping has different degrees of strength and persistence. The danger of this view is that it makes this poem 禪くさい, makes it stink of Zen.

Before I explain the poem, let me say four things:

(a) A poor *haiku* of Bashô is better than the best of Kikaku, Buson, or Issa. In this respect, English and Japanese poetry differ very much. When we read an English poem it is pleasant and profitable to know the author, but not essential. But it is necessary to know, for example, that Bashô is the writer of a certain *haiku,* for several reasons. First and most obviously, *haiku* are very short. Second, if we know that Bashô wrote the *haiku,* we summon up the whole of our poetic energies as we read it. Third, our knowledge of Bashô's choice of poverty; his profound realisation of the impermanence of all things; his tender love of human beings; his view of poetry as insight into reality, not mere art or literature; his desire for the naked, unadorned truth, — this knowledge enables us to look with Bashô's eyes at what he saw,—the moon, the flowers, the faces of his disciples; to listen with his ears to what he heard,—the voices of the cicada, the dripping of the rain, the silence of the sky.[2] Last, however deep we delve into the

[1] In *Zen Buddhism and its Influence on Japanese Culture,* page 147.
[2] Compare Wordsworth, of his sister:
> She gave me eyes, she gave me ears,
> And humble cares and delicate fears,
> And love and thought and joy.

meaning, however high we may soar with it, we feel *safe*, with the same feeling that we have towards things, towards nature itself. We trust in the unaffected sincerity of Basho.

(b) Partly due to the influence of Masaoka Shiki, the modern view of *haiku* has swung away from Bashô towards the typical English attitude, as expressed in *The Friend of Man,* an essay on walking-sticks, by A. A. Milne.

> Our stick must be propped in the sand while from a suitable distance we throw stones at it. However beautiful the sea, its beauty can only be appreciated properly in this fashion. Scenery must not be taken at a gulp; we must absorb it unconsciously. With the mind gently exercised as to whether we scored a two on the band or a one just below it, and with the muscles of the arm at stretch, we are ideally receptive of beauty.

That is to say, it avoids all so-called religious notions and reasonings, all didacticism and moralising; it registers any and every emotion. The danger here is first, a deficiency of passion, and second, its correlative, an exclusively pluralistic view of the world, in which we scarcely ever see what Emerson calls "the Ever-blessed One," the unity of life which is the nature of the individual thing itself.

Further, to correct the generalisations made above, it is instructive to compare two poems, both of early summer, Bashô's,

> The voice of the cuckoo!
>   And the tall
>   Irises.

ほととぎす啼くや五尺のあやめ草

and Davies'

> A rainbow and a cuckoo Lord!

.   .   .   .   .   .

> May never come together again :
>   May never come
>   This side the tomb.

In the English poem the feeling of warmth and gratitude to
life, ("Lord") and its impermanence ("this side the tomb")
are expressed in order to enhance the soft round voice of the
cuckoo and the soft round arc of the rainbow.   The Japanese
poem is very plain, only the sharp shrill voice of the unseen cuckoo[1] and the sharp green spears of the flags and
their purple flowers.

There is a faint touch of morbidity, of self and self-love
in the English poem which we do not find in such poems as
Wordsworth's *To the Cuckoo* or *Daffodils*.   Our feelings are at
the same time pushed forward and pulled back ; there is no
complete self-abandonment. Compare Bashô's poem, when the
impermanence of life is the *subject ;* vastly inferior to Davies'
though it be, it has not this double meaning :

> The Festival of the Dead :
>   But from the Burning-ground arises smoke,
>   Even today.

魂まつりけふも燒場のけぶりかな

(c) Of all poems about frogs or animals, in this poem of
Bashô the actual living creature has least connection with the
poetical meaning. So Charles Lamb, who wrote the cannibal-
istic essay, *Roast Pig,* and who says in a letter to John Clare,
August 31, 1832, of frogs,

The nicest little rabbity things you ever tasted.   Make
Mrs Clare pick off the hind quarters, boil them plain, with
parsley and butter.   The forequarters are not as good.
She may let them hop off by themselves,

[1] A different bird from the English cuckoo.

would be just as qualified to understand the poem as anyone
e'se. But this must be modified a little. Neither this poem
nor any other, as poetry, teaches the love of animals or any
other moral quality; a man may dislike all animals, all living
things, all things, and still be a poet. Keats may speak of becoming a sparrow "pecking at the gravel outside the window,"
with his mouth full of sparrow-pie. Nevertheless, just as in
art the significant form is enriched by the subject-matter, so in
this poem, love of old things, of ponds, of water, of frogs, of
the infinite range of the sounds of water, makes a great difference to the overtones of the poem. "Overtones" is used
here in its strict musical sense, that is, it does not mean that
things not mentioned in the poem, such as serenity or silence,
are suggested. "Love" also, means the whole energy of the
personality, untrammeled by likes and dislikes, desire and disgust.

(d) The time of the poem. Most people take this as being
the day-time, but it is suggested that early evening is better
for two reasons. First, the world is quieter and the sound of
the water more noticeable; second, evening is more in accord
with the spirit of 古池や, the *old* pond. Against this it may
be urged that without being told the time specifically or indirectly, we have no right to do anything but take it as referring to the day-time. We might compromise perhaps, by
taking the time as five or six o'clock in summer, when the evening hush begins.

I give two meanings, according as we take the poem to
be what was seen and heard by Bashô, or as heard only.

(i) It is just the old pond and the frog and the 'plop' and
no more and no less. "No more" means there is no symbolism, no mysticism, no diving into infinity, no listening to the

voice of Universal Nature. "No less" means that the mind
is spread out in a smooth glassy surface; the mind is green
("a green thought in a green shade") with goggle eyes and
webbed feet. It is "Plop!" The real pond, the real frog, the
real jumping were seen, were heard, were seen-heard, when
Bashô's eyes were flicked open by the 'plop' of the water.
This is the state of being undivided from a thing, from all
things, a state in which we are as Divine as God Himself, described by Eckehart:

> Gott ist ungeschieden von allen Dingen, denn er ist ihnen
> inniger als sie sich selbst. So soll auch der Mensch von
> allen Dingen ungeschieden sein . . . Denn Gottes Gottheit
> liegt darin dass er von allen Dingen ungeschieden ist.
> *Darum nimmt auch der Mensch, der ungeschieden ist von*
> *allen Dingen, die Gottheit da, wo Gott die Gottheit selber*
> *nimmt.*

(ii) At the moment of the 'plop,' the sound and the
silence, the movement and the stillness, were perceived un-
separated, uncontrasted, unantagonised, as they were before
the Spirit of God brooded over the Chaos. And if you have
seen one piece of reality, you have seen all, for the parts are
not less than the whole. Montaigne says,

> Et si vous avez vécu un jour, vous avez tout vu. Un
> jour est égal à tous jours. Il n'y a point d'autre lumière,
> ny d'autre nuit. Ce Soleil, cette Lune, ces Etoiles, cette
> disposition, c'est celle même que vos aïeux ont jouyé, et
> qui entretiendra vos arrière-neveux.
> Non alium videre patres: aliumve nepotes
> Aspicent.

Suzuki says, "This leap is just as weighty a matter as the fall
of Adam from Eden." This is true enough, but this is mysticism. If we say, The fall of Adam from Eden is just as weighty

a matter as the leap of the frog, this is Zen. Mysticism and Zen overlap, but are distinct. Mysticism sees the infinite meaning in the (apparently) trivial thing; Zen sees the thing, the fall of Adam, your own fall out of the window, *and no more*. True, everything is in the thing, but it is not seen as everything, but as the thing. Let me make this clear in some examples.

The servant has given the dog a bone. He comes into the room carrying it. He is blind and deaf to everything else, his world is the size and shape and colour and taste of the bone. I sit and look at the dog, and for a few moments there is nothing between me and the dog and the bone, nothing separating, nothing joining us. You could, as the phrase goes, knock me down with a feather, or rather, you could not knock me down with a club, burn me in fire or drown me in water, because I am not there at all. Then I *re-collect myself*, my eternal life is over and this life continues as before. I look up at the blue sky. I look and look until my very soul is without form and void, until my soul itself is blue and the sky colourless. One last example from Chinese poetry, the best translation (Waley's) of the best poem in the world:

> Swiftly the years, beyond recall,
> Solemn the stillness of this fair morning.
> I will clothe myself in spring-clothing,
> And visit the slopes of the Eastern Hill.
> By the mountain-stream a mist hovers,
> Hovers a moment, then scatters.
> There comes a wind blowing from the south
> That brushes the fields of new corn.

邁邁時運穆穆良朝　襲我春服薄言東郊
山滌餘霭宇曖微霄　有風自南翼彼新苗

(陶淵明)

CHAPTER XVI

PANTHEISM, MYSTICISM, ZEN

PART II

Pseudo-pantheists betray themselves at every turn, often through disclosure of their dualism or their disgust and hatred of something.   So with Pope's famous lines,

> All are but parts of one stupendous whole,
> Whose body Nature is, and God the soul,

in the first line we have unity, broken into two in the second. It continues,

> That, changed through all, and yet in all the same,

sticking the two parts together again,

> Great in the earth, as in the ethereal frame,
> Warms in the sun, refreshes in the breeze,
> Glows in the stars and blossoms in the trees,
> Lives through all life, extends through all extent,
> Spreads undivided, operates unspent:
> Breathes in our soul, informs our mortal part,
> As full, as perfect in a hair as heart;

which begins to sound like the real thing, but then in the next lines,

> As full, as perfect in vile man that mourns
> As the rapt Seraphim that sings and burns,

he lets the cat out of the bag with his version of the missionary hymn,

> Where every prospect pleases,
> And only man is vile.

Man is not vile: man is divine, like all other things and more divine than they, in that he perceives their divinity. To the pure all things are pure. To the divine all things are divine.[1]

In Richard Jefferies we find the same underlying choice between the beautiful and the ugly, the charming and the disgusting. To Zen such an attitude is inconceivable but it is the negation of pantheism also. In *The Story of My Heart* (the title is enough to give the game away), he writes,

> The rich blue of the unattainable flower of the sky drew my soul towards it, and there it rested, for pure colour is rest of heart.

This is good, and very good, but he proceeds,

> By all these I prayed; I felt an emotion of the soul beyond all definition; with these I prayed, as if they were the keys of an instrument, of an organ, with which I swelled forth the notes of my soul, redoubling my own voice by their power,

and this is bad, very bad. This concentration on self, on the soul, the psyche, limits while it seems to open an infinite vista.

> Had any shepherd accidentally seen me lying on the turf, he would only have thought I was resting a few minutes. I made no outward show. Who could have imagined the whirlwind of passion that was going on within me as I reclined there!

From this self-absorbtion, this spiritual masturbation, arise all evil habits of thought, misanthropy and sensuality.

---

[1] Wird sie (die Seele) dann Gott? Spräche ich das, das klänge unglaublich für die, deren Sinn dazu zu swach und die es darum nicht verstehen. (Eckehart)

Unless of the human form, no pictures hold me; the rest
are flat surfaces. The potters, the architects, meaningless,
stony. No prayer with these.

He speaks lovingly of the grass, the bees, the yellow wheat,
and then says suddenly what he really felt:

There is nothing human in nature.

Contrast Wordsworth:

For I have learned
To look on nature, not as in the hour
Of thoughtless youth; but hearing oftentimes
The still sad music of humanity.

He utters the old complaint, that

All nature, all the universe we can see, is absolutely
indifferent to us. The trees care nothing for us.

It is time someone put a stop to this kind of maudlin talk.
Is water to gush from the rock when I am thirsty? Is the
stone to move out of the way lest I trip over it, the sun to
pause in heaven to prolong my joys, and to fall like a thunder-
bolt below the horizon when I am sad? Must nature blubber
with me, and the leaves clap their hands with our joy? And
this from Jefferies of all men, who himself had no sympathy
with Nature, who hated it fanatically, who speaks of " the dis-
torted fishes, the ghastly cuttles, the hideous eel-like shapes,
the centipede-like things," and says of them, " They have no
shape, form, grace or purpose." The toad is a thing of horror,
the snake "is utterly opposed to the ever present Idea in the
mind." The dog's head is almost as repellent to the hand as
the toad is to the eye. The neck of the horse he will pass, but
the hind legs are " anti-human." (Man is truly the impudent

animal.)[1]   He is full of the most absurd ideas and self-contra-
dictions, speaking of "the effortless creed of Confucius"; "all
asceticism is the vilest blasphemy," on one page, and, "I would
submit to a severe discipline and to [sic] go without many
things cheerfully, for the good and happiness of the human
race," on the next.   He says all diseases are preventible.   "It
is perfectly certain that all accidents are preventible."   He
hopes succeeding generations will be able to be idle, that nine-
tenths of their time will be leisure time, and then, poor fellow,
says, "I will work towards that end with all my heart."   No
one can stand outside tradition, outside Christianity or Buddhism, without falling into these aberrations and eccentricities
of thought and feeling.

> For none of us liveth to himself, and no man dieth to him-
> self.

Coleridge is another of those on the black list, partly for
insincere imitation of Wordsworth, partly for his own native
lack of religion and poetry.   He is at the other extreme of
Jefferies, unable to free himself from the cruder interpretations
of the Christian dogma; that is to say, everything is taken unpoetically and alternates in the most disagreeable and dis-
concerting manner with Platonism, Pantheism and Words-
worthianism.   In *Religious Musings,* composed at the end of
1794, the argument is the following hotch-potch:

Introduction.   Person of Christ.   His prayer on the Cross.
The process of his Doctrines in the mind of the Individual.

[1] On a moonlight night we have a chance to "see ourselves as others
(the moon) see us":

         The full moon, and under the trees
            Their shadows—how beautiful
                  Compared to mine!   (Baishitsu, d. 1853)
         名月や草木に劣る人のかげ   (梅　室)
See Cowper, *The Task,* V, 6-23.

Character of the Elect. Superstition. Digression to the present War. Origin and Uses of Government and Property. The present State of Society. The French Revolution. Millennium. Universal Redemption. Conclusion. He expresses the division of the unity of being in the following odious lines:

> Lovely was the death
> Of Him whose life was Love! Holy with power
> He on the thought-benighted Sceptic beamed
> Manifest Godhead, melting into day
> What floating mists of dark idolatry
> Broke and misshaped the omnipresent Sire:

Coleridge is so sickening, in poetry so vulgar, in religion so sanctimonious, that I cannot bear to give any more extracts; read also *Frost at Midnight* which is Wordsworth minus poetry.

Mrs. Browning often has a similar kind of poetical bad manners. What really distinguishes Chaucer, Milton, Shakespeare, and Wordsworth from the rest, is that they may fall, and do, into insipidity, into prose, into nonsense, but never into vulgarity. They could never by any conceivable slip of the mind or pen, write the following lines from *Human Life's Mystery*:

> We vibrate to the pant and thrill
> Wherewith Eternity has curled
> In serpent-twine about God's seat;

In *Aurora Leigh* there are many lines in which the matter is good but not the manner, and that of course, means the matter itself has some rotten place inside. What is wrong at bottom is the duality, which is most pernicious precisely when it apes a unity. In the middle of the 7th book she speaks, rightly, of the artist,

> Who paints a tree, a leaf, a common stone
> With just his hand, and finds it suddenly
> A-piece with and coterminous to his soul,
> Why else do these things move him, leaf or stone?

But then the fatal division comes in :

> The bird's not moved, that pecks at a spring-shoot;
> Nor yet the horse, before a quarry a-graze;
> But man, the two-fold creature, apprehends
> The two-fold manner, in and outwardly,
> And nothing in the world comes single to him.

Again in the 5th Book :

> There's not a flower of spring
> That dies ere June, but vaunts itself allied
> By issue and symbol, by significance
> And correspondence, to that spirit-world
> Outside the limits of our space and time,
> Whereto we are bound.

"Allied," "symbol," "significance," "correspondence," "*that*
spirit world,"—all these expressions separate where they seem
to unite. When Mrs. Browning philosophises, it is only as Dr.
Johnson says, a dog walking on its hind legs. When she expresses her primary intuitions simply, they are often humorous,
and sometimes profound, as for example,

> If we say a true word, instantly
> We feel 'tis God's, not ours,

but immediately she begins to gabble and spoil it all :

> and pass it on
> Like bread at sacrament we taste and pass
> Nor handle for a moment, as indeed
> We dared to set up any claim to such !

Look at a more painful example, a few lines before:

> Earth's crammed with heaven,
> And every common bush afire with God:
> But only he who sees takes off his shoes.

The first two lines are by no means the language of Zen, and as for the third line Zen would point out that the shoes are equally holy.   Nevertheless, it is magnificient poetry expressing the all-enveloping spirituality of matter, and the truth that everything depends on how we look at things.   But the next three lines! — as if she were composing an example of bathos for a text book of rhetoric:

> The rest sit round it and pluck blackberries,
> And daub their natural faces unaware
> More and more from the first similitude.

Give me the blackberry-eaters, with their shoes on, and no cant or humbug.

There are other mystics whose direct apprehension of truth is to some extent confounded by dogmas (taken literally) or by what is more difficult to avoid, the habits of thought and vocabulary of their age.   An example of the former is the Roman Catholic, Robert Southwell, martyred at Tyburn, 1594-5 at the age of 24, after three years of torture in the Tower of London.   Each of his poems has something, some aspect of Zen in it.   In *Times Go By Turns,* the instability of human life, yet its sufficiency:

> Thus with succeeding turns, God tempereth all,
> That man may hope to rise yet fear to fall.

In *Loss In Delay,* the "Do it now!" principle:

> Good is best when soonest wrought,

and the principle of not acting according to principles, but according to the circumstances, with a whole mind,

> Out of season, out of price.

The Burning Babe, perhaps the most remarkable of all English religious poems, reminds one of the Old English *The Rood,* where the cross itself speaks of the sufferings of Christ.

THE BURNING BABE

As I in hoary winter's night stood shivering in the snow,
Surprised I was with sudden heat which made my heart to
glow;
And lifting up a fearful eye to view what fire was near,
A pretty babe all burning bright did in the air appear,
Who scorched with exceeding heat such floods of tears did
shed,
As though His floods should quench his flames with what
his tears were fed;
Alas! quoth He, but newly born in fiery heats of fry,
Yet none approach to warm their hearts or feel my fire
but I!
My faultless breast the furnace is, the fuel wounding thorns,
Love is the fire, and sighs the smoke, the ashes shame and
scorns;
The fuel justice layeth on, and mercy blows the coals;
The metal in this furnace wrought are men's defiled souls;
For which, as now on fire I am, to work them to their good,
So will I melt into a bath, to wash them in my blood:
With this He vanished out of sight, and swiftly shrunk away,
And straight I called unto mind that it was Christmas-day.

This is full of the most shocking mixed metaphors and contradictions, to which Southwell has a Shakespearean indifference. With some changes of metaphor it could be equally well applied to Buddha, when we think of the years of anguish of mind and body he suffered before his enlightenment. To bring the poem down to its lowest and most understandable level, we may say that virtue, Zen, truth, babes, are infectious, contagious. So are all things, everything is infectious. Yes, but virtue more than vice, Zen more than wabbling, truth more than error, Christ more than Judas. "A pretty burning babe shedding tears": he is pretty because "Beauty is truth, truth beauty," burning, because "Zen is boiling oil over a fire," a babe because truth is simple. So Goethe says:

Ich sage immer und wiederhole es, die Welt könnte nicht bestehen, wenn sie nicht so einfach wäre. Dieser elende Boden wird nun schon tausend Jahre bebaut, und seine Kräfte sind immer dieselbigen. Ein wenig Regen, ein wenig Sonne, und es wird jeden Frühling wieder grün.

And in the following well-known passage, he uses the simile of children to express this directness and naturalness of truth:

Alles Denken zum Denken hilft nichts: man muss von Natur rightig sein, so dass die guten Einfälle immer wie freie Kinder Gottes vor uns dastehen und uns zurufen: da sind wir!

"Shedding tears" is what St. Thomas of Aquinus calls grief, as distinct from mercy. In mercy we stand outside, in grief for ourselves or for others, there is a complete identification with the other person and no feeling of *my* sympathy for *him*.

Mercy is compassion for another's unhappiness, and therefore regards someone else, not ourselves, except by likeness. But as it is grief that we feel towards ourselves, as when we suffer a cruelty, so it is grief, not mercy, we feel in the sufferings of persons who are so joined as to be part of us.[1]

These "floods of tears" are of the essence of Zen, however

[1] Quoted in *Poetic Experience*, Thomas Gilby, page 80. This is a book worth buying; not a book to be borrowed.

stoical and heroic it may otherwise seem. "But newly born,"
implies what the mystics call the Eternal Birth of Christ. The
expression "washed in blood" is a very strange one and shows
the power that experience gives to the mind to combine in
thought what words divide. Intellectually impossible to conceive and esthetically disgusting, this phrase, which seems to
occur first in *Revelation* I, 5, "Unto him that loved us and
washed us from our sins in his own blood," is used to express
the most profound and fundamental truth of the Christian
religion, the redemption of the world by the voluntary suffering of good men.   Buddhists therefore should not despise this
apparently repulsive phrase, for it represents equally the fundamental of Buddhism.   And if anyone thinks "the bread of
life" is poetical and "the blood of the Lamb" is odious, let
him remember Herbert's words:

> Look on meat; think it dirt, then eat a bit,
> And say withal—"earth to earth I commit."

The poem *I Dye Alive* was written in prison, probably during intervals of torture and under the shadow of the scaffold:

> O life! what letts thee from a quicke decease?
>   O death! what draws thee from a present praye?
> My feast is done, my soul would be at ease,
>   My grace is saide; O death! come take away.

"My grace is saide"; this is the attitude of Zen. Grace, that
is, thanks, is said, said once for all for everything past, present,
future in the history of the universe; and said somewhere at
the bottom of the mind as we receive all the gifts of God one
after another.

> I live but such a live as ever dyes;
>   I dye, but such a death as never endes;

> My death to end my dying life denyes,
>   And life my living death no whitt amends.

Southwell is speaking of his life in death just before execution,
but as Victor Hugo says, we are all sentenced to death with
an indefinite reprieve, and what Southwell said of himself at
that time is equally true of everyone at each moment as it
comes. We do not live, we do not die, we live-die. What is
the relation of this living-dying and the actual death and dissolution in time which we all suffer? Simply that the living-
dying stops. We stop living and we stop dying.

> Thus still I dye, yet still I do revive;
>   My living death by dying life is fedd;
> Grace more than nature keeps my hart alive,
>   Whose idle hopes and vague desires are deade.

"Grace" and "nature" is of course a false distinction; "idle
hopes" and "vague desires" also is a mistake, but one hardly
likes to point this out to a man about to die a degrading death.
All hopes are idle, all desires are vain; human life is useless
and profitless. Thus hopes are not idle, desires not vain, since
these words, being universally applicable, have no meaning;
hopes are hopes, desires are desires, human life is human life,
no more, no less.

> Not where I breath, but where I love, I live;
>   Not where I love, but where I am, I die;
> The life I wish, must future glory give,
>   The deaths I feele in present daungers lye.

The first two lines rise up like a wave to Zen, the last two
fall back towards the dogma of a future state of the soul. The
next poem, *Of the Blessed Sacrament of the Aulter,* is very good
indeed. There are very few religious poems in English which
surpass this in profound thought, sincerity and dignity.

The angells' eyes, whome veyles cannot deceive,
  Might best disclose that best they do descerne;
Men must with sounde and silent faith receive
  More than they can by sense or reason lerne;
God's poure our proofes, His workes our witt exceede,
  The doer's might is reason of His deede.

"Sense or reason" cannot grasp things as wholes but only the
parts.   "The doer's might is reason of His deeds," Southwell
applies to God only, but it applies equally to us when there
is Zen in our activity.   It is the true meaning of "Might is
Right."   This natural flowing of the action out of our deepest
self, this inevitability, is what characterises the greatest works
of art and the most trivial perfect behaviour.   What Southwell
really says is, "The action is itself the reason of the act."

A body is endow'd with ghostly rightes;
  And Nature's worke from Nature's law is free;
In heavenly sunne lye hidd eternall lightes,
  Lightes cleere and neere, yet them no eye can see;
Dedd formes a never-dyinge life do shroude;
  A boundless sea lyes in a little cloude.

The first two lines express the mind's absolute freedom,
God's absolute freedom.   God is a spirit.   Man is a spirit.
Were there no likeness between them there could be no love,
no knowledge of each other.   In a simple state of culture,
freedom from Nature's law was conceived of as miracle.   Later
this was found to be not merely irrational but an arbitrary
interference that somehow or other could not satisfy our innate
idea of freedom.   Freedom, it was felt, is doing what you like;
but freedom is Zen and Zen means liking what you do.   The
doing and the liking are of course not separate things.   The
action and its indivisible and invariable concomitant, its happiness, is free, is the reason of the activity.   "In heavenly

sunne lye hidd eternall lightes;" this is what Blake saw when
he looked at the sun; what Bashô saw when he looked at the
moon; what I see when I look at my dog. "Dedd formes a
never-dying life do shroude," is not a very satisfactory expression.   The shrouding is done by us, and the form is dead only
in the sense that

> it is not the form that exists but the composite, which is
> determined by the form as a certain kind of thing.[1]

"A boundless sea lyes in a little cloude," is expanded, in Southwell's usual way, into the next four verses.

> The God of hoastes in slender hoste doth dwell,
>   Yea, God and man with all to ether dewe,
> That God that rules the heavens and rifled hell,
>   That man whose death did us to life renewe:
> That God and man that is the angells' blisse,
>   In forme of bredd and wyne our nurture is.

The pun in the first line, like some of Hood's, and the play on
words in

> We thought her dying when she slept,
>   And sleeping when she died

has an extraordinary power in it.   It is the best I know.

> Whole may His body be in smallest breadd,
>   Whole in the whole, yea whole in every crumme;
> With which be one or be tenn thousand fedd,
>   All to each one, to all but one doth cumme;
> And though ech one as much as all receive,
>   Not one too much, nor all too little have.

From this verse we see how to read the story of the Feeding of the Multitude.   It is a parable, like that of the walking

[1] Gilby, *Poetic Experience*, p. 7.

on the water, which Goethe said he loved better than any
other. We find it in the mediaeval problem how many
devils could stand on the head of a pin. It is resurrected by
Chesterton in *The Holy of Holies*.

> Speller of the stones and weeds,
> Skilled in Nature's crafts and creeds,
> Tell me what is in the heart
> Of the smallest of the seeds.

> God Almighty, and with Him
> Cherubim and Seraphim,
> Filling all eternity—
> Adonai Elohim.

There is the same thing in the *Yuima Kyō*,[1] where Yuima ac-
comodates thousands of people in his one small room.

> One soule in man is all in everye part;
>   One face at once in many mirrhors shynes;
> One fearfull noyse doth make a thousand start;
>   One eye at once of countless things defynes;
> If proofes of one in many, nature frame,
>   God may in straunger sort performe the same.

This kind of argument, popularised by Drummond in his
Natural Law in the Spiritual World, is weakening to Southwell's declaration. If someone says, "Death rather than dishonour!" we believe it and, for a moment, could act on it.
When we begin to think about it, analyse it, argue for and
against it, it loses all its power to move us.

> God present is at once in everye place,
>   Yett God in every place is ever one;
> So may there be by gifts of ghostly grane,
>   One man in many rooms, yett filling none;
> Sith angells may effects of bodyes shewe,
>   God angells' gifts on bodyes may bestowe.

[1] See Suzuki, *Essays in Zen Buddhism, First Series,* pages 86-7.

There is something very beautiful in the first two lines both in the thought and the expression of it. The idea of the last two lines seems to be this. In the Old Testament we have several examples of the materialisation of angels, spirit manifesting properties of matter. So we may expect the reverse operation, the spiritualisation of matter, in which the body may exhibit, as in the miracles of the Gospels, the properties of pure spirit, that is to say, may be freed of the limitations of time and space.

The unity of God and man is expressed also by Herbert in *Affliction*.

My heart did heave and there came forth ' O God! '
By that I knew that Thou wast in the grief,
To guide and govern it to my relief,
    Making a scepter of the rod :
        Hadst Thou not had Thy part,
Sure the unruly sigh had broke my heart.

To understand the truth of the first two lines we must remember Wordsworth's

There is a comfort in the strength of love;
'Twill make a thing endurable, which else
Would overset the brain, or break the heart.
                              (*Michael*, ll. 448-450)

There is a comfort in the depth of the emotion, if it is deep enough to go down to where God is.   This idea of Christ suffering with us and we with him, is that of Amida's 18th vow, recorded in the *Daimuryôjukyô* (大無量壽經) :

If I become a Buddha and any one living being of the ten quarters, desiring with deep sincerity, faith and joy, to be born into my realm, is not so born, I will not accept Perfect Understanding.

設我佛を得たらんに、十方の衆生至心に信樂し
て、我國に生んと欲し、乃至十念せんに、若し生
ぜずんば正覺を取らじ、云云。

In Christian terms this means that Christ will not ascend to
Heaven while one sinner remains in Hell.   Thus he shares in
his own person, our grief and pain.   Our rod is his rod.   But
his rod is a sceptre, and thus our rod is that same sceptre. We
suffer, but we are the master of our suffering which is also our
relief.   "Foul is fair and fair is foul."

> But since Thy breath gave me both life and shape,
> Thou know'st my tallies; and when there's assign'd
> So much breath to a sigh, what's then behinde?
>   Or if some yeares with it escape,
>   The sigh then onely is
> A gale to bring me sooner to my blisse.

This verse is a little difficult.   What I think Herbert means is
this: God, who gave me the vital energy which both supports
life and gives it form, in this case, a human form, knows my
capacities and when he allots to me such a violent emotion, I
perceive an indication of my nearness to the Source of Things,
to Reality, to God Himself. Suppose you say such intense grief
burns life away, shortens it; I answer, so much the better.

> Thy life on earth was grief, and Thou art still
> Constant unto it, making it to be
> A point of honour now to grieve in me,
>   And in Thy members suffer ill.
>   They who lament one crosse,
> Thou dying dayly, praise Thee to Thy losse.

At this vital point Christianity and Buddhism coincide.   Not
one Cross, but many ; not one Buddha, but many.   And yet it
is one huge Cross, one great Buddha, for

The whole creation groaneth and travaileth together.

This unity of Nature and Man is stated directly by Wordsworth, in *Lines Written in Early Spring,*

> To her fair works did Nature link
> The human soul that through me ran,

and indirectly, but using a similar metaphor of 'linking,' by
Bashô, in

> Ah, hanging bridge!
> Ivy-ropes
> Entwine existence!

栈やいのちをからむ蔦かつら

Love is both the cause and the effect of this union, this realisation of original unity, as Wordsworth says in *The Excursion,*
I, 194,

> the lesson deep of love which he
> Whom Nature, *by whatever means,* has taught
> To feel intensely, cannot but receive.

Thus Bashô's devotion to Nature and Dante's to Beatrice are
an identical state of mind. Now we can see how Nature, by
whatever means, in flowers or in those whom we love, teaches
us, we see how

> One impulse from a vernal wood
> May teach you more of man,
> Of moral evil and of good,
> Than all the sages can.

So when Bashô says

> The harvest moon!
> Among us, none
> Has a face of beauty.

明月や座に美しき顔もなし

we are not to take this in the literal, comparative meaning,
but in the sense of

> La vista sua face ogni cosa umile,

(*La Vita Nuova,* par. xxvii, the sonnet beginning, Vede per-
fettamente ogni salute.)   The beauty of moon or woman when
perceived purely, without desire of possession, has the effect
of dissolving our pride.   Dante says again,

> Negli occhi porta la mia donna Amore;
> > Perche si fa gentil ciò ch'ella mira:
> > Ov' ella passa, ogni uom vêr lei si gira,
> > E cui saluta fa tremar lo core,

> Sicchè bassando il viso, tutto smuore,
> > E d'ogni suo difetto alor sospira:
> > Fuggon dinanzi a lei superbia ed ira:
> > Aiutatemi, donne, a farle onore.

> Ogni dolcezza, ogni pensiero umile
> > Nasce nel core a chi parlar la sente;
> > Ond' è laudato chi prima la vide.

> Quel ch'ella par quand' un poco sorride,
> > Non si può dicer, nè tener a mente,
> > Si è nuovo miracolo gentile.

(In English, with all the music, that is, half the meaning gone,)

> Love in my lady's eyes is dwelling,
> > Softening all those on whom she looks;
> > Where'er she walks all men turn to behold her,
> > And her salute makes throb their hearts.

> Lowering his face, he pales
> > And sighs at all his weakness;
> > Before her flees all pride and wrath:
> > O help me, ladies, that I do her honour!

All sweetness, and humble thoughts,
  Rise in the heart of him who hears her speak;
  Thus he is praised who sees her first.

That which she appears when faintly smiling,
  No one can tell, nor hold in mind—
  Such is the miracle so rare and sweet!

Compare Masefield's lyric at the end of *The Everlasting Mercy:*

    O lovely lily clean,
    O lily springing green,
    O lily bursting white,
    Dear lily of delight,
    Spring in my heart agen
    That I may flower to men.

Just as the beauty of Beatrice, springing up in the heart of Dante, united him to her, so the beauty of the cherry blossoms, ever-blooming in the mind of Bashô, united him to his old friend.

    Our two lives:
      Between them is the life
        Of the cherry flowers.

    命二つの中に活たる櫻かな

CHAPTER XVII

"RELIGIOUS" POETRY

There is only one thing more dismal than an anthology of religious poetry, and that is a book of jokes. This is not because religious poetry is on the whole poor in quality, both as religion and as poetry, but because "it has designs upon us," like the book of jokes. It wants to push us into the arms of Jesus; it wants to push us off this planet into space, into infinity, into eternity. Once you understand that religion is poetry and poetry is religion, you can never talk about "religious" poetry, you can never take religion and poetry to be two different things, as Professor Suzuki does in his *Zen Buddhism and its Influence on Japanese Culture*. He translates Kikaku's

雨蛙芭蕉にのりて戰ぎけり

> The tree-frog
>> Riding the bashô-leaf,
>>> Sways and quivers.

and says of this frog,

In it and through it one can read the gravest religious truth.

He quotes

> By a little kitten
> Sniffed at,
> Creeps the slug unconcerned.

by Saimaro (才麿) a contemporary of Bashô and Kikaku. The

original, 猫の子に嗅れてゐるや蝸牛, does not say "creeps,"
or "unconcerned"[1]; it is only,

> Sniffed at
>> By a kitten—
>>> The snail!

There is not an atom of truth, not a particle of poetry, not a
spark of Zen here; only sentiment and sentimentality, seen by
Saimaro, or as Suzuki himself says, "a bit of human playful-
ness and sweetness." He then gives Buson's famous verse,
(translated once before in the present book, and differently,)

> The butterfly
>> Resting upon the temple bell,
>>> Asleep.

The surroundings, the historic associations, the quiet sunshine have calmed the mind, emptied it and prepared it for
this slight thrill of surprise at finding a butterfly in such an
unlikely place. The colour (supposing it to be a white butterfly, the commonest,) the delicacy, the lightness, the feeling that
it may be gone the next instant—all this is brought out in contrast with the dark colour, the weight, solidity, rigidity of the
massive bell. *And this is all.* But Professor Suzuki says,[2]

> The haiku is not merely descriptive, it is of religious
> connotation. Human life after all is not any better than
> that of the butterfly, it gains its meaning only when it is
> connected with something far more enduring and all-sus-
> taining. The playfulness, however, Buson the poet had in
> mind comes from the butterfly's utter unawareness of any
> sudden event which may shake the very foundation of its
> existence. The noon hour is come and the monk may

[1] To take や as "unconcerned" is just possible as an explanation,
but not as a translation.
[2] Page 263.

strike the bell and send out a series of terrific vibrations.
This kind of uncertainty always clings to all forms of life.
Man tries to avert it by so-called science, but his greed
asserts itself, and all scientific calculations are upset. If
nature does not destroy, man destroys himself. There is
a great deal of philosophy at the back of this epigrammatic
utterance of Buson.[1]

This reminds us of the Duchess in *Alice in Wonderland*:

" Tut, tut, child," said the Duchess, " Everything's got a
moral if only you can find it."

Buson himself, after he had composed the poem, may have had
such thoughts of the contrast of active and passive, the symbolism of life and death in the butterfly and the bell. I hope
not. But we are all prone to this kind of thing, this sentimen-
talising, unless we remember that poetry, like religion, must
be ascetic, must have the element of poverty in it. In poetry
also,

> Blessed are the poor in spirit.

Wordsworth, the most ascetic of English poets (Hardy
comes a close second,) fell into this poetico-sentimentality
rarely. One example, a conscious one, is in *Lines Written in
Early Spring*:

> And 'tis my faith that every flower
> Enjoys the air it breathes.

1 What he should have said of Buson's *haiku*, is what he says of "A
Fishing Boat," by Baen, facing page 270:

Mere suggestiveness, to my mind, is not enough to describe this. The
idea of " All in One, One in All" must be recognised here. When an
object is picked up, everything else, One and All, comes along with it,
not in the way of suggestion, but all-inclusively, in the sense that *the
object is complete in itself*. (My italics.)

> The budding twigs spread out their fan,
> To catch the breezy air;
> And I must think, do all I can,
> That there was pleasure there.

Nobody wants to know what Wordsworth's faith, his philosophy was, or what he thought about this or that. We can all think as well as Wordsworth, or better. We cannot approach his power, in the year 1798, of

> a heart
> That watches and receives.

Wordsworth, up to the age of 30 would have been surprised. not to say puzzled, if you had asked him to write a religious poem. As he lay dying, Bashó's disciples asked him to write a religious poem (a death-poem). He said with profound truth that every poem he had written since the age of forty had been his death-poem, a religious poem. Symbolism, pantheism, mysticism, religiosity, these are not Zen. Zen is poetry. Compare Coleridge's milk and water, wishy-washy

> He prayeth best who loveth best
> The things both great and small,
> For the good God who loveth us,
> He made and loveth all

with a real religious poem, by Taigi. The circumstances of the poem are thus well described by Mr. Miyamori in *An Anthology of Haiku:*

> The poet was walking home along the road by night. A dog barked at him. He wanted to throw a stone at it. So he looked all round for a stone on the road bathed in an icy bright winter moon; but to his mortification, he could not find one.

This is the poem itself:

> Not a single stone
>> To throw at the dog,—
>> The wintry moon!

犬を打つ石のさてなし冬の月

If you wish to know where the religion is in this, think of the lines in *Expostulation and Reply*,

> Nor less I deem that there are powers
> Which of themselves our minds impress.

"Of themselves." Here again, man's extremity, (just that moment of ego-lessness when mental and physical action is suspended), is God's opportunity—something, Something, some Power, slides imperceptibly into the mind in the form of cold moonlight.

> Think you, mid all this mighty sum
> Of things forever speaking,
> That nothing of itself will come,
> But we must still be seeking?

Zen, religion, poetry, "comes of itself." What then about

Ask, and it shall be given you; seek, and ye shall find; knock, and it shall be opened unto you.

How we can we seek and yet not seek? This Gordian knot is cut for us by Rôshi, Chapter XI:

Thirty spokes makes a wheel; but it is the empty space at the centre that gives it its use. Clay is moulded into a vessel, but the empty space is the useful part. So we see that the existence and use of things has its basis in non-existence.

(Following the interpretation of Inoue Shuten, *Rôshi no Shin Kenkyu*, pp. 80-84)

三十幅は一轂をともにす、その無なるに當つて
車の用あり。埴を挺して以つて器となす、その
無なるに當つて、器の用あり。故に有の以つて
利たるは無の以つて用をなす（が故）なり。

We are to ask fervently, to seek passionately, to knock madly
— but it must be for nothing. When our self is all asked,
sought, knocked away, everything is given, found, opened.
We empty ourselves and God fills us. Emerson says,

> When half-gods go,
> The Gods arrive.

Nature abhors a vacuum.

Christian Religious poetry (not mere verse) gains much
and loses nothing from an interpretation according to Zen.
Let us take two poems, at the extremes of feeling, of mildness
and ferocity, Herbert's *Love,* and Isaac Watts' *The Day of
Judgement.* Without twisting the thoughts or spoiling in any
way the original meaning of the poet, let us re-read them in
the light of Zen, and universalise them.

LOVE

Love bade me welcome! Yet my soul drew back,
        Guilty of dust and sin.
But quick-eyed Love, observing me grow slack
        From my first entrance in,
Drew nearer to me, sweetly questioning,
        If I lacked anything.

A guest, I answered, worthy to be here:
        Love said, you shall be he.
I the unkind, ungrateful? Ah, my dear,
        I cannot look on thee.
Love took my hand, and smiling did reply,
        Who made the eyes but I?

> Truth Lord, but I have marred them: let my shame
>   Go where it doth deserve.
> And know you not, says Love, who bore the blame?
>   My dear, then I will serve.
> You must sit down says Love, and taste my meat:
>   So I did sit and eat.

"Love," here means Love, not love, the opposite of hate; it means Nature, Reality, God, Life. "Guilty of dust and sin." This dust and sin is not in the actions, which *must* be, objectively speaking, dusty and sinful, in a dusty and sinful world, but in the will. This defection, this apostasy of the will is expressed in "drew back." "Quick-eyed Love." How quick all things are, quick to bless, quick to curse. We fall over and swifter than thought, the ground smites us hip and thigh. But the ground is equally quick to support us when we fall, lest we fall further. How quick the pain and yet how quick nature runs to help us. So in the next poem, *The Day of Judgment,* we have

> the gaping waters,
> Quick to devour them,

but they are just as quick to uplift us, to quench our thirst, as to kill us with dropsy. "If I lacked any thing." What do we lack? Nothing at all. What do we possess? Nothing at all. "I the unkind, the ungrateful." In general, the spirit of the Pharisee, and that of the Publican who beat on his breast, is the same. Pride and humility are only the back and front of the same thing; true repentance wipes the slate clean. Further remorse is only masochism, an excuse for non-action. "Who made the eyes but I?" If we grasp this, there is no excuse for false humility:

> I am the doubter and the doubt.

"I have marred them." How can we follow our instincts when

we have such bad ones? "Who bore the blame?" God is to blame for everything, but we are God. Christ dies for us, not once, but daily, eternally. Yet we are one with Christ and he with us. God, Christ is to blame, and we are to blame in so far as we realise the vicarious responsibility of our (original) unity with the Godhead. We are guilty of sin just as Christ was and God is. We are innocent of it in so far as we bear anything and everything for the sake of others.

The intellect beats its wings in vain against the bars of this intellectual cage, but as soon as we say, "Innocent or guilty, I do the will of God," that is, "My dear, then I will serve," all the problem disappears. But even so, we cannot serve God. God serves us, God serves in us. "Taste my meat." What is the taste of this meat? This, with the answer, will make a *Mondô,* and everyone must answer for himself. "So I did sit and eat." No gibble-gabble, no humming and hawing; just sit when you sit, eat when you eat, nothing poetical, nothing religious in it, and yet it is the poetical life, the religious life, the life of Zen.

THE DAY OF JUDGMENT

When the fierce North-wind with his airy forces
Rears up the Baltic to a foaming fury;
And the red lightning with a storm of hail comes
        Rushing amain down,

How the poor sailors stand amazed and tremble!
While the hoarse thunder like a bloody trumpet,
Roars a loud onset to the gaping waters
        Quick to devour them.

Such shall the noise be, and the wild disorder
(If things eternal may be like these earthly)
Such the dire terror when the great Archangel
        Shakes the creation;

Tears the strong pillars of the vault of Heaven,
Breaks up old marble, the repose of princes,
Sees the graves open, and the bones arising,
            Flames all around them.

Hark, the shrill outcries of the guilty wretches!
Lively bright horror and amazing anguish
Stare thro' their eyelids, while the living worm lies
            Gnawing within them.

Thoughts, like old vultures, prey upon their heart-strings,
And the smart twinges, when the eye beholds the
Lofty Judge frowning, and a flood of vengeance
            Rolling before Him.

Hopeless immortals, how they scream and shiver,
While devils push them to the pit wide-yawning,
Hideous and gloomy, to receive them headlong
            Down to the centre!

Stop here, my fancy : (all away, ye horrid
Doleful ideas!) come, arise to Jesus,
How He sits God-like! and the saints around Him
            Throned, yet adoring!

O may I sit there when he comes triumphant,
Dooming the nations! then ascend to glory,
While our Hosannas all along the passage
            Shout the Redeemer.

Now is the Day of Salvation, *now* is the Day of Judgment.   As
the 6th Patriarch says,

An ordinary man is Buddha; desire and passion is enlightenment.   One thought of folly makes a man an ordinary man.   The next enlightened thought, and he is a
Buddha.

凡夫即ち佛、煩惱即ち菩提、前念迷へば即ち
凡夫、後念悟れば即ち佛。   (第二章)

This means that at every moment we are saved or damned, at

every moment[1] there are hosannas or the sound of the bloody trumpet. We are either "throned yet adoring," or screaming and shivering.

> Things are in the saddle
> And ride mankind.

If we are in this condition (and how few are not), the living worm lies gnawing within us.   The man next door, the newspapers, our money in the bank—everything "preys upon the heart-strings."

> My apprehensions come in crowds;
> I dread the rustling of the grass;
> The very shadows of the clouds
> Have power to shake me as they pass.

This is not only the condition of Margaret, it is the story of *Anna Karenina, Crime and Punishment,* of *Hamlet, Lear* and *Othello,* where desire, passion, greed, lust, in a word, attachment to things good and bad,

> Tears up the strong pillars of the vault of Heaven,
> Breaks up old marble, the repose of princes,

and we hear "the shrill outcries of the guilty wretches and watch their "lively bright horror and amazing anguish."

[1] There is an expansion of this thought in the following passage from Hermann Hesse's *Siddhartha:*

Der Sünder, der ich bin und der du bist, der ist Sünder, aber er wird einst wieder Brahma sein, er wird einst Nirvana erreichen, wird Buddha sein—und nun siehe: dies "Einst" ist Tauschung, ist nur Gleichnis! Der Sünder ist nicht auf dem Weg zur Buddhaschaft unterwegs, er ist nicht in einer Entwickelung begriffen obwohl unser Denken sich die Dinge nicht anders vorzustellen weiss.   Nein, in dem Sünder ist, ist jetzt und heute schon der künftige Buddha, seine Zukunft ist alle schon da, du hast in ihm, in dir, in jedem den werdenden, den möglichen, den verborgenen Buddha zu verehren. Die Welt, Freund Govinda, ist nicht unvollkommen, oder auf einem langsamen Wege zur Volkommenheit begriffen: nein, sie ist in jedem Augenblick vollkommen, alle Sünde trägt schon die Gnade in sich, alle kleinen Kinder haben schon den Greis in sich, alle Säuglinge den Tod, alle Sterbenden das ewige Leben.

> There is no rest for the wicked,

and "the wicked" means here not robbers and murderers, but all us ordinary, greedy, self-seeking creatures, who want pleasure without pain, profit without loss, life without death. Bacon says in his *Of Marriage and Single Life,*

> He that hath a wife and children hath given hostages to fortune,[1]

but he who has *anything,* has given hostages to fortune. Only he who has nothing has all things; he has everything and nothing can be taken away from him. This is the attitude expressed in,

> For gods delight in gods,
>   And thrust the weak aside;
> To him who scorns their charities,
>   Their arms are open wide.

The devils who push us into the pit and the angels that raise us to paradise, are the same; and what are they? All the things in the world.

> The wings of Time are black and white
> Pied with morning and with night,

but to the eyes of God there is no day or night, He needs no light to see nor darkness for slumber. So we, if we can only take these devils (all the apparently hostile things), as they are (that is, as God sees them), they are ministering angels, and we are raised aloft on the waves that "gape to devour us." Love, God, Nature, Reality, has no mercy, only justice and truth, tit for tat, an eye for an eye, a tooth for a tooth.

[1] Compare the Japanese proverb, "Children are a cangue in the three worlds." (子は三界の首枷)

Heaven and earth are merciless,

天 地 不 仁 （第 五 章）

says Rôshi. The "flood of vengeance" is always rolling; it is unescapable. The wages of sin is death; the wages of goodness is life. God is "the frowning judge," Fudô, with the uplifted sword. God is love, Kwannon, with a thousand arms to save.

I would like to quote some lines from Herbert's *Advice to Churchgoers,* which has more common sense and humour than any other religious poem known to me.

In church

God is more there, than thou.

Not only in church but in every place, wherever we are, God is more there than we, — in two ways. First, in the simple sense that "In Him we live and move and have our being;" second, in the more profound sense that "In us He lives and moves and has his being." The "I" which looms so large to us is a hallucination, a bubble that the truth is constantly pricking, a scum on the clear water of eternity, a delirium of "life's fitful fever."

All equal are within the church's gate,

and outside it also. The fundamental principle of religion is respect, respect for self, for other human beings, for animals, and for inanimate things. Christ had the "disciple which Jesus loved," and so also have we, and so must we, as human beings, but Heaven has no favourites, and beyond our human likes and dislikes, there must be for us also the Ground of Existence ("within the Church's gate,") where all things are equal.

> Who marks in church-time others' symmetry,
> Makes all their beauty his deformity.

Human beauty is one of the chief causes of moral ugliness, but beauty is in the eye of the beholder. "If thine eye be single, thy whole body shall be full of light." When we can talk with the same *degree* (not kind) of interest to an old lady as to her pretty niece, what a blessed state this is!

> Do not grudge
> To pick out treasures from an earthen pot,

or a chamber-pot. To God, a man is the same, on a chamber-pot or on a throne. All men are naked under their clothes. A tiger seems a nobler animal than a bed-bug. There seem to be vessels of honour and vessels of dishonour, and in this short life we can hardly escape this feeling, but at the back of our minds, in the bottom of our hearts, there must be the full realisation that there is no difference between birth and death, the entrance and the exit, good morning and good night, the dining-room and the lavatory.

There is a short piece of writing by Rikeiho[1] (Yikyubo, in Korean) 1168-1241 A.D., poet, musician and Prime Minister, which illustrates this fact of the equality of things:

A friend of mine came and said, "Yesterday evening I saw some rascal beat to death a dog which was wandering about there. It was such a pitiful sight, and I was so upset by it, I resolved never to touch dog's flesh again." I said to him, "Last night I saw a man sitting by the fire cracking lice and burning them. I was so upset I made up my mind never to kill another louse." My friend said indignantly, "A louse is a very small thing; what I saw was a big animal done to death and because I felt so grieved, I told you about it. Why do you answer me so

[1] See a later page.

facetiously?" I replied, "All things with life and breath, from common men to oxen, horses, pigs, sheep, down to insects, mole-crickets and ants, — all, without exception, love life and hate death. Do you imagine for a moment that big animals only dislike to die and the little ones don't mind it? Thus the death of a louse is no different from that of a dog. This is quite clear; why should you suppose I was talking flippantly? Bite your own ten fingers and see. The thumb hurts; but how about the rest of the fingers? In one body there is no distinction between large and small members. All that has blood and flesh feels the same pain. So it is with all things that have received life and breath: how can you think that one hates death and another finds it pleasant? Now you go home and quietly meditate on this, and when you see that the horns of a snail are the same as those of a bull, the wren of equal value with the mighty Rukh, then come, and we'll talk of religion again."

蝨 犬 說　(東國李相國集卷第二十一說序)

客有謂予曰。 昨晚見一不逞男子。 以大棒子
椎遊犬而殺者。 勢甚可哀。 不能無痛心。 自
是誓不食犬豕之肉矣。 予應之曰。 昨見有人
擁熾爐捫蝨而烘者。 予不能無痛心。 自誓不
復捫蝨矣。 客憮然曰。 蝨微物也。 吾見庬然
大物之死。 有可哀者故言之。 子以此爲對。
豈欺我耶, 予曰。 凡有血氣者。 自黔首至于
牛馬猪羊昆虫螻蟻。 其食生惡死之心。 未始
不同。 豈大者獨惡死。 而小則不爾耶。 然則
犬與蝨之死一也。 故舉以爲的對。 豈故相欺
耶。 子不信之。 盍齕爾之十指乎。 獨拇指痛
而餘則否乎。 在一體之中。 無大小支節。 均
有血肉。 故其痛則同。 況各受氣息者。 安有
彼之惡死而此之樂乎。 子退焉。 冥心靜慮。
視蝸角如牛角。 齊斥鷃爲大鵬。 然後吾方與
之語道矣。

> The worst speak something good: if all want sense,
> God takes a text, and preacheth patience.

All *does* want sense. Things just are, events just occur. All things are senseless. They have no meaning beyond the fact of the things themselves. This is the region Christians get to when they are asked, "Who made God?" "God takes a text and preacheth patience." This is one of the most beautiful thoughts in English literature. The practical meaning is the same as, "We suffer fools gladly," but "God takes a text and preaches,"—this is wonderful! It is Wordsworth's

> Let nature be your teacher,

but taking "nature" in the true sense of all that exists. For God is always speaking through the most trivial things as well as the greatest. In the *Introduction* to the 8th Case of the *Hekiganroku,* it says,

At one time, one blade of grass is as effective as a sixteen foot golden Statue of Buddha. At another time, a sixteen foot golden Statue of Buddha is as effective as a blade of grass.

有時將一莖草作丈六金身用。　有時將丈六金
身作一莖草用。　　　　　　　(碧巖錄、第八則)

God is always preaching, through the biggest fool or knave, as through the greatest saint or genius. This is the meaning of Emerson's

What you are, speaks so loudly I cannot hear what you say,

that is, Reality speaks so loudly in you I can't hear what you are saying to distract me from it.

And lastly:

God sent him, whatsoe'er he be.

Nero and Caligula, Judge Jeffreys, all the monsters of antiquity, as well as Marcus Aurelius; the germs of cholera, the scorpion, as well as the puppy and the kitten.

There is a poem of Vaughan which I wish to quote and comment on, even though I do not more than half-understand it. It contrasts the false life with the true.

QUICKNESS

False life! a foil, and no more, when
    Wilt thou be gone?
The foul deception of all men,
That would not have the true come on!

Thou art a moon-like toil; a blind
    Self-posing state;
A dark contest of waves and wind,
A mere tempestuous debate.

Life is a fixed discerning light,
    Doth vivify
And shine and smile, and hath the skill
To please without eternity.

Thou art a toilsome mole, or less,
    A moving mist.
But life is, what none can express,
A quickness, which my God hath kissed.

The false life is a foil to the true, that is, sin and imperfection are the material out of which the true grows by contrast. Wordsworth expresses the "that would not have the true come on," more indulgently, in

To make her foster-child, her inmate, Man,
    Forget the glories he hath known,
And that imperial palace whence he came.

"A moon-like toil"; whether we take it as the phases of the
moon or the ebb and flow of the tides caused by the moon,
this means the dull, monotonous round of mechanical pleasures and meaningless pains.   "A blind, self-posing state" is
the senseless, automatic life, which is at the mercy of every
event, happy in success, doleful in failure.   "A dark contest
of waves and wind," again, expresses the state of being blown
about by every wind of doctrine, being tossed up and down by
the waves of circumstance.   "Life is a fixed, discerning light."
Here there is an echo of Shakespeare on love:

> It is an ever-fixèd mark
> That looks on tempests and is never shaken.

"A knowing joy" is what Bacon spoke of when he said,

> No pleasure is comparable to the standing on the vantage
> ground of truth.

"The skill to please without eternity," is the property of all
existing things.   Eternity, infinity, are not necessary to the
true life, which is complete, with which we can be satisfied
and pleased, at any moment, in any place.   "*A quickness which
my God hath kissed.*"   This remarkable line expresses briefly
the nature of Reality as we see it.   Our words make mincemeat
of it, yet it can be expressed in words, if we look beyond the
words into the fact.   Life, that is, living, has two elements in
it which we call material and spiritual, higher and lower,
human and divine, — a foolish distinction, but intellectually in-
evitable.   The word "quickness" suggests mere animal living,
mere existence.[1]   "Which my God hath kissed," is the enlightened life, conscious of itself and its divinity.   This "kiss"

[1] Though we say "mere" existence, it is hard enough to grasp, for
as Ekai says in the *Introduction* to the *Mumonkan*, while we are fumbling
and hesitating, life like a race-horse has flashed past the window.   (設或
躊躇也似隔窗看馬騎.)

of God may take the forms that Stevenson describes in the following lines:

> Lord, Thy most pointed pleasure take
> And stab my spirit broad awake;
> Or, Lord, if too obdurate I,
> Choose Thou, before that spirit die,
> A piercing pain, a killing sin,
> And to my dead heart run them in!

The life of Zen is the God-kissed life.

There are one or two more specifically religious poems worth noting in connection with Zen. The first verse of Traherne's *Thoughts:*

> A delicate and tender thought
> The quintessence is found of all He wrought;
> It is the fruit of all his works,
> Which we conceive,
> Bring forth and give,
> Yea, and in which the greater value lurks.
> It is the fine and curious flower
> Which we return and offer every hour;
> So tender is our Paradise,
> That in a trice
> It withers straight and fades away,
> If we but cease its beauty to display.

The word "thought" here has, not the hard, intellectual connotation, but the tender meaning of those momentary half-timid, half-bold essays and flights of the soul towards some ideal region. The universe flowers in us when we have such thoughts. The aged Komachi, in *Sotoba Komachi,* says,

Though I too am a withered tree of no worth, my heart has flowers, that may be offered to Buddha.

われも賤しき埋木なれど心の花のまだあれば
手向になどかならざらん。

These flowers of the soul are to be returned and offered every
hour, they are offerings before the altar of Reality. But, "so
tender is our Paradise," that the flower that blooms in a
moment, will fade and wither in a moment.   The identical
truth is expressed in the second chapter of the *Rokusodankyô*:

At every moment, in every place, if we are free from
foolish desires and act wisely, we have Wisdom (Paradise).
One foolish thought, and Paradise is lost; one wise thought
and salvation is again ours.

一切處所、一切時中、念念愚ならず、常に智慧
を行ずれば、即ち是れ般若の行なり、一念愚な
らば即ち般若絶す、一念智なれば即ち般若生
す。　　　　　　　　　　　（六祖壇經、第二章）

The thought of the thing is far above the thing itself, in value.
Christ's thought of the lilies of the field transcended in beauty
that of the flowers themselves.   Eckehart also says:

Das geringste Vermögen, dass es in meine Seele gibt,
ist weiter als der weite Himmel.

There is a poem of Matthew Arnold that I cannot forbear
quoting. Like Wordsworth's *We are Seven*, it has not a "poetical" line in it, yet it is more affecting than many great poems.

EAST LONDON

'Twas August, and the fierce sun overhead
Smote on the squalid streets of Bethnal Green,
And the pale weaver, through his windows seen
In Spitalfields, looked thrice dispirited.

I met a preacher there I knew, and said:
'Ill and o'erworked, how fare you in this scene?'
'Bravely!' said he; for I of late have been
Much cheered by thoughts of Christ, *the living bread*.'

O human soul! so long as thou canst so
Set up a mark of everlasting light,
Above the howling senses' ebb and flow,

To cheer thee, and to right thee if thou roam—
Not with lost toil thou labourest through the right!
Thou mak'st the heaven thou hop'st indeed thy home.

"Thoughts of Christ, the living Bread"; these are the flowers
of the mind that grow in the squalour of Bethnal Green. All
the flowers that bloom in heaven have their roots here. God
is the root and God is the flower. God lives in us and blossoms
in us. This is the meaning (to jump back three centuries) of
the prayer of the *Sarum Primer:*

God be in my head,
And in my understanding;
God be in mine eyes,
And in my looking;
God be in my mouth
And in my speaking;
God be in my heart
And in my thinking;
God be at my end
And at my departing.

This is a prayer for Zen.

Of all the poets, Milton seems farthest from Zen: religion
without pantheism, poetry without mysticism, interest in mankind but none in men, seeing Nature as a picture, but no real
love of it as alive. This lack of Zen is connected closely with
his want of Christian charity, notorious unsatisfactoriness as
a husband and father, intolerant politics, and above all, his
pride, not to say arrogance. He never forgets himself, except
perhaps at the organ, where even his hard heart was "dissolved
into ecstasies." God he seems to meet as an equal, as if he
realised that his poetry would reflect glory on the Creator. He

has the impudence to attempt (and fail) "to justify the ways of God to Man." But there is another side to the question. Milton says a poet "ought himself to be a true poem" (*Apology for Smectymnus*), and Pope also,

> For modes of faith let graceless zealots fight;
> He can't be wrong whose life is in the right.

Milton belonged to both classes: he was a graceless zealot, but his life was in the right. Zen takes a man as he is, and raises him to his highest power. It does not necessarily improve his morals, still less his intelligence. This is the point of Suzuki's bull-fighter.[1] Zen makes a bull-fighter a good bull-fighter, or rather, it makes him *a* best bull-fighter, though not *the* best. If such a man did Zazen and actually studied Zen under a master, no doubt he would change bull-fighting for needle-work. But this would be an *indirect* result of Zen, in that for-getfulness of self implies sympathy, sympathy means universal sympathy and therefore with bulls, who as far as possible should be given a chance to live a natural life out on the mountains — not teased to death in an enclosure to make a Spanish holiday. Milton was like this bull-fighter, like his own angel-fighter, Satan. Satan is full of Zen, because in him Milton expresses the Zen which his actual life was full of:

> Yet I argue not
> Against Heaven's hand or will, nor bate a jot
> Of heart or hope; but still bear up and steer
> Right on.

This reminds us of words spoken seven hundred years before, at the Battle of Maldon:

> Mind shall be the firmer, heart the keener,
> Mood shall be the braver as our might lesseneth.

[1] See *Zen Buddhism and its Influence on Japanese Culture*, page 90.

This unreasonable, inverse proportion of might and mood, has
something of Zen in it.   The well-known haiku of Bashô has
the same meaning:

> Nothing in the voice of the cicada
> Intimates
> How soon it will die.

やがて死ぬけしきは見えず蟬の聲　　芭 蕉

if we take it according to Prof. Suzuki's interpretation,[1] to
mean that it does not "bate a jot of heart or hope", but continues to sing its best until the last moment of its life.   Bashô
also exemplified it in his life, every poem a death-poem.

This then is the Zen of Milton, of Satan:

> To be weak is miserable,
> Doing or suffering.

Active or passive, half-heartedness is misery, whole-hearted-
ness, no-heartedness is bliss,

> and in my choice
> To reign is worth ambition, though in hell:
> Better to reign in hell than serve in heaven.

Zen means to reign in hell *and* heaven.

> A mind not to be chang'd by place and time.

The actions change according to circumstances but the mind
itself does not change in its nature.   It is like water that takes
the shape of any vessel but remains water.   This mind has a
unity, a wholeness, because it is like water, the same in every
part, though different in form and function.   This kind of
mind, (that of the Grand Duke Charles Augustus) Goethe describes to Eckermann (Thursday, Oct. 23, 1828):

[1] 禪と日本文化、182 頁。

Er war ein Mensch aus dem Ganzen, und es kam bei ihm alles aus einer einzigen grossen Quelle.   Und wie das Ganze gut war, so war das Einzelne gut, er mochte thun und treiben was er wollte.

Milton says further,

> The mind is its own place, and in itself
> Can make a heaven of hell, a hell of heaven.

"The mind is its own place," that is, the mind has no locality in space, it is not inside the skull of a certain person. We may say, in the same way, "The mind is its own time." It is time-less, out of time, creates the time it lives in.   Kanzan[1] says,

> The years of a man's life do not reach a hundred,
> But his griefs are those of a thousand years.

人 生 不 滿 百　 常 懷 千 載 憂　 寒 山

Look once more at the following lines:

> Which way shall I fly
> Infinite wrath and infinite despair?
> Which way I fly is hell; myself am hell,

and compare them to

> The water a cow drinks turns to milk;
> The water a snake drinks turns to poison.

牛 飲 水 成 乳　 蛇 飲 水 成 毒　 (槐安國語)

Water is the same everywhere: everything depends on your-self as to whether it shall become milk or poison, heaven or hell.   Again, in the 38th Case of the *Hekiganroku,* we have

---

[1] Kanzan (寒山) was a monk of the Tō (Tang) dynasty, whose poems were collected and published after his death by Dôgen (道翹) of Kokusei-ji (國清寺).

To meet with ill fortune is to meet with good fortune.
To meet with submission is to meet with an enemy.

受 災 如 受 福　　受 降 如 受 敵

(碧 巖 錄、第 三 十 八 則、頌 着 語)

The first line means that actually, ill fortune and good fortune
are only fortune: we make it ill or good ourselves. The second
line is Blake's

> Bless relaxes, damn braces.

There is more Good in evil than in good, and we may say
à la Shinran Shônin, "Even from good (good fortune), we can
get some Good,—how much more from evil (ill fortune)."[1] So
Satan says,

> Our torments also may in length of them
> Become our elements.

We create, uncreate, and recreate daily the world in which we
live, justifying Mephistophiles' words,

> Am Ende hängen wir doch ab
> Vom Creaturen die wir machten.

We are never to question the goodness of God, that is to say,
our innate ability to get the Good from our daily life. Not
music or art or poetry or Zen, but

> to know
> That which before us lies in daily life
> Is the prime wisdom.

Then we shall neither curse God and die, nor justify his ways
to men:

[1] What Shinran, (1173-1262) the founder of the Shin Sect of Buddhism, actually said, was, "Even good men will go to Paradise, let alone
he bad." (善人なをもて往生をとくゝいはんや惡人をや。 歎異鈔、第三條。)

> Accuse not Nature: she hath done her part;
> Do thou but thine.

Our attitude must be that expressed in:

> Nor love thy life nor hate but what thou liv'st
> Live well; how long or short permit to heaven.

The lines quoted show Milton's natural Zen. Such a man, like the 6th Patriarch, E-Nô, needs no master to teach him. As the pine tree can grow on the rocks, so Milton could nourish himself on a childish cosmology and maintain his soul on impossible creeds. No wonder that we are drawn to Satan, and feel no inspiration, no poetry, no life, no freedom, in God, Christ, Michael, Adam and the rest, a rabble of Zen-less creatures wandering in a "cave of ghosts." From the point of view of Zen we can appreciate deeply the last three lines of Wordsworth's sonnet to Milton:

> So didst thou travel on life's common way,
> In cheerful godliness; and yet thy heart
> The lowliest duties on herself did lay.

There is another definition of Zen for you. Zen is cheerful godliness,—we could almost say simply, Zen is cheerfulness, for cheerfulness means reigning in Hell; godliness means reigning in Heaven, not so difficult a thing.

The Pulley, of Herbert, may seem at first sight to have little or no Zen in it; it appears to be a nice, slightly sentimental Christian poem with no specially deep meaning. But if we read it more sympathetically and try to reach the original state of feeling from which the poem sprang, it then represents something fundamental in human nature, namely, the desire of the mind for real things; not for wisdom or honour, beauty or strength, but for a complete knowledge of existence.

When God at first made man,
Having a glasse of blessings standing by,
'Let us,' said He, 'poure on him all we can;
Let the world's riches, which dispersed lie,
    Contract into a span.'

So strength first made a way,
Then beautie flow'd, then wisdom, honour, pleasure;
When almost all was out, God made a stay,
Perceiving that, alone of all His treasure,
    Rest in the bottome lay.

'For if I should,' said He,
'Bestow this jewell also on My creature,
He would adore my gifts instead of Me,
And rest in Nature, not the God of Nature:
    So both should losers be.

'Yet let him keep the rest,
But keep them with repining restlessnesse;
Let him be rich and wearie, that at least,
If goodnesse leade him not, yet wearinesse
    May tosse him to My breast.'

What Herbert calls Nature, that is, music, art, poetry, virtue, science,—these are not enough. The aim of the soul is not Beauty, Goodness, Truth, but beatitude, a lively peace, what Herbert names "the breast of God," "the God of Nature." What man wants is things, all things, all things as One Thing, a complete union of himself with that One Thing, with Life, Reality, God. This condition of active rest is the state of Zen, in which nothing is omitted, not the ugliest, filthiest, falsest, most sinful thing; all is included in me and I in it. "Contract into a span," is very good. All the glory and power of the universe is contracted, concentrated, into a single thought, a single emotion of one human being. "So both should losers be." Not only man but God also loses by our restlessness.

This comes from the original identity of Man and God, parabolically shown in the Incarnation, but experienced, unnoticed,
every day by each one of us in his moments of com-passion,
sym-pathy with persons, animals or things.   The pun in the
first line of the last verse, (it is not accidental here) is worth
thinking about.   This kind of pun, unnecessary and meaningless to the thought of the poem itself, is at first only annoying,
but after a time, especially if one reads Japanese *Nô* plays in the
original, where they are continual and continuous, it begins to
have a peculiar, inexplicable value, somehow suggesting to the
mind the underlying connection between all things, between
" shoes and ships and sealing wax, and cabbages and kings."

The picture by Baen (Ma Yuan, 馬遠) may be taken as an
illustration of the thought of Herbert's poem.   It is a picture
of a fisherman intent on his work among the rushing waves.
If we think that the work is arduous, that man faces the elements with courage, this is morality.   If we think of the spac-
ing of the picture, this is beauty.   If we think of the justness
of the drawing, this is truth.   If we think of it as a symbol of
humanity and nature, man and the universe, this is religion.
But these, as Herbert says, are not enough.   And if we think
of loneliness, or repose, or the Infinite, we are not thinking of
the picture at all, we are thinking about ourselves, our own
emotions.   We must look at the picture so that, *what it is
speaks so loudly we cannot hear what it says.*   What the picture
is, gives us rest; so long as we do not think of the meaning,
we have the same active rest, resting activity, as the artist had
at the moment he painted the picture.   We look at the picture,
the roaring of the waves in our ears, yet unheard; the rope
cutting our fingers and straining the muscles of the back, but
unnoticed; self-forgetful in intent labour; overhead, the grey
sky, beneath, the grey waters, rocked with the motion of the

boat in the midst of the void,—all this in a timeless moment, and afterwards, "Am I man who dreamed he became a picture, or a picture dreaming it is a man?"

Last, let me give Herbert's well-known *The Collar:*

I struck the board, and cry'd, 'No more;
   I will abroad.'
  What, shall I ever sigh and pine?
My lines and life are free; free as the rode,
  Loose as the winde, as large as store.
   Shall I be still in suit?
  Have I no harvest but a thorn
  To let me bloud, and not restore
What I have lost with cordiall fruit?
   Sure there was wine
  Before my sighs did drie it: there was corn
   Before my tears did drown it.
  Is the yeare onely lost to me?
   Have I no baye to crown it;
No flowers, no garlands gay? all blasted,
   All wasted?
  Not so, my heart; but there is fruit,
   And thou hast hands.
  Recover all thy sigh-blown age
On double pleasures; leave thy cold dispute
Of what is fit and not; forsake thy cage,
   Thy rope of sands,
Which pettie thoughts have made; and made to thee
  Good cable, to enforce and draw
   And be thy law,
  While thou didst wink and would not see.
   Away! take heed;
   I will abroad,
Call in thy death's-head there, tie up thy fears;
   He that forbears
  To suit and serve his need
   Deserves his load.
But as I rav'd and grew more fierce and wilde
   At every word,

> Me thought I heard one calling, 'Childe';
>   And I reply'd, 'My Lord.'

This is the essence of all religion; the hardness of iron, the softness of wool, the blueness of the distant mountains, the coldness of water,—it is the will of God, the will of Nature, receive it without hesitation.

CHAPTER XVIII

NON-ATTACHMENT

PART I

This word suggests to an ordinary Englishman something like the character of Harold Skimpole in *Bleak House,* a kind of drone who tries to get all the honey of life with none of its poison, the rose without the thorns. Mr. Skimpole explains himself:

> "I covet nothing," said Mr. Skimpole, in the same light way. "Possession is nothing to me. Here is my friend Jarndyce's excellent house. I feel obliged to him for possessing it. I can sketch it and alter it. I can set it to music. When I am here, I have sufficient possession of it, and have neither trouble, cost, nor responsibility."

This non-attachment comes from a deep, cold selfishness, which avoids all love and sympathy because it may lead to pain. There seems to have been more than a touch of this in Goethe's attitude towards other people. Eckermann says, speaking of himself, Sunday, May, 2, 1824,

> "Und dann trage ich in die Gesellschaft gewöhnlich meine persönlichen Neigungen und Abneigungen und ein gewisses Bedürfniss zu lieben und geliebt zu werden. Ich suche eine Persönlichkeit die meiner eigenen Natur gemäss sei; dieser möchte ich mich gern hingeben und mit den andern nichts zu thun haben."

This carrying into one's relations with other people likes and dislikes, is to be avoided, and to desire to be loved is wrong

however natural it may seem. But his desire to love, to bestow affection and good upon another is beyond praise.
Goethe's reply, however worldly wise, sounds calculating, as
though the aim of life were to receive only. There is nothing
we can disagree with, yet the heart rebels against it.

"Es ist eine grosse Thorheit, zu verlangen, dass die Menschen zu uns harmonieren sollen. Ich habe es nie gethan.
Ich habe einen Menschen immer nur als ein für sich be-
stehendes Individuum angesehen, dass ich zu erforschen
und dass ich in einer Eigentümlichkeit kennen zu lernen
trachtete, wovon ich aber durchaus keine weitere Sym-
pathie verlangte."

It is too true to be good. Neither Buddha nor Christ were as
wise as this.

There is another kind of non-attachment similar to the
above, but based on the belief (which is itself again based on
the same cold-heartedness), that all the things of this world are
of no account compared with those of the next and that we
must set our minds entirely on things above. This can justify
itself equally from the Sutras and the Bible.

Love not the world, neither the things that are in the
world; if any man love the world the love of the Father is
not in him.   And the world passeth away and the lust
thereof but he that doeth the will of God abideth for ever.
                                            (*John*, 2, 15.)

In the *Hôkukyô* (*Dhammapada*) we are told the same thing:

Love not anything:
Hate and envy arise from this same love.
He who loves nothing, hates nothing,
Is free from all evil bonds.

愛しきをおもふ思想を捨てよ。
にくみ、ねたみはこれにもとづく。

愛し、憎しの思想捨てなば、
我をなやます絆はあらじ。   (法句經、211)

From love comes grief,
From love comes fear:
He who knows not love, knows no grief,
Free from love, he is free from fear.

戀し、愛しは憂を招き、
愛し戀しは畏を起す。
戀しを離れ、愛しを去らば、
憂もあらじ、畏もあらじ。   (213)

The New Testament forbids us to love the world because
it is impermanent, the Sutra because it will be a cause of pain,
but we shall be making a fatal mistake if we are not careful
with the meaning of word "love," in the Bible and in the
Buddhist scriptures.   In the Bible, love means passionate self-
identification. In this way we are to understand the two great
commandments, "Love God and thy neighbour as thyself,"
and in this sense John's injunction is plain: do not give yourself with passion to all those things which the world counts so
dear, money, position, fame, power, not to speak of the lower
and debasing pleasures.   From the point of view of Zen, however, we would interpret it rather differently and say: "Love
the world, and love the things of the world, all of them without exception, but do not love them for the pleasure they give
you or hate them for the pain they bring you.   That is to say,
love them without attachment."   In the Buddhist writings,
"love" means this attached love, it is the "love" of "the love
of money is the root of all evil."   It has, religiously speaking, a
bad meaning, it means attachment, bondage.   When we think
of the worse side of the love of Nancy for Bill Sykes, of Dombey
for his son, of Jude for Sue, Alec for Tess, Romeo for Juliet,
Lear for Cordelia, Hamlet for his mother, we can get some

idea of the meaning of "attachment." "The worse side" does not mean the physical as opposed to the spiritual: far from it. It means the selfish, directly or indirectly self-seeking side, as opposed to pure love, which means giving, not for the pleasure of giving, like Mrs. Jellyby, but simple, thoughtless, instinctive giving, like Mark Tapley's, without reference to past, present or future. In pure love (which no doubt does not exist at all except in our imagination), the giver is not aware that he gives, nor of what he gives, nor to whom he gives, still less of whether it is appreciated by the recipient or not. There is a trinity here, a single action with the three parts undifferentiated in its activity. To be without attachment does not mean to look at things like a mirror or a camera. It means to look at them as God looks at them. This is humorously and graphically illustrated by Stevenson, in a fable called *The Two Matches*.

One day there was a traveller in the woods in California, in the dry season, when the Trades were blowing strong. He had ridden a long way, and he was tired and hungry, and dismounted from his horse to smoke a pipe. But when he felt in his pocket he found but two matches. He struck the first, and it would not light.

"Here is a pretty state of things!" said the traveller. "Dying for a smoke; only one match left: and that certain to miss fire! Was there ever a creature so unfortunate? And yet," thought the traveller, "suppose I light this match, and smoke my pipe, and shake out the dottle here in the grass—the grass might catch on fire, for it is dry like tinder; and while I snatch out the flames in front, they might evade and run behind me, and seize upon yon bush of poison oak; before I could reach it, that would have blazed up; over the bush I see a pine tree hung with moss; that too would fly in fire upon the instant to its topmost bough; and the flame of that long torch—how would the trade wind take and brandish that through the inflam-

mable forest! I hear this dell roar in a moment with the
joint voice of wind and fire, I see myself gallop for my
soul, and the flying conflagration chase and out-flank me
through the hills; I see this pleasant forest burn for days,
and the cattle roasted, and the springs dried up, and the
farmer ruined, and his children cast upon the world. What
a world hangs upon this moment!" With that he struck
the match, and it missed fire.

"Thank God!" said the traveller, and put his pipe in
his pocket.

The moral of this fable is not, of course, that we are to add
up the pros and cons of each action, all the permutations and
combinations of possible contingencies, but that we are to
"thank God" for everything.

> Receiving trouble is receiving grace:
> Receiving happiness is receiving a trial.

受災如受福、受降如受敵。 (禪林句集)

How are we to attain this state? By getting rid of our own
particular likes and dislikes, and being empty, yet "filled with
the spirit." "When the half gods go," that is when Mr. Blyth,
alias that fascinating girl, alias that odious old woman, alias
that filthy sink, goes, "the gods arrive": the girl is still pretty,
the old woman still ugly, the sink still dirty, but there is a difference. What is this difference? I have become like the
ghost in *Hamlet;* and the girl and the old woman and the sink
must say of me, like Marcellus of the ghost,

> We do it wrong, being so majestical,
> To offer it the show of violence,
> For it is, as the air, invulnerable,
> And our vain blows malicious mockery.

There is a story of two monks on a journey who came to

a river with no bridge across it. As they were about to begin
to ford it, a young woman came up.   The first monk was just
going to offer to carry her across, when the second said to her,
" Get on my back and I'll carry you over."   She did so and
parted from them gracefully on the other side.   After the two
monks had walked on for a few miles, the first monk, unable
to contain himself any longer, burst out, " What did you mean
by carrying that girl across the river? You know monks are
allowed to have nothing to do with women ! "   The other said,
with a smile, " You must be tired, carrying that girl all this
way.   *I* put her down as soon as we got to the other side of
the river."   Things are beautiful but not desirable; ugly but
not repulsive; false, but not rejected; dirty, but ourselves no
cleaner.

> The fallen flowers voluntarily (we suppose) float
>   away down the stream;
> The flowing water receives them involuntarily
>   (we suppose) and carries them down the stream.[1]

落花意あつて流水に隨ひ、
流水情なくして落花を送る。

(從容錄、五十二)

These two lines represent our arbitrary ascription of emotion
to nature.   We fancy the flowers fall reluctantly; we think
the stream receives them coldly; but it is not so.   The flowers
are not reluctant, they are not willing, the stream does not receive them coldly or warmly.   We too are to be the same, but
are not to imitate the stream or the flowers, but be human beings in the same complete, vital way that the flowers blossom
and the stream flows.   Though the self, the selfish self, must
disappear, emotion remains and this emotion is love.   Here is

[1] From 大乘文字禪、by 織田善雄、同文館。

both the meeting and the parting point of Zen and ordinary Buddhism. Ordinary Buddhism teaches us to love all existing things. Zen says, " Get rid of the self and act from the Self ! " It is like the two sides of a mountain which, however separated at the base, meet at the top. There is this difference also, that the Zen side is short but exceedingly steep and difficult. The ordinary Buddhist side is long, the slope gradual. Nevertheless they are the same in the end, for the nature of the universe (that is, of the Self) is Good as taught in the Eki Kyô (易經):

> Active and Passive follow each other in the
> Harmony of Goodness.

一 陰 一 陽 之 謂 道 繼 之 者 善 也。

This in the justification, the basis, of the *Auguries of Innocence*. Everything is bathed in love like the ether. The world is like a spider's web; touch one part and the whole quivers. So we have,

> Scoop up the water and the moon is in your hands:
> Hold the flowers and your clothes are scented with them.

掬 水 月 在 手、 弄 花 香 滿 衣。 (禪林句集)

So Dickens, in *Bleak House*, speaking of the beggars and outcasts of the slums of London, whom he calls Tom:

> But he has his revenge. Even the winds are his messengers, and they serve him in these hours of darkness. There is not a drop of Tom's corrupted blood but propagates infection and contagion somewhere. It shall pollute, this very night, the choice stream of a Norman house, and his Grace shall not be able to say Nay to the infamous alliance. There is not an atom of Tom's slime, not a cubic inch of any pestilential gas in which he lives, not one obscenity or degration about him, not an ignorance, not a wickedness, not a brutality of his committing but shall

work its retribution, through every order of society up to
the proudest of the proud, and to the highest of the high.
(Chap. XLVI)

Dickens is also among the mystics, for this is Blake's *London :*

> How the chimney-sweeper's cry
> Every black'ning church appals;
> And the hapless soldier's sigh
> Runs in blood down palace walls.

And Dickens' own profound sense of the love that moves the
sun and the other stars, that in his own breast was the light
of his life and work, he expresses in the famous lines at the
end of the next chapter, on Jo, the crossing sweeper's death:

Dead, your Majesty. Dead, my lords and gentlemen.
Dead, Right Reverends and Wrong Reverends of every kind.
Dead, *men and women, born with Heavenly compassion in
your hearts.* And dying thus around us every day.

But this Heavenly compassion, that is the life of every
creature, this Goodness, unlike Dickens himself, has no sentimentality. There is nothing miraculous, exceptional, lawless
about it. The Universe is Good as we manifest the nature of
water (and of our bodies), whether we float on it or drown in
it. What Zen wishes us to do is to let go of the ordinary goodness of philanthropy and duty, and the badness of tyranny and
cruelty, and live always in this Goodness, dissolved in it, sub-
limed in it. Zen says, as in the *Shinjinmei,* all forms of dualism, right and wrong, good and bad, gain and loss—get rid of
them all, forget them !

This is good for me, that is bad for me, this is so, that
is not so,—we must be free from all such thoughts.

得 失 是 非, 一 時 放 却。　　(信 心 銘)

In this, Zen shows (shall we say, betrays) its partial derivation from Rôshi. On this point Rôshi is as paradoxical and violent as Zen itself.

When the Way was not followed, arose goodness and virtue.

大 道 癈、 有 仁 義。　　(第 十 八 章)

Get rid of goodness, dispense with virtue, and people will behave as they should, feel as they should.

絕 仁 棄 義、 民 復 孝 慈。　　(第 十 九 章)

The attitude of Zen is, Follow the Self, and all these things, goodness, purity, compassion, will be added unto you. That is, do not attach yourself even to goodness, to ideals, to Zen it-self. Thus Rôshi says of the Way (=Zen) in Chapter 34,

All things depend on It; It brings them into being, but does not leave them in the lurch. It completes Its work, but lays no claim to have done anything. It cherishes and upholds all things, but does not behave as a master.

大 道 汎 兮、 其 可 左 右。　萬 物 恃 之、 以 生 而 不 辭。
功 成 不 名 有。　愛 養 萬 物、 而 不 爲 主。

Flow like the river, be firm as the rocks, pliant as the willow, eternal as the sky, transitory as the dew-drops, for man is all these, and more.

There is a Korean poem by Rikeihô[1] (李奎報), concerning this attachment to the Way, to Zen, to the Truth, that is, to the Moon:

Desiring to possess the moon,
A monk once ladled it out with the water into a vessel,
But, reaching the temple with it, found
That when he poured the water out, the moon was gone.

山 僧 貪 月 色。　井 汲 一 瓶 中。
到 寺 方 應 覺。　瓶 傾 月 亦 空。

[1] See page 256.

One of Issa's *haiku* has the same thought:

> Whose is it then,
>> My children,
>>> This red, red moon?

赤い月これは誰のぢや子供達

In the *Kongô Kyô* it is expressed in a less picturesque but more unmistakable way:

> Buddha asked, "Subodai. What do you think about this: has the Buddha attained to Perfect Enlightenment? Is there any Truth for him to teach?" Subodai answered, "According to the teaching of the Buddha, the World-Honoured One, there is nothing we can call Perfect Enlightenment, neither is there any Truth for the Buddha to teach. Why not? Because we are not to adhere to the teaching of the Buddha, nor is it to be taught."

須菩提。 於意云何。 得阿耨多羅三藐三菩提
耶如來有所說法耶。 須菩提言。 世尊、如我解
佛所說義。 無有定法名阿耨多羅三藐三菩提。
亦無有定法如來可說。 何以故。 如來所說法。
有定法如來可說。 何以故。 如來所說法。 皆
不可取。 不可說。　　　　　　　　　　（第七章）

In the Bible, both the New and the Old Testament, there is not much talk of freedom or bondage, except in regard to sin. Christ says,

> Verily, verily, I say unto you, Everyone that committeth sin, is the bondservant of sin.

But are there not also the bondservants of goodness, slaves of ideals, those who ruin themselves and others for the sake of one or another of the virtues? Othello was the bondservant of purity (but "To the pure all things are pure"); Hamlet, of

---

1 In 海東詩選、滙東書館、京城。

justice (but "Vengeance is Mine, saith the Lord, I will repay");
Lear, of simple love[1] (but "Love covereth a multitude of sins").
For this reason we are told, in Zen,

If you meet a Buddha, kill him!
If you meet Daruma or any other great master, kill him!

逢 佛 殺 佛、 逢 祖 殺 祖。

Christ has the same feeling:

If any man come to me and hate not his father and mother
and wife and children and bretheren and sisters, yea, and
his own life also, he cannot be my disciple,

but he does not universalise it as Zen does to include all things,
even God himself. That is to say, there is in the Bible no actual meditation on what we may call absolute freedom; there
is a kind of tacit assumption that God could not, for example,
tell a lie. There are one or two passages, it is true, in the Old
Testament, which point towards this absolute freedom, a real
omnipotence of God, but they seem quite out of the current of
Jewish thought. We have in *Amos* III, 6,

Shall a trumpet be blown in the city, and the people not
be afraid? Shall there be evil in a city, and the Lord hath
not done it?

and in *Isaiah* XLV, 6, 7,

I am the Lord and there is none else. I form the light and
create darkness: I make peace, and create evil: I the
Lord do all these things.

Orthodox commentators struggle desperately with this verse;
some say that "evil" here means "calamity." But to bring

[1] Though knaves flatter, we are not, like Cordelia, to refrain from
praising, even in chorus with them.

calamity upon human beings too ignorant, too weak to extract the good from it, makes God a cause of useless cruelty, and what else is evil? Some say that this is a declaration of the fact that Jehovah combines the attributes of Ahuramazda and Ahriman in the dualistic system of Zoroaster. This is better, but why not interpret it in the light of *Habakkuk* 1, 13,

Thou art of purer eyes than to behold evil,

where God transcends both good and evil, for God cannot see good and evil, but only Good.

In Wordsworth we often find attachment to goodness:

> Yea, to this hour I cannot read a tale
> Of two brave vessels matched in deadly fight
> And fighting to the death, but I am pleased,
> *More than a wise man ought to be.*

(Recluse: 721-4)

but in Nietzsche we find, equally often, attachment to the idea of non-goodness:

Der Krieg und der Mut haben mehr grosse Dinge getan als die Nächstenliebe.

However, in the same chapter we hear the true voice of Zen:

Ihr sagt, die gute Sache sei es, die sogar den Krieg heilige? Iche sage euch: der gute Krieg ist es, der jede Sache heiligt,

and in Wordsworth also, when he speaks of anguish and death, (*Excursion*, I, 921-4):

> I stood, and leaning o'er the garden wall
> Reviewed that Woman's sufferings: *and it seemed*
> *To comfort me* while with a brother's love
> I blessed her in the impotence of grief.

CHAPTER XIX

NON-ATTACHMENT

PART II

The attitude of Christ towards the problem of freedom is utterly different from that of all the rest of the Bible. This attitude is expressed more implicitly than explicitly, and partly for this very indirectness, we feel in another world, the world of the spirit, where

> Stone walls do not a prison make,
> Nor iron bars a cage.

Nevertheless there are three passages that express superlatively the nature of freedom, and we will take them in this and the succeeding two chapters. First,

Judge not, that ye be not judged.

"Judge not" means, "Do not allow your judgements to be static: be like water that 'judges' the shape of every vessel into which it is poured but does not lose its nature, its fluidity and mobility." Judge as bad but do not reject. Shakespeare says of the pimp, the most despicable of all the creatures in the universe,

> Truly, sir, I am a poor fellow that would live.

Judge as good but do not desire. This is illustrated by one of Wordsworth's poems, *Two April Mornings,* woefully misinterpreted by Lafcadio Hearn, because he did not understand Zen. Here is the poem:

TWO APRIL MORNINGS

We walked along, while bright and red
Uprose the morning sun;
And Matthew stopped, he looked, and said,
" The will of God be done! "

A village schoolmaster was he,
With hair of glittering grey;
As blithe a man as you could see
On a spring holiday.

And on that morning, through the grass,
And by the steaming rills,
We travelled merilly, to pass
A day among the hills.

" Our work " said I, " was well begun,
Then from thy breast what thought,
Beneath so beautiful a sun,
So sad a sigh has brought? "

A second time did Matthew stop;
And fixing still his eye
Upon the eastern mountain-top,
To me he made reply,

" Yon cloud with that long purple cleft
Brings fresh into my mind
A day which I have left
Full thirty years behind.

" And just above yon slope of corn
Such colours, and no other,
Were in the sky, that April morn,
Of this the very brother.

" With rod and line I sued the sport
Which that sweet season gave,
And, to the churchyard come, stopped short
Beside my daughter's grave.

"Nine summers had she scarcely seen,
The pride of all the vale;
And then she sang; she would have been
A very nightingale.

"Six feet in earth my Emma lay;
And yet I loved her more,
For so it seemed, than till that day
I e'er had loved before.

"And turning from her grave, I met,
Beside the churchyard yew,
A blooming Girl, whose hair was wet
With points of morning dew.

"A basket on her head she bare;
Her brow was smooth and white;
To see a child so very fair,
It was a pure delight!

"No fountain from its rocky cave
E'er tripped with foot so free;
She seemed as happy as a wave
That dances on the sea.

"There came from me a sigh of pain
Which I could ill confine;
I looked at her and looked again:
And did not wish her mine!"

Matthew is in his grave, yet now,
Methinks I see him stand,
As at that moment, with a bough
Of wilding in his hand.

Why did he not wish her his? Lafcadio Hearn explains, that first, no person can take the place of a dead child; second, the new person would be a reminder of the former; third,

it would be a sort of unkindness to the dead to allow any living person to take the empty place.

Such sentimental and superstitious explanations are indeed far from the truth, but typical of Hearn, who, except for the macabre and horrible, cheapens everything he touches. Matthew gives the reason himself in the fourth verse from the end:

> It was a pure delight,

or rather, a purified delight.   He did not wish her his because he had gone beyond the possessive stage of love, and towards his own daughter he had this same love, purified by grief.   He did not wish her his, and he did not wish his own daughter his,—only pure love for the dead girl and pure delight in the living.   When you love one person properly, you love all.   If you *really* love your own dog, you love all dogs, all living creatures.   This is the same truth that Detective Bucket tells Esther about the pretended non-attachment of Mr. Skimpole, so devoted to the pleasures of life; and adds the following rule, which may justly be called a rule of Zen:

> " Fast and loose in one thing, Fast and loose in everything.
> I never knew it fail.   No more will you.   Nor no one."

Lack of desire in one (desirable) thing, lack of desire in all.   Lack of judging in one thing, lack of judging in all.   Judge as good, as beautiful, but do not wish it yours.

Precisely the same thought is expressed in *The Fountain:*

> " And Matthew, for thy children dead
> I'll be a son to thee!"
> At this he grasped my hand, and said,
> " Alas! that cannot be."

So Bashô says, realising like Matthew the eternal Nature of things,

> The morning-glory!
>   But this too
>   Can never be my friend.

朝顔やこれもまた我友ならず

"Judge not;" why not? Because there is no judge, no criminal, no crime. This is the teaching of the *Kongô Kyô:*

1. These (those who are enlightened) have no (false) idea of an ego, an individual, a being, a soul.

是諸衆生無我相人相衆生相壽者相。(第六章)

2. Cherish thoughts that are dwelling on nothing whatever.[1]

應無所住而生其心。   (第十章)

"Dwelling on nothing," means there is nothing to judge. We cannot judge the stream; it will not appear in court, it is too busy flowing.

What is the meaning of "that ye be not judged"? If you reject things, they will reject you. If you cling obstinately to things, things will cling obstinately to you. If you are an enemy of Nature, Nature is your enemy. If you divide the world into two, you will be nipped between the two, as in a pair of nut-crackers.

Loving and loathing; accepting and rejecting; grasping

[1] There are many translations of this famous line: the one given above is Suzuki's in his *Manual of Zen Buddhism.* Others are:

1. Awaken one's thoughts where there is no abode whatever. (also Suzuki's.)
2. We should use a mind dwelling upon Nothing.
3. One should use one's mind in such a way that it will be free from attachment.
4. Awaken the mind without fixing it anywhere.
5. Use the mental faculties spontaneously and naturally, but unconstrained by any preconceptions arising from the senses.

and disdaining; longing and spurning; this is the disease
of the mind.

違 順 相 爭。　是 爲 心 病。　　　(僧　璨)

The opening line of this poem of Sôsan says the same thing:

The Way of Perfection is not difficult; only, it does not
like choosing.

至 道 無 難。　唯 嫌 揀 擇。

Christ also says it, but more violently :

Whoever shall say, 'Thou fool!', shall be in danger of hell
fire.

(Or as Zen would express it, "*is* in hell fire.")

We are told to avoid this attitude.   But how is it possible,
when we are choosing (pleasure, comfort, wisdom, goodness
etc.) every moment of the day?   No one chooses pain, unless
to gain some greater bliss with it.   If we are cold we choose
a fire, if our leg itches we choose to scratch it.   Would not the
cessation of choosing mean the cessation of life itself?   To
answer this we must first consider the question.   What is religion? or to put it more concretely, what is a man's religion?
A man's religion is what he thinks about his relation to the
universe; or rather, it is what he feels about this relation; or
better, it is what he *does* about this relation; or best, it is *how*
he acts.   The style is the man.   Spenser says in Book 2 of the
Faerie Queene,

> For a man by nothing is so well bewrayed
> As by his manners,

and Emerson,

> The greater man, the greater courtesy.

Thus we see that the all important thing is not, killing or

giving life, drinking or not drinking, living in the town or the country, being lucky or unlucky, winning or losing. It is *how* we win, *how* we lose, *how* we live or die, finally, *how we choose.* We all do the same things, eating, drinking, getting up, going to bed, avoiding pain, pursuing pleasure. We walk, and our religion is shown (even to the dullest and most insensitive person), in how we walk. Or to put it more accurately, living in this world means choosing, choosing to walk, and the way we choose to walk is infallibly and perfectly expressed in the walking itself. Nothing can disguise it. The walk of an ordinary man and of an enlightened man are as different as that of a snake and a giraffe. What is the difference? We may express it briefly, though not very intelligibly, by saying it is a question of balance; the one has it, the other not. This "balance" is Johnson's "life led according to Nature," it is the manner an enlightened person acts in those particular circumstances. We can feel it by experience, see it in others, or guess at it by natural analogies:

The mirror reflects the tapers of the golden pavilion;
The mountain echoes the bell of the moon-tower.

鏡 分 金 殿 燭，山 答 月 樓 鐘。 (禪 林 句 集)

AT THE SEA-SIDE

When I was down beside the sea,
A wooden spade they gave to me
To dig the sandy shore.

My holes were empty like a cup,
In every hole the sea came up,
Till it could come no more.

This, from Stevenson's *A Child's Garden of Verses,* expresses that inevitability (another word for "balance"), which is the

essence of all music, poetry and art, and also the art of living.
Christ says,

> Be ye perfect, even as your Father is perfect,

for balance, inevitability, perfection, are convertible terms and
are to be applied, not, like moral and aesthetic judgements, to
one aspect of the case but to the whole, — to the person,
circumstances, action, cause, effect. All these become a unity
when the person makes them so by his own internal unity.
This is expressed by Stevenson in the last line of the *Whole
Duty of Children:*

> A child should always say what's true,
> And speak when he is spoken to,
> And behave mannerly at table:
> At least as far as he is able.

This does not imply weakness or imperfection in his words
and actions. The first three lines mean, "Be perfect"; the
last line, that he is not to attach himself to some impossible,
ideal, unreal mode of behaviour. It is only a bad carpenter
who blames his tools. A good carpenter is not attached to
them: he can be a perfect carpenter with a few rusty nails and
a blunt chisel. We are to be like Mr. Carker, the villain of
Dombey and Son;

> He did each single thing as if he did nothing else.

This non-moral, a-moral manner of living is illustrated in a
fable of Stevenson called *Faith, Half-faith, and No Faith At
All.* Faith, the priest, is the man who believes, or pretends to
believe, in revealed religion, revealed to a certain number of
people at a certain time and place. Dante is the greatest ex-
positor of this kind of belief. Half-faith, the virtuous person,

is the man who talks about Goodness, Beauty, Truth, with capital letters, who says that all religions are true. Many Buddhists and most scientists belong to this class. No-Faith, the rover, is the man who lives by Zen.

In the ancient days there went three men upon pilgrimage; one was a priest, and one was a virtuous person, and the third was an old rover with his axe.

As they went, the priest spoke about the grounds of faith.

"We find the proofs of our religion in the works of nature," said he, and beat his breast.

"That is true," said the virtuous person.

"The peacock has a scrannel voice," said the priest, "as has been laid down always in our books. How cheering!" he cried, in a voice like one that wept. "How comforting!"

"I require no such proofs," said the virtuous person.

"Then you have no reasonable faith," said the priest.

"Great is the right, and shall prevail!" cried the virtuous person. "There is loyalty in my soul; be sure, there is loyalty in the mind of Odin."

"These are but playings upon words," returned the priest. "A sackful of such trash is nothing to the peacock."

Just then they passed a country farm, where there was a peacock seated on a rail; and the bird opened its mouth and sang with the voice of a nightingale.

"Where are you now?" asked the virtuous person. "And yet this shakes not me! Great is the truth, and shall prevail!"

"The devil fly away with that peacock!" said the priest; and he was downcast for a mile or two.

But presently they came to a shrine, where a Fakeer performed miracles.

"Ah!" said the priest, "here are the true grounds of faith. The peacock was but an adminicle. This is the base of our religion." And he beat upon his breast, and groaned like one with colic.

"Now to me," said the virtuous person, "all this is as little to the purpose as the peacock. I believe because I see the right is greater and must prevail; and this Fakeer might carry on with his conjuring tricks till doomsday, and it would not play bluff upon a man like me."

Now at this the Fakeer was so much incensed that his hand trembled; and, lo! in the midst of a miracle the cards fell from up his sleeve.

"Where are you now?" asked the virtuous person. "And yet it shakes not me!"

"The devil fly away with the Fakeer!" cried the priest. "I really do not see the good of going on with this pilgrimage."

"Cheer up!" cried the virtuous person. "Great is the right, and shall prevail!"

"If you are quite sure it will prevail," says the priest.

"I pledge my word for that," said the virtuous person.

So the other began to go on again with a better heart.

At last one came running, and told them all was lost: that the powers of darkness had besieged the Heavenly Mansions, that Odin was to die, and evil triumph.

"I have been grossly deceived," cried the virtuous person.

"All is lost now," said the priest.

"I wonder if it is too late to make it up with the devil?" said the virtuous person.

"Oh, I hope not," said the priest. "And at any rate we can but try. But what are you doing with your axe?" says he to the rover.

"I am off to die with Odin," said the rover.

Odin is the "That," the Nature of things, of the 29th Case of the *Hekiganroku:*

A monk said to Daizui, "In the Age of Fire, everything in the Universe will be destroyed by Fire. Will "That" (the Buddha-nature of all things, the Nature of the Universe) be annihilated or not?" Daizui answered, "It will be annihilated!"

僧問大隋、劫火洞然、大千俱壞、未審、這箇壞、
不壞、隋曰、壞。

So we are not to be attached to Goodness or Beauty or Truth,
nor to Odin, to Reality, to the Absolute, to Zen.   We are to
live with life and be annihilated with annihilation:

> He who bends to himself a Joy,
> Doth the wingèd life destroy;
> But he who kisses the Joy as it flies,
> Lives in eternity's sunrise.

And Emily Dickinson, even nearer to Daizui than Blake,

> In insecurity to lie
> Is joy's insuring quality.

The misery (often disguised as happiness) that comes from
attachment, is marked on every face; it is the theme of novels
dramas, poetry.   Attachment is "the root of all evil."   The
condition of the "attached" man is described by Spenser (recording his own experiences in the English court,) in *Mother
Hubbard's Tale:*

> To lose good dayes, that might be better spent;
> To wast long nights in pensive discontent;
> To speed today, to be put back tomorrow;
> To feed on hope, to pine with feare and sorrow.

Another aspect is described by Shakespeare in *King John.*
Constance is speaking of her son Arthur:

> Grief fills the room up of my absent child,
> Lies in his bed, walks up and down with me,
> Puts on his pretty looks, repeats his words,
> Remembers me of all his gracious parts,
> Stuffs out his vacant garments with his form.

King Philip rightly says,

> You are as fond of grief as of your child,

that is to say, as fond of yourself, of your own emotions, as of your son.   This is the tragedy of Mr. Dombey, in *Dombey and Son,* of whom Dickens says,

> For all his starched, impenetrable dignity and composure, he wiped blinding tears from his eyes; and often said, with an emotion of which he would not for the world, have had a witness, "Poor little fellow!"
> It may have been characteristic of Mr. Dombey's pride, that he pitied himself through the child.

Othello is one of the greatest examples of this kind of attachment (to oneself disguised as another person,) for in Othello himself it is exacerbated by the poetical faculty, the imagination, which is the greatness of Othello.   The trouble is that Othello does not "regulate his imagination by reality":

> I had rather be a toad,
> And live upon the vapours of a dungeon,
> Than keep a corner of the thing I love
> For others' uses.

This idea of complete, ideal, unshared possession of Desdemona is an impossible one:

> For none of us lives unto himself, and no man dieth to himself.
> For whether we live, we live unto the Lord; and whether we die, we die unto the Lord: whether we live therefore, or die, we are the Lord's.

But this ideal attachment he has made the whole motive force of his existence,

> But there, where I have garner'd up my heart,
> Where either I must live, or bear no life,—

Without it, life is meaningless, it stagnates.

> O, now for ever
> Farewell the tranquil mind! farewell content,
> Farewell the plumed troop, and the big wars,
> That make ambition virtue! O farewell!
> Farewell the neighing steed, and the shrill trump,
> The spirit-stirring drum, the ear-piercing fife,
> The royal banner, and all quality,
> Pride, pomp and circumstance of glorious war!
> And, O you mortal engines, whose rude throats
> The immortal Jove's dread clamours counterfeit,
> Farewell! Othello's occupation's gone!

It was this condition that Confucius had in mind when he said:

> The Superior Man is not a utensil,

子曰、君子不器 （論語、二、十二。）

which is capable of one use only. This stagnation of life is the real tragedy of this world, for it is the waste of life. There are many tragic forms. In the play of *Othello* we have the three types, Iago, Desdemona, Othello. Iago is the tragedy of the exercise of (intellectual) power heedless of reality; Desdemona, of unmerited anguish; Othello, of the damming of a life by a spurious imagination, by *judging,* by separating himself from the (supposed) sinner, and condemning her. Zen sets out to help men to avoid this last kind of tragedy. To Zen the tragic figure of the Gospels is not Christ, nor the Roman soldiers who crucified him, nor Mary the mother of Christ weeping before the cross, but the disciples, as exemplified in Peter and his three denials, Pontius Pilate and his lying question, "What is truth?" (One can lie in a question just as much as in an answer.) Othello does not, cannot, understand what the Duke says in his presence:

What cannot be preserved when fortune takes,
Patience her injury a mockery makes.
The robbed that smiles steals something from the thief.

This was Ryôkan's attitude when a thief broke into the house.

The thief
    Left it behind—
        The moon at the window.

盗人にとりのこされし窓の月

Ryôkan stole the moon from the thief, and smiled in seventeen
syllables. In Othello this disease of possession is so acute that
it can be cured only by killing the patient. It is of the greatest
importance to notice that this disease of attachment could not
be cured, and in fact, is not cured, by his discovery of Desdemona's innocence and faithfulness. We may learn as we
watch the tragedy unfold, but the hero himself learns nothing.
This is true also of Antony, Hamlet, and Macbeth.

In complete contrast to Othello with his "love" of Desdemona,

Damn her, lewd minx! O, damn her!
Come, go with me apart; I will withdraw
To furnish me with some swift means of death
For the fair devil,

we have the words of Lovelace:

If I have freedom in my love,
    And in my love am free,
Angels alone that soar above
    Enjoy such liberty.

Freedom does not mean some kind of absolute pure freedom
in a vacuum. It does not mean spiritual freedom in material
bondage. It means an activity of the mind, that is, of the soul,

that is, of the body, at all times and in all places, which is in accordance with its own nature and with that of the circumstances.   This is what Johnson speaks of in *Rasselas,*

the simple and intelligible maxim, — that deviation from nature is deviation from happiness.
To live according to nature, is to act always with due regard to the fitness arising from the relations and qualities of causes and effects; to concur with the great and unchangeable scheme of universal felicity; to co-operate with the general disposition and tendency of the present system of things.

Though Johnson is here making fun of these vague abstractions, we find him, in Boswell's *Life of Johnson,* endorsing this attitude in his own person.

When I, in a low-spirited fit, was talking to him with indifference of the pursuits which generally engage us in a course of action and enquiring a *reason* for taking so much trouble, " Sir," said he in an animated tone, " it is driving on the system of life."

This "driving on the system of life," this " co-operation with the general disposition and tendency of the present system of things," is thus expressed in the *Saikontan.*[1]

Fishes swim in the water, but do not think of it; birds fly in the wind, but are not aware of it.

魚 得 水 逝 而 相 忘 乎 水。   鳥 乘 風 飛 而 不 知 有 風。

Fear or hatred (they are almost inseparable,) of the world is a form of attachment to it.   It is commoner than generally suspected, found, to some extent, in the hearts of everyone of us.   The following anecdote, probably imaginary, was written

[1] 菜根譚, literally, vegetable roots talkings, that is, Meditations of a Simple Lifer, by Kôjisei, (1575–1619) a man who blended Taoism, Confucianism and Buddhism into a spiritual unity of outlook on the world.

by Kutsugen himself (about 1000 years before the Tô (Tang) era.) Giles has translated this in *Gems of Chinese Literature*, Prose, page 34, in some places simplifying, in other places over-elaborating it.

When Kutsugen was dismissed from office he went to Kôtan, and sat sighing by the river. He looked like a skeleton, so pale and emaciated was he. A fisherman, seeing him there, said to him, "Are you not the Prime Minister? What may you be doing here?"

Kutsugen replied, "The whole world is filthy; I alone am clean. Everybody is drunk; I alone am sober. This is the reason I was dismissed." The fisherman said, "A sage is not bound to things, is not the slave of circumstances, but follows them, acts in accordance with them. If the whole world is filthy, you must jump in the muddy water and splash about in it. If all men are drunk, drink with them. What is the good of meditating so profoundly and idealistically?" Kutsugen said, "I have heard that when a man has washed himself he dusts his hat, and when a man has bathed his body, he shakes his clothes. How can he who has purified himself put on his old dirty clothes again? I would rather jump in this river and feed my body to the fishes. I will not allow my purity to be sullied by the defilements of this world!"

The smiling fisherman gave a chuckle, and rowed away; he sang, keeping time with his oar,

"If the water of Sôrô is clear, I will
wash the ribbon of my hat;
If it is dirty, I will wash my feet in it."

This was all he said, and was gone.

屈原既放	游於江潭	行吟澤畔
顏色憔悴	形容枯槁。	漁父見而問之曰
子非三閭大夫與	何故至於斯。	屈原曰
舉世皆濁我獨清	衆人皆醉我獨醒	是以見放。
漁父曰	聖人不凝滯於物	而能與世推移
世人皆濁	何不淈其泥	而揚其波

衆人皆醉　何不餔其糟　而歠其醨
何故深思高舉　自令放爲。　屈原曰
吾聞之　新沐者必彈冠　新浴者必振之
安能以身察察　受物之汶汶者乎　寧赴湘流
葬江魚之腹中　安能以皓皓之白　而蒙世俗之塵埃乎。
漁父莞爾而笑　鼓枻而去。　乃歌曰
滄浪之水清兮　可以濯吾纓　滄浪之水濁兮
可以濯吾足　遂去不復與言。

The real point of the story lies in the fact that Kutsugen afterwards drowned himself because he could not regain office. The physician did not take his own medicine. Those who speak do not (necessarily) know; those who know cannot (always) speak. Mere head knowledge of Zen is as useless as medicine in a bottle, or the stable door after the horse has run out.

Attachment means asking for something, asking, not with the mouth but with the inmost heart. The following story illustrates this point. All my life I wanted a friend, and I thought I had found one at last in a monk of the Myôshinji, Keijô, Korea. Overjoyed with this thought, I went one day to the temple, but he treated me quite coolly, just like anybody else, and I went home quite wretched, feeling I did not want a friend anyhow, (sour grapes). That evening he came to the house and I told him what had happened and how I had felt. With a malicious twinkle in his black eyes he said, "That's because you wanted something from me!" (それはブライズさんは我に求める心があるから) The same idea is expressed in a poem of Hakurakuten:

WATCHING FISH AT PLAY

As I wandered round the lake and gazed at the fishes
　　　　　　　　　　　　　　　gliding to and fro,

I came across some boys fishing in a boat.
Both they and I loved the fish,—but our state of mind
was different:
I had come to feed the fish, they to catch them.

觀　　遊　　魚

遶 池 閒 步 看 魚 遊。　正 值 兒 童 弄 釣 舟。
一 種 愛 魚 心 各 異。　我 來 施 食 爾 垂 鉤。

The boys wanted to get something from the fish, Hakurakuten
wanted to give something to them. It may be objected that
both the boys and the poet wanted something, the boys the
fish themselves and the poet the sight of their beauty; that
what they received was the material, and he the spiritual.
This is not so. The boys were concerned with profit and loss,
fish and no fish, big, juicy fish, and skinny, bony fish. The
poet was in that condition which Bashô described in an already
quoted poem:

> Unseen today
>   In misty showers, and yet
>   Today, how beautiful, Mt. Fuji![1]

霧 し ぐ れ ふ じ を 見 ぬ 日 ぞ お も し ろ き

If this were written

霧 し ぐ れ ふ じ を 見 ぬ 日 も お も し ろ し

"when unseen *also,* on a misty, showery day," all the spiritual
meaning would disappear, destroyed by the introduction of the
comparative element. The cherry flowers bloom and the poet

---

[1] This is the real meaning of Unmon's
> Every day is a good day,
> 日 日 是 好 日
that is, every day is a Good day.

receives their beauty into his heart. But when they fall, he sees them fall without regret, for he does not ask them to bloom and does not ask them not to fall. So with Hakuraku-ten; he watched the fish as God watches them and all things, he watched them as another poet who said,

>Beneath a dome of fallen rock,
>   That in the current looms,
>The fishes glide, like birds at night,
>   In colder, greener, glooms.
>
>And there, in darkest mystery,
>   With slow expressive grace,
>They move in rhythmic line and curve
>   Within that holy place.
>
>O joyful dance in shadows dim!
>   O rock of sombre hue!
>O coiling wave and curling stream,
>   Ever the same yet new!

CHAPTER XX

NON-ATTACHMENT

PART III

The truth shall make you free.

In *Othello* the Duke says:

> When remedies are past, the griefs are ended
> By seeing the worst, which late on hopes depended.[1]
> To mourn a mischief that is past and gone
> Is the next way to draw new mischief on.

What is the worst? Sin, suffering, death. If only we can be lifted up by these waves, instead of being submerged by them, we shall be free. Free from what? Free from the illusion that we are not free. Our illusions that we are not (now) free, are our hopes. Our hopes, for a better condition than we are now in, are not only the cause of grief, but the grief itself. There is a story of Rôshi, who was riding towards a city with an attendant. Seeing the city in the distance, the attendant spurred on his horse. Rôshi called him back, saying "Here also it is good," and rode steadily on. Dr. Johnson in *Rasselas* has the same thought.

> If you are pleased with the prognostics of good, you will be terrified likewise with tokens of evil. (Chap. XIII)

Looking forward always is a form of superstition, an attachment to the future; whatever we have, to want more, where-

---

[1] "Which late on hopes depended," qualifies "griefs."

ever we are, to wish to be somewhere else, as Ruskin says.
And Browne, in *Love's Labours Lost,* states,

> At Christmas I no more desire a rose,
> Than wish a snow in May's new-fangled mirth.

This must be our fundamental state of mind every moment of
the day.   But of all things in this world, this love of truth is
the most uncommon.   Long ago Confucius said,

> I have never seen a man who loved virtue as much as he
> loved beauty,

吾 未 見 好 德 如 好 色 者 也。　(論 語 九、十 七)

and

> I have never seen a man able to perceive his own faults,
> and inwardly reproach himself.

吾 未 見 能 見 其 過 而 內 自 訟 者 也。

(論 語 五、二 十 六)

As Blake says in the *Proverbs of Hell,*

> The fox condemns the trap, not himself.

We condemn the universe for being what it is but

> God's in his Heaven,
> All's right with the world

even though it seems full of traps for the wary as well as for
the unwary.   There is a fable of Stevenson which portrays the
man who will sell all that he has to gain the pearl of great
price, who will lose his life to gain it, illustrating the fact that
non-attachment is the condition of attaining to the truth, that
Freedom shall make you true.

THE TOUCHSTONE

The King was a man that stood well before the world;
his smile was sweet as clover, but his soul withinsides was
as little as a pea.   He had two sons; and the younger son
was a boy after his heart, but the elder was one whom he
feared.   It befell one morning that the drum sounded in
the dun before it was yet day; and the King rode with his
two sons, and a brave array behind them.   They rode two
hours, and came to the foot of a brown mountain that was
very steep.

"Where do we ride?" said the elder son.

"Across this brown mountain," said the King, and
smiled to himself.

"My father knows what he is doing," said the younger
son.

And they rode two hours more, and came to the sides
of a black river that was wondrous deep.

"And where do we ride?" asked the elder son.

"Over this black river," said the King, and smiled to
himself.

"My father knows what he is doing," said the younger
son.

And they rode all that day, and about the time of the
sunsetting came to the side of a lake, where was a great
dun.

"It is here we ride," said the King; "to a King's
house, and a priest's, and a house where you will learn
much."

At the gates of the dun, the King who was a priest
met them; and he was a grave man, and beside him stood
his daughter, and she was as fair as the morn, and one
that smiled and looked down.

"These are my two sons," said the first King.

"And here is my daughter," said the King who was a
priest.

"She is a wonderful fine maid," said the first King,
"and I like her manner of smiling."

"They are wonderful well-grown lads," said the

second, "and I like their gravity."

And then the two Kings looked at each other, and said, "The thing may come about."

And in the meanwhile the two lads looked upon the maid, and the one grew pale and the other red; and the maid looked upon the ground smiling.

"Here is the maid that I shall marry," said the elder. "For I think she smiled upon me."

But the younger plucked his father by the sleeve. "Father," said he, "a word in your ear. If I find favour in your sight, might not I wed this maid, for I think she smiles upon me?"

"A word in yours," said the King his father. "Waiting is good hunting, and when the teeth are shut the tongue is at home."

Now they were come into the dun, and feasted; and this was a great house, so that the lads were astonished; and the King that was a priest sat at the end of the board and was silent, so that the lads were filled with reverence; and the maid served them smiling with downcast eyes, so that their hearts were enlarged.

Before it was day, the elder son arose, and he found the maid at her weaving, for she was a diligent girl. "Maid," quoth he, "I would faith marry you."

"You must speak with my father," said she, and she looked upon the ground smiling, and became like the rose.

"Her heart is with me," said the elder son, and he went down to the lake and sang.

A little after came the younger son. "Maid," quoth he, "if our fathers were agreed, I would like well to marry you."

"You can speak to my father," said she; and looked upon the ground, and smiled and grew like the rose.

"She is a dutiful daughter," said the younger son, "she will make an obedient wife." And then he thought, "What shall I do?" and he remembered the King her father was a priest; so he went into the temple, and sacrificed a weasel and a hare.

Presently the news got about; and the two lads and

the first King were called into the presence of the King who was a priest, where he sat upon the high seat.

"Little I reck of gear," said the King who was a priest, "and little of power. For we live here among the shadow of things, and the heart is sick of seeing them. And we stay here in the wind like raiment drying, and the heart is weary of the wind. But one thing I love, and that is truth; and for one thing will I give my daughter, and that is the trial stone. For in the light of that stone the seeming goes, and the being shows, and all things besides are worthless. Therefore, lads, if ye would wed my daughter, out foot, and bring me the stone of touch, for that is the price of her."

"A word in your ear," said the younger son to his father. "I think we do very well without this stone."

"A word in yours," said the father. "I am of your way of thinking; but when the teeth are shut the tongue is at home." And he smiled to the King that was a priest.

But the elder son got to his feet, and called the King that was a priest by the name of father.

"For whether I marry the maid or no, I will call you by that word for the love of your wisdom; and even now I will ride forth and search the world for the stone of touch." So he said farewell, and rode into the world.

"I think I will go, too," said the younger son, "if I can have your leave. For my heart goes out to the maid."

"You will ride home with me," said his father.

So they rode home, and when they came to the dun, the King had his son into his treasury. "Here," said he, "is the touchstone which shows truth; for there is no truth but plain truth; and if you will look in this, you will see yourself as you are."

And the younger son looked in it, and saw his face as it were the face of a beardless youth, and he was well enough pleased; for the thing was a piece of a mirror.

"Here is no such great thing to make a work about," said he; "but if it will get me the maid I shall never complain. But what a fool is my brother to ride into the world, and the thing all the while at home!"

So they rode back to the other dun, and showed the mirror to the King that was a priest; and when he had looked in it, and seen himself like a King, and his house like a King's house, and all things like themselves, he cried out and blessed God. "For now I know," said he, "there is no truth but the plain truth; and I am a King indeed, although my heart misgave me." And he pulled down his temple, and built a new one; and then the younger son was married to the maid.

In the meantime the elder son rode into the world to find the touchstone of the trial of truth; and whenever he came to a place of habitation, he would ask the men if they had heard of it. And in every place the men answered: "Not only have we heard of it, but we alone, of all men, possess the thing itself, and it hangs in the side of our chimney to this day." Then would the elder son be glad, and beg for a sight of it. And sometimes it would be a piece of mirror, that showed the seeming of things; and then he would say, "This can never be, for there should be more than seeming." And sometimes it would be a lump of coal, which showed nothing; and then he would say, "This can never be, for at least there is the seeming." And sometimes it would be a touchstone indeed, beautiful in hue, adorned with polishing, the light inhabiting its sides; and when he found this, he would beg the thing, and the persons of that place would give it him, for all men were very generous of that gift; so that at the last he had his wallet full of them, and they chinked together when he rode; and when he halted by the side of the way he would take them out and try them, till his head turned like the sails upon a windmill.

"A murrain upon this business!" said the elder son, "for I perceive no end to it. Here I have the red, and here the blue and the green; and to me they seem all excellent, and yet shame each other. A murrain on the trade! If it were not for the King that is a priest and whom I have called my father, and if it were not for the fair maid of the dun that makes my mouth to sing and my heart enlarge, I would even tumble them all into the salt sea, and go home and be a King like other folk."

But he was like the hunter that has seen a stag upon a mountain, so that the night may fall, and the fire be kindled, and the lights shine in his house; but desire of that stag is single in his bosom.

Now after many years the elder son came upon the sides of the salt sea; and it was night, and a savage place, and the clamour of the sea was loud. There he was aware of a house, and a man that sat there by the light of a candle, for he had no fire. Now the elder son came in to him, and the man gave him water to drink, for he had no bread; and wagged his head when he was spoken to, for he had no words.

"Have you the touchstone of truth?" asked the elder son; and when the man had wagged his head, "I might have known that," cried the elder son. "I have here a wallet full of them!" And with that he laughed, although his heart was weary.

And with that the man laughed too, and with the fuff of his laughter the candle went out.

"Sleep," said the man, "for now I think you have come far enough; and your quest is ended, and my candle is out."

Now when the morning came, the man gave him a clear pebble in his hand, and it had no beauty and no colour; and the elder son looked upon it scornfully and shook his head; and he went away, for it seemed a small affair to him.

All that day he rode, and his mind was quiet, and the desire of the chase allayed. "How if this poor pebble be the touchstone, after all?" said he: and he got down from his horse, and emptied forth his wallet by the side of the way. Now, in the light of each other, all the touchstones lost their hue and fire, and withered like stars at morning; but in the light of the pebble, their beauty remained, only the pebble was the most bright. And the elder son smote upon his brow. "How if this be the truth?" he cried, "that all are a little true?" And he took the pebble, and turned its light upon the heavens, and they deepened about him like the pit; and he turned it on the hills, and the hills were cold and rugged, but life ran in their sides so that his own life bounded; and he turned it on the dust and he beheld the dust with joy and terror; and he turned it on himself, and kneeled down and prayed.

"Now, thanks be to God," said the elder son, "I have found the touchstone; and now I may turn my reins, and ride home to the King and to the maid of the dun that makes my mouth to sing and my heart enlarge."

Now when he came to the dun, he saw children playing by the gate where the King had met him in the old days; and this stayed his pleasure, for he thought in his heart, "It is here my children should be playing." And when he came into the hall, there was his brother on the high seat and the maid beside him; and at that his anger rose, for he thought in his heart. "It is I that should be sitting there, and the maid beside me."

"Who are you?" said his brother. "And what make you in the dun?"

"I am your elder brother," he replied. "And I am come to marry the maid, for I have brought the touch-stone of truth."

Then the younger brother laughed aloud. "Why," said he, "I found the touchstone years ago, and married the maid, and there are our children playing at the gate."

Now at this the elder brother grew as gray as the dawn. "I pray you have dealt justly," said he, "for I perceive my life is lost."

"Justly?" quoth the younger brother. "It becomes you ill, that are a restless man and a runagate, to doubt my justice, or the King my father's, that are sedentary folk and known in the land."

"Nay," said the elder brother, "you have all else, have patience also; and suffer me to say the world is full of touchstones, and it appears not easily which is true."

"I have no shame of mine," said the younger brother. "There it is, and look in it."

So the elder brother looked in the mirror, and he was sore amazed; for he was an old man, and his hair was white upon his head; and he sat down in the hall and wept aloud.

"Now," said the younger brother, "see what a fool's part you have played, that ran over all the world to seek what was lying in our father's treasury, and came back an old carle for the dogs to bark at, and without chick or child. And I that was dutiful and wise sit here crowned with virtues and pleasures, and happy in the light of my hearth."

"Methinks you have a cruel tongue," said the elder brother; and he pulled out the clear pebble and turned its light on his brother; and behold the man was lying, his soul was shrunk into the smallness of a pea, and his heart was a bag of little fears like scorpions, and love was dead in his bosom. And at that the elder brother cried out aloud, and turned the light of the pebble on the maid, and, lo! she was but a mask of a woman, and withinsides she was quite dead, and she smiled as a clock ticks, and knew not wherefore.

"Oh, well," said the elder brother, "I perceive there is both good and bad. So fare ye all as well as ye may in the dun; but I will go forth into the world with my pebble in my pocket."

The "piece of a mirror" typifies the ordinary superficial view of the world,—the soul is eternal, good and evil are irreconcilable contraries, virtue always prospers, my umbrella is God's umbrella. This is what Confucius had in mind when he declared (rather strongly for him),

The "Good men" of the villages are the thieves of Virtue.

子曰、鄉原德之賊也。 (論語十七、十三。)

Mencius, explaining this, as though he were commenting on the two Kings and the younger brother in the fable above, says,

Confucius means, 'I hate the imitation of reality. I hate tares, for they will be mistaken for corn. I hate

glibness,[1] for it will be mistaken for righteousness. I hate
bluntness, for it will be mistaken for sincerity. I hate the
music of Tei for it will be mistaken for real music. I hate
reddish-blue, for it will be mistaken for vermilion. I hate
the " good men" of the villages for they will be mistaken
for the really virtuous.'

孔子曰。 惡似而非者。 惡莠。 恐其亂苗也。
惡佞。 恐其亂義也。 惡利口。 恐其亂信也。
惡鄭聲。 恐其亂樂也。 惡紫。 恐其亂朱也。
惡鄉原。 恐其亂德也。 (孟子、七、二、三十七、十三。)

"It had no beauty and no colour." The truth is like health,
or the air we breathe; we don't realise it when we have it, it
seems so common and tasteless. Confucius, when he perceived
the truth, could not express it in words, and yet did so:

> Standing by a stream, Confucius said, 'It flows on and
> on like this, never ceasing day or night.'

子在川上曰、 逝者如斯夫不舍晝夜。

(論語 九、十六。)

The commentators explain this as referring to 天地之化, the
course of nature, and make Confucius wish to continue his
moral striving as unceasingly as the flowing of the stream.
Mencius also (IV, ii, 18) falls into the same error. This kind
of misinterpretation of his words was no doubt the reason for
Confucius' cry,

> I wish never to speak,

子曰、 予欲無言。

The statement "It flows on and on without ceasing day or
night," is quite plain, in fact too plain. People won't take it
just as it is. They don't like the penny plain; they want the
twopence coloured. It is a wonder, when one comes to think

[1] This and what follows is a free version of the *Analects* XVII, 17, 18.

of it, that Zen, which has no dogmas, no badges, no uniforms, no flags, nothing but an open secret to give away, should have continued to exist for more than a few score years.   There must be, after all, a large number of human beings that Stevenson describes so well, "like the hunter that has seen a stag upon a mountain, so that the night may fall, and the fire be kindled, and the lights shine in his house; but desire of that stag is single in his bosom." "In the light of each other, all the touchstones lost their hue and fire."   So with Christianity and Buddhism, Determinism and Free Will, Materialism, Spiritualism, Confucianism, Positivism, Taoism, Communism and all the rest of the -isms,—they are mutually destructive. "But in the light of the pebble their beauty remained, only the pebble was most bright." When we understand what Zen is, all those -isms become full of beauty and truth.   Then Christianity, with all its unnecessary ornamentations, is enough; there is no need to know a syllable about Buddhism. The *Analects* of Confucius are enough, without the Bible or the Sutras.   Or simple devotion to one's family, to one's country is enough, or the *Origin of Species* will provide us with all we need.[1]   Whatever it may be, however foolish, prejudiced,

1 Popular proverbs alone express all the essential meaning of a man's experiences.   Here are some examples chosen from the first few pages of Everyman's *Dictionary of Proverbs*.

1. A coward's fear may make a coward valiant. (When it goes down deep enough to reach the unity of the mind.)

2. Beggars must not be choosers.   (Who is not a beggar? the same meaning as the following.)

3. Comparisons are odious. (All Zen is contained in this proverb. Zen is the comparison-less life.)

4. He who hesitates is lost. (Even when you "Look before you leap," there must be no hesitation in your looking.)

5. He that hath nothing is frightened at nothing. (Absolute poverty is absolute freedom.)

6. In every country the sun shineth in the morning. (This we understand when we have the "touchstone."   This is the real "Buddhist peace.")

obscene,—anything will do, for, as Blake said,

Everything possible to be believ'd is an image of truth.

The expression of this thought in Zen is both more simple and more transcendental. When we are free of relativity,

We sleep with both legs outstretched, free of the true, free of the false.

長 伸 兩 脚 睡 無 僞 亦 無 眞　　　(禪 林 句 集)

This is why, when he turned the light of the pebble on the heavens, "they deepened round him like the pit." The universe is not limited between any pair of contraries, it is thus illimitable. The hills were "cold and rugged," (no sentimentality about Nature), but "life ran down their sides." He beheld the dust with "joy and terror," no philosophic calm, Buddhist peace, passive meditation here. When he turned the light of the pebble on himself, he kneeled down,—what else could be do? He prayed. What for? To whom? To what? Prayer is union with God, when there is no sense of two but of one only. Not so much "He prayed," but as in the creation of Adam, "He became a living prayer."

CHAPTER XXI

NON-ATTACHMENT

The wind bloweth where it listeth and thou hearest the sound thereof, but canst not tell whence it cometh, and whither it goeth: so is everyone that is born of the spirit.

The absolute freedom of life, its unpredictability, is here stated in general terms. As a particular example we may take the following from the *Hekiganroku*:

A monk asked Kyôrin, "What is the meaning of Daruma's coming from the west (that is, the essence of religion)?" Kyôrin answered, "I am stiff with sitting so long."

僧問香林。 如何是祖師西來意。 林云。 坐久成勞。
(碧巖錄、十七)

Where did this answer come from? And how far, during the following eight hundred years, has it gone? Kyôrin was born of the spirit and we can understand him to the extent that we are born of the spirit, and only to that extent. We may quote Blake and say

One thought fills immensity,

and explain Kyôrin as expressing this one thought. But we remain with the one thought. We do not fill immensity. We have a thought of immensity, but it is only a poor, flabby little thought.

There is a passage from a poem ascribed to Taliessin, a semi-mythical Welsh poet of the sixth century AD., which helps us to understand the meaning of "born of the spirit."

The wind without flesh, without bone, without veins, without feet, is strong; the wind has no wants, but the sea whitens when he comes out of nothing. He is in the field, he is in the wood, without age, without old age. He was not born, he has never been seen, he will not come when desire wishes. He is loud voiced, he is mute. He is uncourteous, he is vehement, he is bold. He is bad, he is good. He is yonder, he is here. He comes from the heat of the sun, and he comes from the coolness of the moon.

Let us take this phrase by phrase and elucidate Christ's "born of the spirit" with the help of some of the text-books of Zen. You may think some of these comparisons are fanciful. Remember first, that it is necessary to understand *both* separately before you criticise the comparison; and second, that when we compare the wind and the spirit, the material with the immaterial, we are not using the wind as a symbol. The wind and the spirit are both the working of Nature, of God, of Reality, the same in every place, the same yesterday, today and forever.

Without flesh, without bones, without veins, without feet, the wind is strong.

Kyôgen said, "This is what it's like. Here is a man up a tree, holding on to a branch by his mouth; neither his hands nor feet can touch the tree. A man at the foot of the tree calls out to him, 'What is the essence of Buddhism?' If he does not answer he denies the other man (the knowledge of the Truth). If he answers he will fall and lose his life. In such a case, if you were that man, what would you do?"

香嚴和尙云、如人上樹、口啣樹枝、手不攀枝、

脚 不 踏 樹、 樹 下 有 人、 問 西 來 意、 不 對 即 違 他
所 問。 若 對 又 喪 身 失 命、 正 恁 麼 時 作 麼 生 對。
(無 門 關、 第 五 則)

The wind has no bones. Have you any bones, any precious
bones? Which do you love more, your bones or the truth?
The wind, though invertebrate, is strong. Are you strong?
Blake says,

> Man's perceptions are not bounded by Organs of Percep-
> tion. (That is, he is not bounded by his hands and feet.)

> He perceives more than Sense (tho' ever so acute) can dis-
> cover. The Desire of Man being Infinite, the possession is
> Infinite, and himself Infinite.

He is not bounded by a tree nor by death or the fear of it.
This is why he is strong. Seppô (雪峰) was one of these strong
men. He picked up the terrestrial globe between finger and
thumb, and found it as large as a grain of millet.

盡 大 地 撮 來 如 粟 米 粒 大   (碧 巖 錄、五)

The wind has no wants.

We can compare this to Jôshû's declaration to the congregation of monks; he is quoting from the *Shinjinmei* (信心銘):

> The Way is not difficult; only there must be no wanting
> or not wanting.

趙 州 示 眾 云。 至 道 無 難。 唯 嫌 揀 擇, (碧 巖 錄、二)

This is all very well, but what shall we say of Browning's *The
Statue and the Bust,* and Blake's

> Sooner murder an infant in its cradle, than nurse unacted
> desires,

where we are told not only to have wants, and violent ones,

but that it is a sin not to put them into action? As pointed
out above, the state of wanting which is the root of all evil is
the condition of the mind when its desires obstruct, diminish,
diffuse the energy of the personality. It is this kind of the
wanting of the instincts which both Jôshû and Blake are de-
nouncing. To give a simple illustration: you arrange to go
out for a picnic on Sunday and make all the necessary pre-
parations. Sunday morning dawns with a drizzle. You spend
the morning peering out of the window at the sky and waste
a whole day. This, you will say, explains Jôshû's "wanting,"
but how about Blake's unacted desires? Does he mean that
we are to go out for a picnic even though it is pouring with
rain? Blake speaks of the necessity of acting desires, but this
does not mean every fleeting, foolish whim and fancy. The
truth is, we do not know what our real desires are. We spend
our lives in attempting to obtain things we really do not want
at all. This is why Blake says

If a fool persists in his folly he will become wise,

and find out what his desires truly are.

In the contest of the poems in the *Rokusodankyô,* Jinshu's
poem shows his earnest desire to purify his passions, control
his desires, and obtain the state of mind where all his wants
were for the good only:

> The body is the Tree of Salvation
> The mind is a clear mirror.
> Incessantly wipe and clean it!
> Let no dust fall on it!

> 身是菩提樹、
> 心如明鏡臺。
> 時時勤拂拭、
> 勿使惹塵埃。

E-Nô's poem expresses *his* want, his desire, his choice, which is also a non-wanting, a non-desiring, a non-choosing.   Does the feather *want* to sail along in the wind?   Or is it blown unwillingly?   Did you want to be born or not?   In Christian terminology, E-Nô's poem expresses his view that the all-important thing is that our will shall become the will of God, or rather, that we should realise that from the beginning, our will and God's will was exactly the same, only custom, the intellect, self-full-ness, blinded our eyes to it.

> Salvation is nothing like a tree,
> Nor a clear mirror;
> Essentially, not a "thing" exists;
> What is there then for the dust to fall on?

菩 提 本 無 樹、
明 鏡 亦 非 臺、
本 來 無 一 物、
何 處 惹 塵 埃。

The sea whitens when he comes out of nothing.

E-Nô says, "Be free.   Don't be bound by your choosings and wantings.   Never mind your sins.   Act your desires.   Act your Desire.   Do not abide in delusion, do not abide in enlightenment.   Do not let the mind dwell on goodness or evil. Things and the self are void."   The mind changes ("whitens") moment by moment, but the wind of circumstances that disturbs it comes from the void, "with whom there is no variableness, neither shadow of turning."   Thus the "desire" of Blake is the "non-desiring" of Jôshû, for no, yes, wanting, not wanting, relative, absolute,—all these are only the whitening of the waves of the sea of words.

A monk asked Fûketsu,   "Both speaking and silence belong

to the relative world: how can we escape these two errors?"
Fûketsu said,

> I always think of Kônan in March;
> Partridges chirp among the scented blossoms.

風穴和尙因僧問。　語默涉離微如何通不犯。
穴云長憶江南三月裏，　鷓鴣啼處百花香。
(無門關、二十四)

Fûketsu did not speak, he was not silent. A voice came out
of the Nothing; the question was answered. Christ, in the
same way, tells his disciples to transcend speaking and non-
speaking:

> But when they deliver you up, take no thought how
> or what ye shall speak; for it shall be given you in that
> same hour what ye shall speak.

This was a little above their heads. Christ here forgot his
own maxim, "Cast not your pearls before swine," and acted
on a better one, "Fear not to sow because of the birds."

He is in the field, he is in the wood.

On the one hand the ideal is an "ever fixèd mark"; on
the other it has this elusive chameleon-like quality that St.
Paul describes in

> I am made all things to all men.

You think the wind is in the field, but as soon as you are there,
you see the trees in the wood are tossing their heads, while
here is "not a breath of wild air."

> Jôshû asid, "Can we get in harmony (with the Way)?"
> Nansen answered, "If you try to approach it, you will get
> away from it."

趙 州 云。　還 可 趣 向 否、泉 云。　擬 向 即 乖。
(無 門 關、十 九)

The Way is really rather exasperating.　It is just like the
Looking Glass world; like holding sand in the fist, the harder
you hold it, the more it runs away.　It is like walking the
tight-rope.　Think the rope is laid on the ground and you can
walk on it with ease.　Remember it is suspended in mid-air,
and not a step can you advance.　Think of Zen, of the Void,
of Good and Evil, and you are bound hand and foot.　Think
only and entirely and completely of what you are doing at the
moment and you are as free as a bird.

Without Age, without Old Age; he was not born.

What is life?　Life gives us a chance to live an Eternal Life.
Death means there is no more chance.　Confucius therefore
says,

If a man sees Truth in the morning, he may die in the evening without regret.

子 曰、　朝 聞 道、　夕 死 可 矣。　(論 語、四 八)

The meaning, the object of our life, is this state of being unborn, age-less, immortal, which is our real nature and the
nature of all things.

Sharishi, all things are void; they are unborn, they never
perish.

舍 利 子、是 諸 法 空 相。　不 生 不 滅。　(金 剛 經)

This is the immortality of man that underlies all the parables
and personifications of the Christian and Buddhist religions,
but this immortality is visible only to that inward eye which
is the true bliss of man's eternal solitude.

He will not come when desire wishes.

This is one of the many truths brought home to us by Kurata's *The Priest and his Disciples* (出家とその弟子).[1]   Matthew Arnold says,

> We cannot kindle when we will
>   The fire which in the heart resides,
> The spirit bloweth and is still;
>   In mystery our soul abides.

but Zen will not allow us to have such thoughts, such states of mind.   If you are the master of your fate, the captain of your soul, then when you get into such a condition, you are only a Jonah, not a captain, and you had better chuck yourself off the ship and see how it gets on without you.   When the sick man is mimbling-mambling, the only thing is for the fireman to cleave him to the bed with his hatchet.   Then he will suffer a metamorphosis described in the following lines:

> For long years a bird in a cage,
> Today flying along with the clouds.

多 年 籠 中 鳥、 今 日 負 雲 蟄。   (禪 林 句 集)

He is loud, he is mute.

Bokushû said to a monk, "Where have you come from recently?"   The monk said "Kwats!"   Bokushû said, "So you have given men a 'Kwats,' have you?"   The monk again said, "Kwats!"   Bokushû said, "When you have finished with your 'Kwats, Kwats,' when then?"   The monk was silent.   Bokushû thereupon struck him, crying, "You plundering, empty-headed rascal!"[2]

睦 州 問 僧、 近 離 甚 處。   僧 便 喝。   州 曰、 老 僧 被

---

[1] Translated by Glenn Shaw, a play concerning the life of Shinran.
[2] This striking and abuse may be a mark of approval.

汝一喝。　僧又喝。　州曰、三喝四喝後、作麼生。
僧無語。　州便打曰、這掠虛頭漢。　　　（碧巖錄、十）

Here are two anecdotes illustrating the speaking and the silent
expression of one's own nature, that is of Nature; the first of
General Nogi where Nature is loud, and the second of Admiral
Tôgô, where it is mute.[1]

> General Nogi once went to Normal School of a certain pre-
> fecture. With his snow-white heard and black eyes, he
> stood erect upon the platform. "Teachers, boys, I am
> General Nogi, who, at Port Arther, killed so many of your
> fathers and brothers." And the tears fell from his eyes.

This was speaking, speaking like one of the little children that
Christ made an eternal pattern for proud man.

> Just before the defeat of the Russian Baltic fleet, Admiral
> Tôgô was summoned before the Emperor Meiji. The Em-
> peror said, "Admiral Tôgô, do you expect to win this
> battle?" Tôgô answered, "Yes, sire, I do." But the Em-
> peror still looked unsettled and asked "Are you quite con-
> fident?" Tôgo replied "Quite confident, Your Majesty."
> When he was retiring from the Presence, the Emperor
> called him back and again asked, "You say you will win?"
> Admiral Tôgô answered, "Set your mind at rest; I shall
> destroy the entire enemy fleet." The Emperor smiled.

Just as there are two kinds of speech so there are two kinds
of taciturnity. We do not say Tôgô had the right kind of
taciturnity because he won the Battle of the Japan Sea.
Winning or losing has nothing to do with Zen even though the
chances of winning may be increased by it, for Zen has nothing
to do with chance. When Admiral Tôgô said "I shall destroy
the entire enemy fleet," his mind was raised above the pos-
sibilities of fever, hurricanes, shipwreck and all the accidents

[1] Taken from 本來の面目、菅原時保。

that flesh is heir to.   He looked on the face of the Emperor and his real essence of mind was expressed in all that he did not say.

He is uncourteous.

We see this in Christ's cleansing of the temple, a scene which many Christians do not like to picture, but which is very clear in the light of Zen.   We see it in his treatment of his family, the Pharisees, and often, perhaps too often, of his disciples.   The rudeness of Zen is proverbial, but there are, it goes without saying, two kinds of rudeness.   Here is an example of the Zen kind:

> Suibi was asked by Ryuge, "What is the essence of Buddhism?"   Ryuge replied, "Just hand me that Zenban,[1] will you?"   Ryuge passed it to him, whereupon Suibi struck him with it.

> 龍牙問翠微。　如何是祖師西來意。　微曰、與
> 我過禪板來。　牙過禪板。　與翠微。　微接得
> 便打。　　　　　　　　　　　　　　（碧巖錄、二十）

Rudeness is characteristic of children, old people, idiots, and animals, and therefore highly recommended.

He is vehement; he is bold.

Ordinary impudence, and the impudence of Zen; how shall we distinguish these?   In practice it is easy, since the impudence of Zen is accompanied by goodness, that is, it is not self-seeking. But the fundamental difference is more profound, it is a question of sensitiveness.   Ordinary impudence is due to insensitiveness both of a general kind, and also to the particular persons and circumstances.   Zen impudence is a uni-

[1] A kind of stick for resting the chin on, when weary of sitting long.

versal sensitiveness in which individual sensitivenesses take their proper place, assume their relative importance. We are not swamped by the emotions of the particular case; we know that life is proceeding steadily, at its usual pace, whatever our own circumstances may be. (But it is not that we have two thoughts, one of the individual and one of the universal; this would make a mere battledore and shuttle-cock of the mind.) We feel, to some extent at least, as God feels, and act accordingly; and God is impudent.

For there is no respect of persons with God.

This divine vehemence and boldness, which we feel in Blake, Spinoza, Paul, Mahomet, St Francis, Luther, is not to be obtained through any study or intellectual understanding of Zen, for Zen begins just at the point where the intellect leaves off. This is the idea of the 46th Case of the *Mumonkan*.

Sekisô said, "How can you jump another step from a pole a hundred feet high?"

石霜和尚云、百尺竿頭如何進步。

Christ said,

Destroy this temple and three days I will raise it up again.

He is bad, he is good.

Sometimes we must save life, sometimes take life, sometimes create, sometimes destroy. In his *Criticism* of the 3rd Case of the *Hekiganroku,* Engo says,

If you are a real man, you can freely drive away the farmer's ox, or snatch the food from a starving man.

若是本分人、須是有驅耕夫之牛。 奪飢人之
食底手脚。

Another famous case where morality and Zen seem at variance is the following:

> The monks of the Eastern Hall were having a quarrel with those of the Western Hall about who should own a kitten. Rushing out, Nansen snatched up the kitten and cried, "Now, all of you; if any one of you can say a word of Zen, I will spare the kitten. Otherwise, I will kill it!" They all stood dumbfounded, so Nansen killed it on the spot.

> 南泉和尚、因東西兩堂、爭猫兒。泉乃提起云、大衆、道得即救、道不得、即斬却也。衆無對。泉遂斬之。　　　　　　　　(無門關、十四)

Certainly the S.P.C.A. would never consent to overlook this, but actually it is above criticism. However, to explain it by saying that the Truth, that the enlightenment of the monks, is of greater importance than the life of a kitten, is to miss the point altogether.

He is yonder, he is here.

Describing the state of the enlightened, Hakuin says,

> We see all phenomena as eternal realities, yet as phenomena; whether we go or whether we return, for us there is no movement.

> 無相の相を相として、行くも歸るも餘所ならず
> 　　　　　　　　(白隱禪師坐禪和讚)

This is the irresistible force and the immovable post that puzzles our boyhood; this is the still small voice; the hare that cannot catch up to the tortoise; the colourless bamboo that we see green and paint black.

He comes from the heat of the sun, and he comes from the coolness of the moon.

That is, from everywhere, from everything; and wherever it comes from, it is the wind.

> Baso was ill, and the head monk came and asked him, "How are you feeling recently?"   Baso said, "There is a Sun Buddha and a Moon Buddha."

馬大師不安。 院主問、和向、近日、尊候如何。
大師曰、日面佛月面佛。   (碧巖錄、三)

The Sun Buddha lives 1800 years, the Moon Buddha only one day and night, but wherever life is, it is life.

> It is not growing like a tree
> In bulk, doth make Man better be;
> Or standing long an oak, three hundred year,
> To fall a log at last, dry, bald, and sere.

However long or short your life is, it is a complete one. [1] Whether the wind comes from the heat of the sun or the coolness of the moon, it is the wind; to fill every moment of a life with living, that is to be like the lily, the plant and flower of Light:

> In small proportions we just beauties see;
> And in short measures life may perfect be.

[1] Il git en votre volonté, non au nombre des ans, que vous ayez assey vécu. (Montaigne)

CHAPTER XXII

DEATH

Right up to modern times, but especially in the Elizabethan Age,[1] the minds of men were preoccupied with the thought of death, or rather, with the thought of what would happen after death. Shakespeare himself seems to have shared this emotion, and expresses it with especial force, particularly in *Hamlet* and *Measure for Measure*.

> Ay, but to die, and go we know not where;
> To lie in cold obstruction and to rot;
> This sensible warm motion to become
> A kneaded clod; and the delighted spirit
> To bathe in fiery floods, or to reside
> In thrilling region of thick-ribbed ice;
> To be imprison'd in the viewless winds,
> And blown with restless violence round about
> The pendent world.

This fear naturally causes extreme confusion of thought. In the Bible itself we have on the one hand such passages as,

> For the living know that they shall die but the dead know not any thing. Also their love, and their hatred, and their envy, is now perished: neither have they any more a portion for ever in anything that is done under the sun.

and on the other hand everlasting fire and everlasting bliss after death. In Shelley's *Adonais* there is the same confusion. In the fifty-first verse it says,

1 *See Death and Elizabethan Tragedy*, Spencer.

> From the world's bitter wind
> Seek shelter in the shadow of the tomb.
> What Adonais is, why fear we to become?

but in verse thirty-nine we have been told,

> Peace, peace! he is not dead, he doth not sleep—
> He hath awakened from the dream of life.

This confusion of morbid thought and oversensitive feeling is found the less as we approach Nature.   Montaigne says,

> Regardons à terre les pauvres gens que nous y voyons épandus, la tête penchante après leur besogne, qui ne savent ny Aristote ny Caton, ny exemple, ni précepte : de ceux-là tire Nature tous les jours des effets de constance et de patience, plus purs et plus roides que ne sont ceux que nous étudions si curieusement en l'école.

This natural attitude of human beings towards death is shown in one of the best of Katherine Mansfield's works, *At the Bay*. Old Mrs. Fairfield has been looking back down the years and thinking of the dead.   Kezia, her grandchild, asks,

> "Does everybody have to die?"
> "Everybody!"
> "Me?" Kezia sounded fearfully incredulous.
> "Some day, my darling."
> "But, grandma." Kezia waved her left leg and waggled the toes.
> They felt sandy.   "What if I just won't?"
> The old woman sighed again and drew a long thread from the ball.
> "We're not asked, Kezia," she said sadly.
> "It happens to all of us sooner or later."
> Kezia lay still thinking this over.   She didn't want to die. It meant she would have to leave here, leave every where, for ever, leave — leave her grandma.   She rolled over quickly.

"Grandma," she said in a startled voice.

"What, my pet!"

"*You*'re not to die." Kezia was very decided.

"Ah, Kezia"—her grandma looked up and smiled and shook her head—"don't lets talk about it."

"But you're not to. You couldn't leave me. You couldn't not be there." This was awful. "Promise me you won't ever do it, grandma," pleaded Kezia.

The old woman went on knitting.

"Promise me! Say never!"

But still her grandma was silent. Kezia rolled off the bed; she couldn't bear it any longer, and lightly she leapt on to her grandma's knees, clasped her hands round the old woman's throat and began kissing her, under the chin, behind the ear, and blowing down her neck.

"Say never . . . say never . . . say never—" she gasped between the kisses. And then she began, very softly and lightly, to tickle her grandma.

"Kezia!" The old woman dropped her kitting. She swung back in the rocker. She began to tickle Kezia. "Say never, say never, say never," gurgled Kezia, while they lay there laughing in each other's arms. "Come, that's enough, my squirrel! That's enough, my wild pony!" said old Mrs. Fairfield, setting her cap straight. "Pick up my knitting."

Both of them had forgotten what the "never" was about.

In Wordsworth's *Address to the Scholars of the Village School* (1798) he illustrates his own maxim, uttered under similar circumstances, in *The Excursion* (III, 231), that

> Wisdom is ofttimes nearer when we stoop
> Than when we soar.

(To paraphrase this, we may say, "What cannot be explained to a child, what a child cannot understand, is not true; or if true, is not worth knowing.")

Here did he sit confined for hours;
But he could see the woods and plains,
Could hear the wind and mark the showers
Come streaming down the streaming panes.
Now stretched beneath his grass-green mound
He rests a prisoner of the ground.
He loved the breathing air,
He loved the sun, but if it rise
Or set, to him where now he lies,
Brings not a moment's care.

The last three lines, in their cadences, in their tones and over-tones, express the general meaning of death,

the calm oblivious tendencies
Of Nature, 'mid her plants and weeds and flowers,
And silent overgrowings,

Excursion II, 927.

the truth that all is change, nothing is permanent in ourselves or the outside world. But death comes nearer to us, deeper in meaning. Bridges' *Winter Nightfall* has the same inevitability, but with more pain, more wrenching of the mind.

The day begins to droop,—
Its course is done:
But nothing tells the place
Of the setting sun.

The hazy darkness deepens
And up the lane
You may hear, but cannot see,
The homing wain.

An engine pants and hums
In the farm hard by:
Its lowering smoke is lost
In the lowering sky.

The soaking branches drip
And all night through
The dropping will not cease
In the avenue.

Every line speaks of death: the last three verses, though subdued and resigned, are hardly necessary, but with the human
element "bring the eternal note of sadness in."

A tall man there in the house
Must keep his chair:
He knows he will never again
Breathe the spring air.

His heart is worn with work;
He is giddy and sick
If he rise to go as far
As the nearest rick.

He thinks of his morn of life,
His hale strong years.
And braves as he may the night
Of darkness and tears.

The "horror of the shade" we may meet without fear, without regret, but what for our friends, our father and mother,
our children, our cats and dogs? There is only one answer to
the question "What do you think of death?" and that was the
one given by Christ himself when told of his friend's death,

Jesus wept.

Confucius gave the same answer at the early death of one of
his disciples.

When Gan-en died, Confucius groaned aloud and was inconsolable. The disciples said, "Is not your grief excessive?" Confucius said, "You call it excessive? If I am
not to lament for this man, when am I to grieve?"

顏淵死、子哭之慟、從者曰、子慟矣、曰、有
慟乎、非夫人之爲慟、而誰爲。 (論語、十一、九)

Death is dreadful, grievous; and nothing can or should
alter the fact.   But the more we think about death "in the
quietness of thought," the more value it seems to have for us.
Aldous Huxley, in one of his disagreeable essays, says that
men have lifted up their little legs, and like dogs, made water
on everything — except death.   Seneca also points out that
there is something very exceptional about death.   It is not
merely universal, but, unlike life, cannot be taken away from
man, and therefore we may consider it as *the* gift of God.

> Ubique mors est, optime hoc cavit Deus.
> Eripere vitam nemo non homini potest;
> At nemo mortem.

So Cicero says

> Tota philosophorum vita commentatio mortis est

and the character of every man and his true value may be
known by his attitude to it.   Horace has the following:

> Omnem crede diem tibi deluxisse supremum
> Grata superveniet, quae non sperabitur hora.

" Think every day your last: you will receive with joy hours
on which you have not counted."   Montaigne quotes this and
taking it in a more profound sense than Horace perhaps in-
tended, adds,

> Il est incertain où la mort nous attende, attendons-la par-
> tout.   La préméditation de la mort est prém̂ditation de la
> liberté.   Qui a appris à mourir, il a désappris à servir.   Le
> savoir mourir nous affranchit de toute sujétion et con-
> trainte.

This is Spinoza's

> Liber homo de nulla re minus cogitat quam de morte.

To die is thus not merely the nature but also the duty of man, his true element,[1] and everywhere in Plutarch we have practical examples of this attitude. When Agis, King of Sparta was asked how a man could live in freedom, he answered, "By scorning death!" A Lacedemonian boy taken by the Macedonian general Antigonus and sold as a slave, was ordered by his master to do some menial task. "I will show you that which you have bought!" he cried. "It would be shameful in me to serve, when I have my liberty in my own hand!" and threw himself down from the top of the house. Tacitus tells us of a German chieftain Boiocalus who said to the Romans, "We may lack enough land to live in, but we cannot lack enough to die in!" In a word, death is that which gives life its value, as the blackboard gives meaning to the white chalk-marks on it. This paradoxical fact is expressed in one of Hardy's lyrics, *Last Words to a Dumb Friend,* on the death of his cat.

> Strange it is this speechless thing,
> Subject to our mastering,
> Subject for his life and food
> To our gift, and time, and mood;
> Timid pensioner of us Powers,
> His existence ruled by ours,
> Should—by crossing at a breath
> Into safe and shielded death,
> By the merely taking hence
> Of his insignificance—

[1] Compare Mrs. Gamp, on the (supposed) death of young Bailey: "He was born into a wale," said Mrs. Gamp, with philosophic coolness, "and he lived in a wale; and he must take the consequences of sech a sitiwation."

> Loom as largened to the sense,
> Shape as part, above man's will,
> Of the Imperturbable.

When alive it is only a cat, but in death, it also

> Beacons from the abode where the Eternal are.

Here we have that wonderful truth so difficult to grasp and almost impossible to retain, that

Difference is Identity

差 別 即 平 等

that is, the relative is the absolute, time is eternity, the finite is the infinite. By going away, the cat becomes everpresent; the death of the cat is essential to its eternity; by change, it becomes changeless. But all this is mere words unless you have the experience they express. Unless you love the living cat, the beautiful sentient creature, as Hardy himself did, discrimination and equality remain separate and alien ideas.[1] Hardy concludes the poem thus:

> As a prisoner, flight debarred,
> Exercising in a yard,
> Still retain I, troubled, shaken,
> Mean estate, by him forsaken;

[1] Nietzsche says,
> Was aus Liebe gethan wird, geschieht immer jenseits von Gut und Böse.

And compare also the Spanish copla quoted in Waley's *170 Chinese Poems*, page 28:

> El candil se està apagando,
> La alcuza no tiene aceite—
> No te digo que te vayas, . . .
> No te digo que te quedes.

> The lamp is going out;
> The oil bottle is empty.
> I do not say "Go!"
> I do not say "Stay!"

> And this home, which scarcely took
> Impress from his little look,
> By his faring to the Dim
> Grows all eloquent of him.
>
> Housemate, I can think you still
> Bounding to the window-sill,
> Over which I vaguely see
> Your small mound beneath the tree,
> Showing in the autumn shade
> That you moulder where you played.

Death, then, is meaningless without Love, without Life. Elemental and eternal love alone it is which gives value to physical and mental annihilation in death. That is to say,

Identity is Difference

平 等 即 差 別

the absolute is the relative, eternity is time,[1] the infinite is the finite, unchanging, eternal love endues the ephemeral, insignificant life of the cat with glory.

Concerning that profound saying in the *Analects,* when Confucius was asked about death,

> If you do not know life, how can you know death?

未 知 生、 焉 知 死。 (論 語、十 一、十 二)

Legge says, "Confucius avoids answering the important questions proposed to him," and Waley, "The reply is a rhetorical one and must not be analysed too logically." Looked at superficially, Confucius seems to mean only that we are to consider the condition of the living before that of the dead, with something of the same meaning as John's

[1] Compare Blake: Eternity is in love with the productions of time.

He that loveth not his brother whom he hath seen, how can he love God whom he hath not seen?

I wish, however, to take it in this way: "If you do not know life, how can you know death? If you do not know death, how can you know life?" thus emphasising the thought of the intimate relation which exists between life and death. In actual fact, life and death are not to be separated. From the moment we are born to the moment we die, we have life-death, a stream of mental and physical changes, which at no point can be called life and at no point death, but which at every point is both. Life therefore really means what I have called "life-death." Death means no more life-death.

Further, we can distinguish life and Life, animal life, existence as a living creature, undergoing the process we call life-death; and the Life we live when we love, when we laugh, when we truly grasp an object (poetry), when we forget ourselves entirely and irrevocably (religion). That is to say, life gives us a chance of Life, a chance to live in the eternal world *now*, in "Eternity's glad sunrise." Death is the end of our life and chance to Live. So when Bashô was asked, as he lay dying, for a death-poem, he answered, Rotsu tells us,

From old times it has been customary to leave behind a death-poem, and perhaps I should do the same. But every moment of life is the last, every poem a death poem! Why then at this time should I write one? In these my last hours I have no poem.

芭 蕉 翁 行 狀 記

いにしへより辭世を殘す事は誰誰も有事なれば、
翁にも殘し給べけれど、平生則ち辭世なり、何事
ぞ此節にあらんやとて、臨終の折一句なし。

(小沙彌路通謹書)

Every poem was an expression of his Life, each one equally the first and the last poem of his life. But it must be remembered that Life and life-death are one thing, not two; Life is life-death looked upon absolutely, as if static and immutable, life-death is Life looked upon dynamically, as movement and eternal change.

In Bashô's well known haiku,

> What stillness!
>   The voices of the cicadas[1]
>   Penetrate the rocks.

閑けさや岩にしみいる蟬の聲　　　芭　蕉

is the same "Difference is identity, identity is difference." We say that if there is no sound, there is silence, and if there is no silence, there is sound, and some critics state that the sound of the cicadas intensified the quietness of the scene. This is far indeed from Bashô's experience. We advance beyond that to a realisation of the fact that "If there is no sound, there is no silence; no silence, no sound," but this still means dividing the one fact into two, sound and silence. Bashô's poetical experience transcended this relativity; the sound of the voice of the cicada *is* the stillness. If you understand Rôshi's

These two (the Existent and the Non-existent) are the same but have different names

此兩者（有無）同出而異名。

this presents no difficulties to the mind. In the same way with the poem of the frog, the sound of the water is identical with the silence that was left unspoken. So also with

[1] Plural. The singular would bring the individual cicada too much to the foreground of the mind.

A crow
> Upon a leafless bough:
>> An autumn evening.

枯枝に烏の止りけり秋の暮

The crow on the bare branch of the tree *is* the autumn evening, not its symbol or poetical accompaniment or picturesque point of interest.   The reader may say, "But after all, even though you write "is" in italics, we all know that the crow is one thing and the autumn eve quite another."   Yes, we know it, but the question is, Does God know it?   Or to put it *in other words,* did Bashô know it, at the moment of his poetic experience?   If so, then Christ is not risen and we are yet dead in our sins, *in other words,* the poem is meaningless and we are wasting our time on it.   For a specific example of the teaching of the identity of life and death, let us look at the 55th case of the *Hekiganroku.*[1]

Dôgo went with his disciple Zengen to a certain house to offer condolences for someone's death.   Zengen rapped on the coffin and said to Dôgo, "Is he alive or dead?"   Dôgo replied, "I do not say he is alive; I do not say he is dead."   Zengen then asked, "Why don't you tell me (one way or the other)?"   Dôgo answered "I will not say!   I will not say!"   On their way back to the temple, Zengen said, "Master! do tell me!   If you don't, I'll knock you down!"   Dôgo replied, "Strike me if you like—but you won't get a word out of me."   Zengen thereupon struck him.   Afterwards, when Dôgo was dead, Zengen went to Sekisô, [another of his disciples,] and told him what had happened.   Sekisô said, "I do not say he was alive, I do not say he was dead."   Zengen asked, "Why don't you tell me?"   Sekisô said, "I will not say!   I will not say!"   Zengen suddenly realised the truth.

[1] Fortunately, this is translated in full in Suzuki's *Essays in Zen, Series 2,* pages 219 to 226.   Unfortunately, it seems to have been translated with the intention of showing (what is true,) how extremely difficult the original is.

舉。 道吾、與漸源、至一家弔慰。 源、拍棺云、
生邪死邪。 吾云、生也不道、死也不道。 源云、
爲什麼不道。 吾云、不道不道。 回至中路、源
云、和尚、快與某甲道。 若不道、打和尚去也。
吾云、打即任打、道即不道。 源、便打。 後、
道吾遷化。 源、到石霜、舉似前話。 霜云、生
也不道、死也不道。 源云、爲什麼不道。 霜云、
不道、不道。 源、於言下有省。

We can explain psychologically how Zengen came to a realisation of the meaning of life and death upon the repetition of
the words of Dôgo by Sekisô. We can explain rationally and
logically the identity of life and death.   But we are no nearer
the illumination which Zengen's whole personality experienced
because we are using only a part of ourselves in understanding
it. If it is true, as Unmon says, that

> Even the greatest of men, even those who have absolute
> knowledge, become entangled in words,

古人道沒量大人被語脈裏轉卻。

we can perceive why Dôgo refused to answer the question, and
refrain ourselves from asking it; but that does not mean we
have grasped the fact.   However, we are now in a position to
understand, to some extent, one of Wordsworth's greatest
poems, a poem, however, in which there is not a single line of
poetry, *We are Seven*. It states the problem in the very first
lines:

> —A simple Child,
> That lightly draws its breath,
> And feels its life in every limb,
> What should it know of death?

Let us look first of all at Lafcadio Hearn's answer to this question.

> Nobody could make her understand what death means ex-
> cept by such cruelty as no gentle nature could possibly
> think about.

(Perhaps I have a very horrible nature, but I cannot help
wondering what cruelty one could adopt to make her understand. She had seen her sister lie moaning till she died, she
had seen her brother die, and attended the burial service of
both, heard the earth dropped on their coffins and sat on their
very graves.)

> The child will grieve terribly, may even die of sorrow, but
> this is only because of the knowledge that he will never
> see his mother again, never feel her caress. That is all.
> The really cruel fact is quite unknown.

(What really cruel fact is this which is unknown even when
the child dies of grief?) This is the same sort of canting
humbug which the mother (through the mouth of the child,
who would never think of saying such a thing spontaneously,)
expresses in,

> The first that died was sister Jane;
> In bed she moaning lay,
> Till God released her of her pain;
> And then she went away.

The extraordinary thing about this poem is that it is a question whether Wordsworth himself understood it. Anyway, it
is difficult to believe that he understood it at all, later in life.
Does the child know about death? The answer is given in
Shelley's *Skylark*:

> Waking or asleep
>   Thou of death must deem
> Things more true and deep
>   Than we mortals dream,
> Or how could thy notes flow in such a crystal stream?

Even Hardy gives it, as if unwillingly, unwittingly, in the last
verse of *The Darkling Thrush,* which suddenly began to sing
one dull, winter evening when all was bleak and gloomy.

> So little cause for carolings
>   Of such ecstatic sound
> Was written on terrestrial things
>   Afar or nigh around,
> That I could think there trembled through
>   His happy good-night air
> Some blessed Hope, whereof he knew
>   And I was unaware.

And once more in the same grudging, half-incredulous way, in
An August Midnight:

> A shaded lamp and a waving blind,
> And the beat of a clock from a distant floor:
> On this scene enter—winged, horned, and spined—
> A longlegs, a moth, and a dumbledore;
> While 'mid my page there idly stands
> A sleepy fly, that rubs its hands. . . .

> Thus meet we five, in this still place,
> At this point of time, at this point of space.
> —My guests besmear my new-penned line,
> Or bang at the lamp, and sink supine.
> "God's humblest, they!" I muse.   Yet why?
> They know Earth-secrets that know not I.

That is to say the child, the skylark, the thrush, the insects,
understand the nature of death.   We do not.   We do not understand it because we *try* to understand it, to reason about it,
divide the flow of life into two, life and death, good and bad,
loss and gain.   This is an intellectual convenience that is fatal
whenever we forget (and when do we remember it?) that the
division is artificial, verbal.   However much Wordsworth persists in emphasising the difference between life and death, be-

tween running about in the sunshine and lying in the church-yard beneath the yew-trees, the little girl will not allow herself to be dragged down to his level (from the Absolute to the Relative; in Zen parlance from 第一義 to 第二義) and answers "We are Seven." She does not say "We *were* seven," nor "We *shall be* seven," when united again in paradise. This "We are Seven," is the timeless, "Before Abraham was, I am!"

In Zen this is expressed by

Summer at its height—and snow on the rocks!
The death of winter,—and the withered tree blossoms!

九夏寒岩雪、三冬枯木花。 (禪林句集)

Her world is not only timeless, but placeless, as indicated in Wordsworth's question,

"You say that two at Conway dwell,
And two are gone to sea,
Yet ye are seven! I pray you tell,
Sweet maid, how this may be."

It is beyond rationality, a world in which $7-2=7$. Once you have passed the barrier of life-death, you go safely through the forest of Relativity, says Engo.

跳出生死關驀過荊棘林

"*Quick* was the little maid's reply." To act, to speak, before the mind has time to rationalise and find excuses and reasons, before the emotions have time to colour and discolour—this is Zen. And in the last verse, all Wordsworth's expostulations, explanations, subtraction sums, — "'Twas throwing words away." Zen is

Non-dependence on words and writings;
Direct pointing to the nature of man.

不立文字、直指人心。

It was this direct pointing to his own "essence of mind" which Wordsworth felt instinctively, that was the cause of his writing the poem, bald and babyish as it is. One more phrase in the last verse is worthy of note, "The little Maid would have her will." Everything depends upon the will, that faculty which is the most mysterious of all, and disappears the moment we reason about it. The little girl had a grip of reality and would not relax it for all Wordsworth's protestations. She cared nothing for his heaven and hell, past and present, dead and alive.

> What is death? We are seven!
> What is life? We are seven!

In regard to the problem of death we see the distinction between morality and religion clearly. Confucius says, in a passage already quoted,

> If he hears the Way in the morning, a man may die in the evening without regret.

朝 聞 道、 夕 死 可 矣。　　(論 語、四、八。)

This is morality at its highest point, trembling on the brink of religion. Zen would say rather,

> If a man dies without regret in the evening, he has seen the Way in the morning.

This emphasis on death is in no way morbid. It is simply the Christian

> Unless a corn of wheat fall into the ground, and die, it abideth alone: but if it die, it bringeth forth much fruit.

What is the "fruit" that this death brings? Rôshi, in paragraph 50, expresses it in a way closely corresponding to the spurious passage at the end of Mark, and to many portions of the *Kwannon Kyô*.

He who has grasped life, walks through the land meeting no buffaloes or tigers: in a battle he need not avoid arrows and swords. For a buffalo could not find a place to thrust in his horn, a tiger no place to insert his claws, a soldier none to drive in his weapon. How is this possible? He does not exist in the realm of death. (That is, in the relative, life and death world.)

善攝生者、陸行、不遇兕虎。入軍不避甲兵兕
無所投其角、虎無所措其爪、兵無所容其刃。
夫何故。以其無死地焉。

Christians are thus justified in their insistence on the crucifixion, the death of Christ, as being of greater importance than his life and teachings. In this sense, the personality of Christ has a vaster meaning than that of Buddha. The death of Buddha look place under the Bo-tree. He rose up to save mankind from their ignorance. Christ's death on the cross was the visible consummation, the retrospective and prophetic death of all humanity, all living things.[1] As Antony says of another great man's death, and with no less truth,

> O, what a fall was there, my countrymen!
> Then I, and you, and all of us fell down!

and this not symbolically or parabolically but as an actual fact that is experienced, though unconsciously, whenever we rejoice with those that rejoice, or mourn with those that mourn. But when I say that Christ's death has more meaning than the illumination of Buddha, I am in no sense comparing the two men. I am only saying that when we think of Christ we think of his death and when we think of Buddha we remember his enlightenment and forget the years of anguish he passed

[1] Tennyson, in *Vastness*, says,
He that has nail'd all flesh to the cross, till Self died out in the love of his kind.

through (not less, I think, than that of Christ,) to reach it. And death is truly the gateway of life, not the dissolution of the body and concomitant disintegration of the soul, but the death Paul speaks of in

> So many of us as were baptised into Jesus Christ, were baptised into his death,

what is called in Zen, the Great Death (大死一番). So in *Measure for Measure,* Claudio says

> The miserable have no other medicine
> But only hope:
> I have hope to live, and am prepared to die.

But the Duke, rejecting this relativity, answers,

> Be absolute for death: either death or life
> Shall thereby be the sweeter.

The Great Death, a form of living up to the moment of death, is to "die without regret," death with honour, eternal, timeless life, as opposed to mere life, life with dishonour, i.e. without value, life with regret, "looking before and after." So Brutus says,

> Cowards die many times before their death.

"Cowards" means us ordinary people. If you ask, "How many times do they die?" the answer is, "An infinite number of times," because Shakespeare's words apply to almost the whole of our life, spent as it is in implicit or explicit fears for the future, in a state of unpreparedness for all the slings and arrows of outrageous fortune, which may come at any time and therefore are ever-present,

> quae quasi saxum Tantalo semper impendet.

If only we can die to ourselves just once, once and for all, we can say like the martyr Tankerfield at the stake,

> Be the day short or never so long,
> At length it ringeth to evensong.

Tankerfield suddenly perceived, at the moment of execution, the truth that underlies this apparent platitude, expressed in Zen by

> A long thing is the Long Body of Buddha;
> A short thing is the Short Body of Buddha.

長者長法身、短者短法身。 (禪林句集)

To accept short things as short, long things as long, the passage of time as the passage of time, to realise fully that meeting is the beginning of parting, life is the beginning of death, means to accept Reality, the Absolute, the spiritual Body of Buddha, the will of God. Sôshi criticises scornfully the weeping and wailing which he (for dramatic purposes,) alleges took place at the funeral of Rôshi. He then says, (in paraphrase)

Rôshi happened to be born when it was time for him to be born, and, in the process of Nature, died at his appointed time.   To be overjoyed at his birth or plunged into inconsolable grief at his death was equally vulgar and foolish.   In olden times, a sage who had transcended this relativity of life and death, was said to have attained the state of Cutting the Natural Thread.   Ordinary people fear death for this reason: they do not see that life and death are one process, both present in any single occurence. [For example, the ink must "die" in the ink-pot, before it can "live" on the paper.] Or again, flame is the burning of the wood, life is the dying of the person. Without burning, the destruction of the wood, there is no heat or light.   Without dying, the catabolism of body and per-

sonality there is no life.   The wood is consumed to ashes,
but the fire, the principle of combustion, is immortal.   So
men appear and disappear, but the flame of existence burns
for ever.

適來夫子時也。　適去夫子順也。　安時而處順
哀樂不能入也。　古者謂是帝之縣解指窮於爲
薪、火傳也不知其盡也。

(內篇養生主第三)

Compare this with the lines which Tankerfield quoted on the
scaffold, and then with the following of Wordsworth:

> A slumber did my spirit seal;
>   I had no human fears:
> She seem'd a thing that could not feel
>   The touch of earthly years.

Beauty of mind and body, the poet felt, are eternal, unchanging; age cannot wither her.   This is the world of the spirit,
the Absolute, above all joy and grief, the everlasting flame.

> No motion has she now, no force;
>   She neither hears nor sees;
> Roll'd round in earth's diurnal course
>   With rocks and stones and trees!

This is the agonising every-day world, the Relative.   The wood
is burned away to smoke and ashes.   Yet both are true, and
without the other, each is meaningless, for the Absolute is the
Relative, the Relative is the Absolute.   No wood, no fire; no
fire, no wood.   This nameless and unnameable region is expressed in the last lines of *The Education of Nature*.

> She died, and left to me
> This heath, this calm and quiet scene;
> The memory of what has been,
> And never more will be.

This is the region of Stevenson's poem:

Blows the wind today, and the sun and the rain are flying,
    Blows the wind on the moors today and now,
Where about the graves of the martyrs the whaups are crying,
    My heart remembers how !

Grey recumbent tombs of the dead in desert places,
    Standing stones on the vacant wine-red moor,
Hills of sheep and the homes of the silent vanished races,
    And winds, austere and pure :

Be it granted to behold you again in dying,
    Hills of home ! and to hear again the call ;
Hear about the graves of the martyrs the pewees crying,
    And hear no more at all.

Again in *Evensong,* also written at Vailima :

The embers of the day are red
Beyond the murky hill.
The kitchen smokes : the bed
In the darkly house is spread :
The great sky darkens overhead,
And the great woods are shrill.
So far have I been led,
Lord, by thy will :
So far I have followed, Lord, and wondered still.

The breeze from the embalmèd land
Blows sudden toward the shore ;
And claps my cottage door.
I hear the signal,[1] Lord—I understand.
The night at thy command
Comes. I will eat and sleep and will not question more.

---

[1] Is this Bashô's 水の音, " the sound of the water ? "

CHAPTER XXIII

CHILDREN

And he called to him a little child and set him in the midst
of them, and saith, "Verily, I say unto you, except ye become as little children, ye shall in no wise enter the Kingdom of Heaven."

However often read or quoted, this never loses its charm and
power, partly because we feel, even at a third or fourth remove
of translation, that these words were uttered by a man who
himself had become as a little child.   The fatherhood of God,
the child-hood of man — this is the unique contribution of
Christ to our religious experience.   Compare it to the logic-
chopping, complicated, uninspired and uninspiring epigram
called the Golden Rule: "Do unto others as you would they
should do unto you," which to me personally is and always has
been perfectly meaningless.   When our real child's nature is
appealed to, it is irresistible, for as Ulysses says,

> One touch of nature makes the whole world kin,

that is, we are separated from nothing, we apprehend everything truly, because our own nature begins to work in its
original purity.

In the *Analects,* we are told to respect the young only because
they may equal us in the future.

後 生 可 畏、 焉 知 來 者 之 不 如 今 也。

(論 語 九、 二 十 二。)

but Môshi (Mencius) has something better for us:

The great man is he who does not lose his childlike heart.

孟子曰。 大人者不失其赤子之心者也。

Rôshi, speaking of the man who follows the Way, says,

He is like a child alone, careless, unattached, devoid of ambition.

我獨泊兮其未兆。 如嬰兒之未孩。(第二十章)

But the best example of this state of childlikeness is the passage in the *Rokusodankyô* already quoted:

"Think not of good-evil, think not of good-evil! At this moment what is your real face (nature) Myôjôza?" Emyô suddenly became enlightened.

不思善不思惡。 與麼時那箇是明上座本來目
面。 慧明言下大悟。

What is the nature of a child? What were those divine lineaments which E-Myô suddenly saw?

The answer to this question is contained in Wordsworth's *Characteristics of a Child three Years Old*.

Loving she is, and tractable, though wild;
And Innocence hath privilege in her
To dignify arch looks and laughing eyes;
And feats of cunning; and the pretty round
Of trespasses, affected to provoke
Mock-chastisement and partnership in play.
And, as a faggot sparkles on the hearth,
Not less if unattended and alone
Than when both young and old sit gathered round
And take delight in its activity;
Even so this happy Creature of herself
Is all-sufficient; solitude to her
Is blithe society, who fills the air

With gladness and involuntary songs.
Light are her sallies as the tripping fawn's
Forth-startled from the fern where she lay couched;
Unthought-of, unexpected, as the stir
Of the soft breeze ruffling the meadow-flowers,
Or from before it chasing wantonly
The many-coloured images imprest
Upon the bosom of a placid lake.

Let us take these several characteristics.

1. Loving she is.

This love which springs up in the hearts of children, and which gradually dries away in the desert of life, must have been one of the things Christ wanted his disciples to perceive in the living sermon he set before them.   The complete faith and utter dependence of the child, its trustful affection, which awoke such a response in Christ's own heart, were what enabled him to say in his last agony,

Father, into thy hands I commend my spirit.

Because of this word "Father" and the personification it involves, because Christians do not, in their thoughts and conscious feelings, go beyond God into the region where He too "moves and has his being," Buddhist critics of Christianity say, "Buddhist philosophy and experience go deeper."   As far as the philosophy is concerned this may be so; as for the experience, comparisons are not only odious, but blasphemous, a sin against the Holy Ghost.   Love, the love of God, the love of Christ, the love of Amida, the love of a child, the love which all of us feel sometimes bursting up in our hearts, this love, as Shakespeare says, "mocks comparison."   And there is no other experience but this; it is the beginning and end of all religion. The personification is an intellectual habit or temperamental convenience. It would be well to treat it as a mere question of vocabulary. It has nothing to do with the experience of love itself.

In one of Katherine Mansfield's stories, *The Little Girl,* Kezia finds her father something to be feared and avoided, but after she is taken to his room to sleep and realises his tiredness and loneliness, greater than her own,

"Oh," said the little girl, "my head's on your heart; I can hear it going. What a big heart you've got, father dear."

That is the true Christian experience, Buddhist experience. Children not only have more love in their hearts than adults, it is also indiscriminate, until they are taught by experience, imitation or instruction, to love this and hate that. In Blake's *A Little Boy Lost,* the child says,

> 'And, Father, how can I love you
> Or any of my brothers more?
> I love you like the little bird
> That picks up crumbs around the door.'

This kind of love is socially and conventionally dangerous, and so,

> The Priest sat by and heard the child,
> In trembling zeal he seiz'd his hair:
> He led him by his little coat
> And all admir'd the priestly care.

> And standing on the altar high,
> 'Lo! what a fiend is here' said he,
> 'One who sets reason[1] up for judge
> Of our most holy Mystery.'

John tells us that

There is no fear in love: but perfect love casteth out fear.

[1] Imagination, intuition.

A young child has perfect, indiscriminate, universal love for all things and therefore no fear whatever. As he grows older he make the mistake of supposing that some things are friendly and others antagonistic to him. His religious teaching should show him that the fire that burns him, cooks his dinner; that the fire "loves" him and all other things, without any distinction whatsoever, and that that early indiscriminate love of his was a just and justifiable instinct, a counterpart of the love of God which sends down rain upon the just and upon the unjust, without respect of persons. If I may for once allow myself the luxury, the dissipation, of a comparison between Christianity and Buddhism, I would say that in Christianity the emphasis is on love, "*Perfect love casteth out fear,*" while in Buddhism the emphasis is on fear, fear of birth, sickness, old age and death, the four states of all phenomena (四木目). But if we get rid of fear perfectly, there will naturally and inevitably arise in our hearts, emptied of self, universal love and benevolence, for "*Perfect fearlessness casteth out hate.*" These are the two halves of religion, appealing in different degrees to different people according to their temperament; one of these two is essential to a true, living understanding of life.

> 2. Even so this happy Creature of herself
> Is all sufficient; solitude to her
> Is blithe society.

Paradoxically, this complete dependence results in complete self-sufficiency. Just as

> The river glideth at its own sweet will,

so the child is a perfect microcosm of the universe, in which there is no gain or loss, separation or union. And as

> Whosoever will be chief among you, let him be your servant,

the child is master of the household, its strength made perfect in weakness. Emerson says in his essay on *Self-Reliance,* of children, babies and animals,

> That divided and rebel mind, that distrust of a sentiment because our arithmetic has computed the strength and means opposed to our purpose, these have not. Their mind being whole, their eye is as yet unconquered, and when we look into their faces, we are disconcerted. Infancy conforms to nobody : all conform to it, so that one babe commonly makes four or five out of the adults who prattle and play to it.

This power through weakness is expressed very strongly by Wordsworth in the *Prelude,* (V, 507)

> > Our childhood sits,
> > Our simple childhood, sits upon a throne
> > That hath more power than all the elements.

This same power children share with animals, birds, and other objects of nature. Compare Dansui's

> > Even before His Majesty,
> > > The scarecrow does not remove
> > > > Its plaited hat.

御幸にも編笠ぬがぬ案山子かな　　　　團　水

and Issa's

> > The cherry blossoms!
> > > They have made a daimyô
> > > > Dismount from his horse.

大名を馬からおろす櫻かな　　　　　　一　茶

The nightingale!
    Even before His Lordship,
    That same voice!

鶯や御前へ出ても同じ聲

In the *Green Linnet,* Wordsworth gives us another example of self-sufficiency and bliss in solitude, which is one of the tests of Zen. Speaking of the linnet,

> While birds, and butterflies, and flowers,
> Make all one band of paramours,
> Thou, ranging up and down the bowers,
>   Art sole in thy employment:
> A Life, a Presence like the Air,
> Scattering thy gladness without care,
> Too blest with anyone to pair;
>   Thyself thy own enjoyment.

The same thought of what seems solitariness, but what is in fact a partaking of the divine nature, playing with Stevenson's Unseen Playmate, is found in Emerson's

> Space is ample, east and west,
> But two cannot go abreast,
> Cannot travel it in two:
> Yonder masterful cuckoo
> Crowds every egg out of the nest,
> Quick or dead, except its own.

3. Light are her sallies as the tripping fawn's
   Forth-startled from the fern where she lay couched;
   Unthought-of, unexpected, as the stir
   Of the soft breeze ruffling the meadow-flowers.

Here again we cannot help thinking of Bashô's "sallies":

You light the fire
    And I'll show you something nice—
    A ball of snow!

君火をたけよき物見せん雪丸げ

Now then!
    Let's go snow-viewing
        Until we tumble over!

    いざ行かん雪見にころぶ所まで

Look, children,
    Hail-stones!
        Let's rush out!

    いざ子供はしり歩かん玉あられ

This was the spirit which produced the following poem of
Wordsworth, easy to parody, but impossible to imitate.

Among all lovely things my Love had been;
Had noted well the stars, all flowers that grew
About her home; but she had never seen
A Glow-worm, never one, and this I knew.

While riding near her home one stormy night
A single Glow-worm did I chance to espy;
I gave a fervent welcome to the sight,
And from my Horse I leapt; great joy had I.

Upon a leaf the Glow-worm did I lay,
To bear it with me through the stormy night:
And, as before, it shone without dismay;
Albeit putting forth a fainter light.

When to the Dwelling of my Love I came,
I went into the Orchard quietly;
And left the Glow-worm, blessing it by name
Laid safely by itself, beneath a Tree.

The whole next day, I hoped, and hoped with fear;
At night the Glow-worm shone beneath the Tree:
I led my Lucy to the spot, "Look here!"
Oh! joy it was for her, and joy for me!

So also with the last two lines of the *Daffodils,*

> And then my heart with pleasure fills
> And dances with the daffodils

condemned as bathos by Coleridge.

What is most remarkable about Stevenson's *A Child's Garden of Verses* is that he sees the child's Zen and reflects it back to the child in the form of poetry:

> The friendly cow, all red and white,
>   I love with all my heart;
> She gives me cream with all her might
>   To eat with apple-tart.

The Zen of the cow ("with all her might") appeals to the child's Zen ("with all my heart").

> The rain is raining all around,
>   It falls on field and tree,
> It rains on the umbrellas here,
>   And on the ships at sea.

The rain unites all things into one, as in the next poem, singing does.

> Of speckled eggs the birdie sings
>   And nests among the trees;
> The sailor sings of ropes and things
>   In ships upon the seas.
>
> The children sing in far Japan,
>   The children sing in Spain;
> The organ with the organ man
>   Is singing in the rain.

Auntie's Skirts is nothing more or less than a perfect *haiku*, though Japanese readers and the younger generation of Englishmen could hardly understand it because of the "local colour."

> Whenever Auntie moves around,
> Her dresses make a curious sound;
> They trail behind her up the floor,
> And trundle after through the door.

The Zen of *A Child's Garden of Verses* can be tested by the fact that in most of them it is impossible to think that they were not written by the child himself. The identity with their characters of Shakespeare and Dickens, of Wordsworth with Nature, — these are not deeper, are not more absolute than Stevenson's with the child. The same taking upon himself the spiritual form of a child we see in Issa, in this respect the greatest poet in the world. He himself says,

> Ah! to be
>   A child —
>   On New Year's Day!

正 月 の 子 供 に な つ て 見 た き か な

This attitude of Issa was the same to everything but I will quote here only a few poems relating to childhood itself.

> The child is crying;
>   "Give me it!" she wails—
>   The harvest moon.

明 月 を と つ て く れ ろ と 泣 く 子 哉

But Davies' original is better than my translation:

> The child
> That cries aloud to own thy light:
> The little child that lifts each arm
> To press thee to her bosom warm.

[1] Compare the poems of Bashô on pages 357-8, and contrast his fatherly spirit with the childishness of Issa.

New Year's Presents:
>> The baby also
>>>> Holds out its tiny hands.

年玉やふところの子も手々をして

The kitten is mewing;
>> But the little girl is playing ball,
>>>> And only makes a face at him.

なく猫にあかん目をして手まり哉

The snow having melted,
>> The village
>>>> Is full of children.

雪とけて村一ぱいの子ども哉

Wild persimmons:
>> The mother is eating
>>>> The bitter parts.

しぶいとこ母がくひけり山のかき

But this childlikeness is just as effective when applied to serious things, to death, for example, in *We are Seven.* Compare the last lines of "She dwelt among the untrodden ways,"

>> She lived unknown, and few could know
>>>> When Lucy ceased to be;
>> But she is in her grave, and, oh,
>>>> The difference to me!

with Bashô's poem when he revisited his former home, and remembered his friend and master Sengin of long ago:

>> How many, many things
>>>> They call to mind—
>>>>>> These cherry-blossoms!

（故主蟬吟公の庭前にて）

さまざまの事おもひ出す櫻かな

In Shakespeare, the mind of the child, still kept in the
most terrible and tragic situations, gives us such immortal lines
as the dying Cleopatra s

> Peace, peace!
> Dost thou not see my baby at my breast
> That sucks the nurse asleep?

and Iras'

> Finish, good lady; the bright day is done,
> And we are for the dark.

Another aspect of the nature of children connected with
their "sallies," is their *casualness*,[1] which they share equally
with animals and some of the greatest poets. Coleridge re-
proves Wordsworth with an expression he invented for the
purpose, and which has kept its place in the English language,
matter-of-factness. Just as children cut through all our ideality,
sentimentality, sophistry, with a single word of truth, so
Wordsworth, and with him Vaughan, demolishes our definitions of what poetry is or should be, with a homely phrase of
the deepest religious or imaginative connotation. Take for
example Vaughan's *The Retreate*:

> Happy those early dayes!   When I
> Shin'd in my Angell-infancy
>
> *When yet I had not walkt above*
> *A mile or two* from my first love.

This comes from the same attitude of mind as Bashô's

[1] Cp. Bridges:

> They that in play can do the thing they would
> Having an instinct throned in reasons place,
> —And every perfect action hath the grace
> Of indolence or thoughtless hardihood—
> These are the best.

    It is deep autumn:
        What kind of life
            Is my neighbour's, I wonder?

秋 深 き 隣 は 何 を す る 人 ぞ

which means, what is God doing next door? Again Vaughan
has

> I saw Eternity *the other night*
> Like a great Ring of pure and endless light,
> All calm as it was bright

This intensity of feeling with casualness of expression is the
mark of sincerity; this *continuity* of spiritual vision and daily
life, with no break between, is the life of Zen. In the *Marriage
of Heaven and Hell,* Blake writes,

> The Prophets Isaiah and Ezekiel dined with me, and I asked
> them how they dared so roundly to assert that God spoke
> to them.

Wordsworth's *Michael,* as has been said before, is one whole
poem of matter-of-factness, a great poem which offers the critic
no quotations at all. Even the most pathetic part of the poem,

> many and many a day he thither went,
> And never lifted up a single stone,

has nothing in it to arrest the attention, but as part of the
poem itself it is equal to the most purple of purple patches, and
superior, in the fact that it can never become hackneyed. To
return to Vaughan: in his *Childe-hood* we have the beautiful
line

> By meer playing go to Heaven.

That is what Ryôkan did:

This whole long day
      Of misty spring
            I have spent
In playing ball
      With the children.

かすみ立つながき春日を子どもらと
手まりつきつつけふもくらしつ

If only we had those "white designs," that is to say, the self-lessness, the unselfconsciousness of children, how heavenly our lives would become; but as Vaughan says,

      I cannot reach it; and my striving eye
      Dazzles at it, as at eternity.

There is an interesting story of a man who got in a boat and vowed to go on rowing till he got to Paradise. On his way, he asked some fishermen, "How far is it to Paradise?" They answered "Two thousand miles." On and on he rowed until his arms were like sticks and his back felt red hot. He called to some more fishermen and asked how far it was to Paradise. "Two thousand miles," they answered. Again he rowed on, again he asked the question, and still the same answer "Two thousand miles." Chancing to look round, he saw Paradise sitting in the boat behind him. This is the meaning of "my striving eye dazzles at it." We are spiritually shortsighted, and, like a cat, can see far-off things, infinity or eternity or God, but not the Heaven which is just under our noses. Children see it, and Wordsworth therefore apostrophizes the little child as

      Thou, whose exterior semblance doth belie
            Thy Soul's immensity;
      Thou best Philosopher, who yet dost keep
      Thy heritage, thou Eye among the blind,

> That, deaf and silent, read'st the eternal deep,
> Haunted for ever by the eternal mind—
>> Mighty Prophet! Seer blest!
>> On whom those truths do rest,
> Which we are toiling all our lives to find!
> Thou, over whom thy immortality
> Broods like the day, a master o'er the slave,
> A presence which is not to be put by!

When Coleridge read this, he fairly danced with rage, he frothed at the mouth; to compare him, Coleridge, the real Prophet, the real Seer, the real Philosopher, to a "six years darling of a pigmy size"! It was too absurd, too monstrous!

Now here, not to stop at the daring spirit of metaphor which connects the epithets "deaf and silent," with the apostrophised eye: or (if we are to refer it to the preceding word, philosopher) the faulty and equivocal syntax of the passage; and without examining the propriety of making a "master *brood* o'er a slave" or the *day* brood *at all;* we will merely ask, What does all this mean? In what sense is a child of that age a philosopher? In what sense does he *read* "the eternal deep"? In what sense is he declared to be *"for ever haunted"* by the Supreme Being? or so inspired as to deserve the splendid titles of *a mighty prophet, a blessed seer?* By reflection? by knowledge? by conscious intuition? or by *any* form or modification of consciousness? These would be tidings indeed; but such as would presuppose an immediate revelation to the inspired communication, and require miracles to authenticate his inspiration.

(Biographia Literaria, chap. 22)

I have quoted this at length to show what nonsense a man of intellect, a poet and an intimate spiritual friend of Wordsworth, could write when he comes across the intuitions, as

> Unthought-of, unexpected, as the stir
> Of the soft breeze ruffling the meadow-flowers.

In *The Mother's Return,* the young girl's attitude to life, her instinctive joyful acceptance of all that the intellect fights with, is described:

> No strife disturbs his sister's breast;
> She wars not with the mystery
> Of time and distance, night and day;
> The bonds of our humanity

and only when we have the characteristics of childhood, complete faith in all things, teachableness, self-sufficiency, simplicity and spontaneity, do we realise our own true nature, become free of the bonds of mortality, enter into the Kingdom of Heaven, always beholding the face of God.   As Bashô teaches one of his pupils,

> The man who says,
>   " My children are a burden ! "—
>   There are no flowers for him.

子 に 飽 く と 申 す 人 に は 花 も な し

CHAPTER XXIV
IDIOTS AND OLD MEN

Amiel says,

> Nothing is more characteristic of a man than the manner
> in which he behaves towards fools,

and in the case of Wordsworth we may call his attitude one of
reverence. By "idiots," we mean, of course, not raving luna-
tics or cases of obsession, but what are often called "simple"
people, those whose development has, for some reason or other,
usually physical, been retarded. The fools of Shakespeare are
here excluded, for in their selfconsciousness, and often, pathos
(as in the case of the fool in *King Lear,*) they represent the very
fever and height of the disease of the will from which mankind is suffering and from which Zen desires to release us.
Maggie, in Dickens' *Little Dorrit,* is an example of the kind of
person in whom Wordsworth saw so much poetry. Maggie is
a poor half-wit who has remained in a state of arrested development from the age of ten.

> Maggie laughed and immediately snored. In Little
> Dorrit's eyes and ears, the uncouth figure and the uncouth
> sound were as pleasant as could be.

Here we see the close connection that exists between the child
and the idiot. Little Dorrit is one of the children of this world,
without envy or suspicion, full of faith, hope, and charity, able
to see the truth and beauty to which intellectual and aesthetic

prejudice blinds us.   Chapter 20 of *Roshi*, quoted above, continues,

All other men have plenty; I only seem to have lost all.
I have the mind of an absolute idiot!

衆人皆有餘、而我獨若遺、我愚人之心也哉沌沌兮。

There is a great difference between the apparent, natural stupidity of a man whose inborn Zen causes him to avoid all paradoxical remarks, spectacular actions, dramatic disturbances and interference with other people, and the stupidity that comes from the levelling-down effect of so-called education. Dr. Johnson, (in Boswell's *Life*, under 1763,) tells us with as much truth as wit, of a certain man,

Sherry is dull, naturally dull; but it must have taken him a great deal of pains to become what we now see him. Such an access of stupidity, sir, is not in Nature.

Let us now look at Wordsworth's *The Idiot Boy*.   His mother put him on the pony, to go and fetch the doctor to a sick neighbour,

But when the Pony moved his legs
Oh! then for the poor Idiot Boy!
For joy he cannot hold the bridle,
For joy his head and heels are idle,
He's idle all for very joy.

This joy in such a trivial, ordinary thing as a pony walking, is of the essence of poetry and of religion and of Zen. Compare Bashô's

We gaze
    Even at horses,
        This morn of snow!

馬をさへながむる雪のあしたかな

The mother too has joy in her idiot son, who might well be a source of grief and shame to her; but no, she stands at the door,

> Stands fixed, her face with joy o'erflows,
> Proud of herself and proud of him.

Understand and remember, ALL JOY IS IDIOT JOY! This is the lesson of these four hundred and fifty three lines. In *Michael* again we have,

> Those fields, those hills—what could they less? had laid
> Strong hold on his affections, were to him
> A pleasurable feeling of *blind love,*
> *The pleasure which there is in life itself.*

Never forget, ALL LOVE IS IDIOT LOVE. So Shakespeare says,

> The lunatic, the lover and the poet
> Are of imagination all compact.

In the last lines of the poem we have the words of the Idiot Boy himself, describing his spiritual experience in that memorable night:

> " The cocks did crow to-whoo, to-whoo,
> And the sun did shine so cold ! "
> —Thus answered Johnny in his glory,
> And that was all his travel's story.

For those who find Johnny's words hard to understand or believe, there is following:

> Children and fools cannot lye.

Let us take some examples from Ryôkan.[1] Once he was playing hide-and-seek with some children. When the child who

---

[1] See *Dewdrops on a Lotus Leaf*, by J. Fischer, Kenkyusha. The author shares Ryôkan's beautiful, uncritical simplicity, and the book must be read in this spirit or not at all.

was to find the others was chosen, the others, Ryôkan among them, ran away in different directions and hid themselves. Ryôkan ran to an outhouse, and seating himself on a pile of faggots, covered his head with the long sleeves of his priestly robe. For some reason or other the children stopped playing and left Ryôkan there without saying anything to him. The next morning some one found him there in the same place. "What on earth are you doing here, Ryôkan?" he said. "Hush! —don't speak so loudly—I shall be found!" he whispered.

Another story showing his sublime "idiocy."

Ryokan was on bad terms with a certain Hambei, and the villagers of a certain place determined to take advantage of this to play a trick on Ryôkan. When he entered the village and stood before a certain house begging, a man came out and said to him, "This is Mr. Hambei's house," and Ryôkan fled precipitately. Again he stood begging before another house, and again he was told, "This house is Mr. Hambei's," and off he went. Everywhere it was the same, "This house is Mr. Hambei's," so at last Ryôkan passed through the whole village obtaining nothing. When the villagers realised that Ryôkan believed implicitly all that was told him, because he himself did not lie, they were filled with shame and regret.

Here are three of his *haiku:*

> The sound
>   Of the scouring of the saucepan
>   Blends with the green-frog's voice.

鍋みがく音にまぎるる雨蛙

> The garden grasses:
>   They fall,
>   And lie as they fall.

たふるればたふるるままの庭の草

On rainy days,
>   The monk Ryôkan
>   >   Feels sorry for himself.

雨 の 降 る 日 は あ は れ な り 良 寛 坊

The frogs down in the fields cry, "Poor monk Ryôkan, poor monk Ryôkan!" like the parrot who cried "Poor Robinson Crusoe!" Ryôkan is more famous for his *waka* and *shi*.

I set out
>   To beg my food;
>   >   But the time was spent
>   Gathering violets
>   >   In the fields of spring.

飯 乞 ふ と わ が 來 し か ど も 春 の 野 に
菫 つ み つ つ 時 を へ に け り

What have I
>   To bequeath as legacy?
>   >   The flowers of spring;
>   Hill cuckoos of summer;
>   >   Maple leaves of autumn.

形 見 と て 何 か 殘 さ ん 春 は 花
山 ほ と と ぎ す 秋 は も み ぢ 葉

Last of all, let me quote once more Macbeth's words concerning the meaning of life:

>   >   It is a tale
>   Told by an idiot, full of sound and fury,
>   Signifying nothing.

A few people concur with Macbeth's assertion, but fail to understand it. The majority know it to be true in their heart of hearts, but deny it. Of them, as of Macbeth himself as he utters it, we must say,

> Here you stand,
> Adore and worship, when you know it not;
> Pious beyond the intention of your thought,
> Devout above the meaning of your will.
>   (*Excursion,* IV, 1147)

For it is absolutely true (not relatively) that life signifies nothing whatever; life is life, no more, no less. It is full of sound and full of silence, of fury and of mildness, but of meaning it is totally devoid; yet we cannot say that it is meaningless either. A Zen priest once said to Bashô, "A smattering, a merely theoretical knowledge of Zen, is the cause of grave errors," (なま禪大抵のもとゐとかや) whereupon Bashô has the following *haiku:*

> How admirable,
>   He who thinks not, "Life is fleeting,"
>   When he sees the lightning-flash![1]

稲妻にさとらぬ人の貴さよ   芭 蕉

Life is not fleeting, life is not eternal; life is life, lightning is lightning. But even when we say, "Life is life," we feel that we are saying too much, that is, *saying more than an idiot would say.*

In the extremely inconvenient and inconsistent classification of his poetry, Wordsworth has a special section of Poems Referring to the Period of Old Age. In them there is nothing of the kind of thing we find in Cicero's *De Senectute.* There Cicero rebuts the four alleged infelicities of old age:

> It incapacitates a man for acting in the affairs of the world; it produces great infirmities of body; it disqualifies him for the enjoyment of sensual gratifications; and that it brings him within the immediate verge of death.

[1] Following the interpretation of 服部耕石、芭蕉句集新講。

Wordsworth's attitude is at once more simple and more profound. In the presence of old men, in watching them and listening attentively to them, he had the same experience, the same peculiar sensation, as in the presence of children, idiots, mountains, daffodils. Though no one would call Wordsworth a humble man, he had an absolute humility before these intuitions that came to him in overwhelming strength and number in the year 1798, at the age of twenty seven, decreasing rapidly with the passing of time and practically disappearing by 1812. In a poem written in 1830, *Presentiments*, he looks back on that time:

> The tear whose source I could not guess,
> The deep sigh that seemed fatherless,
> Were mine in early days:

and sees the origin divine of

> A rainbow, a sunbeam,
> A subtle smell that spring unbinds,
> Dead pause abrupt of midnight winds,
> An echo, or a dream.

The poem ends with the significant lines,

> God, who instructs the brutes to scent
> All changes of the element,
> Whose wisdom fixed the scale
> Of natures, for our wants provides
> By higher, sometimes humbler, guides,
> When lights of reason fail.

Wordsworth, like Bach, is always speaking of himself, yet we never feel him in the way; we look through, not at him. Wordsworth seems to think of himself as of the Small Celandine,

> there's not a place,
Howsoever mean it be,
But 'tis good enough for thee,

and so without condescension or affectation he shows us the
spiritual life of beggars, old men and women, children, idiots,
servant girls, and even of rascals and hypocrites.

In *Resolution and Independence,* Wordsworth describes the
Leech-gatherer in extreme old age,

The oldest man he seemed that ever wore grey hairs,

his body bent double, but to Wordsworth's eye, part of nature
itself which gives us "human strength, by apt admonishment."
This old man's continuity with nature, Wordsworth expresses
in three similes:

> As a huge stone is sometimes seen to lie
Couched on the bald top of an eminence,

> Like a sea-beast crawled forth; that on a shelf
Of rock or sand reposeth, there to sun itself,

> Motionless as a cloud the old man stood,
That heareth not the loud winds when they call;
And moveth all together, if it move at all.

The old man, answering Wordsworth's earnest questions about
his life and manner of living, replied that he was a leech-
gatherer, and that he roamed from moor to moor finding them
where he could.

> The old Man still stood talking by my side;
But now his voice to me was like a stream
Scarce heard; nor word from word could I divide.

The meaning of the old man's existence was so strong that
the words became unnecessary and almost inaudible:

What you are, speaks so loudly I cannot hear what you say.

Afterwards, Wordsworth described this state of mind as distinctly as he could.

> While he was talking thus, the lonely place,
> The old Man's shape, and speech—all troubled me;
> In my mind's eye I seemed to see him pace
> About the weary moors continually,
> Wandering about alone and silently.

And, more remote still from the original "troubling" of his spirit,

> I could have laughed myself to scorn to find
> In that decrepit Man so firm a mind.

Like Christ, Wordsworth simply says to us, "Consider the old man of the moors, how he lives." This extraordinary interest of the young man in the old appears again in *The Fountain:*

> We talked with open heart, and tongue
> Affectionate and true,
> A pair of friends, though I was young
> And Matthew seventy-two.

The same beautiful relation transcending the ordinary ideas of affinity comes in the *Hôjôki:*

> At the foot of the mountain [on which my hut stands] there is another humble cottage, where the hill-ward lives. He has a son who often comes to see me when he has nothing to do. Together we go roaming about. He is sixteen and I sixty, but we feel the same about things, and despite the difference of our ages, enjoy each other's company.

また麓に一つの柴の庵あり。すなはち山守が
居る所なり。かしこに小童あり。時時來りて
あひ訪ふ。もしつれづれなる時は、これを友

としてあそびありく。 かれは十六歳、われは
六十、その齢ことのほかなれど、心を慰むるこ
とはこれ同じ。

Old Matthew tells us his view of old age.

> "The blackbird amid leafy trees,
> The lark above the hill,
> Let loose their carols when they please,
> Are quiet when they will.
>
> "With Nature never do they wage
> A foolish strife; they see
> A happy youth, and their old age
> Is beautiful and free."

Matthew's ideal of life, in youth and age, was written after his
death by Wordsworth in the village school of which Matthew
was the school-master. It is another definition of Zen.

> Every hour thy heart runs wild,
> Yet never once doth go astray.

In *The Old Cumberland Beggar,* Wordsworth notes that even
ordinary people feel some faint "troubling" of the mind in
the old man's presence; he has something in him like the angel
which went down at certain seasons into the Pool of Bethesda
and troubled the water.

> The sauntering Horseman throws not with a slack
> And careless hand his alms upon the ground,
> But stops,—that he may safely lodge the coin
> Within the old Man's hat; nor quits him so,
> But still, when he has given his horse the rein,
> Watches the aged Beggar *with a look
> Sidelong, and half-reverted.*

You may say, "That is because he is very, very old." Exactly, but that in no way explains away the "something" we

experience as we look upon his old age. Nothing could be more trite and ordinary than what Wordsworth says of the words of the leech-gatherer :

> But each in solemn order followed each,

but really to experience, for the first time, that words follow one another, is just as thrilling as gazing at the flowers in spring or the mountains in summer.   Further, this old man, the old Cumberland beggar, is not useless, a mere burden of the earth.

> 'Tis Nature's law
> That none, the meanest of created things,
> Of forms created the most vile and brute,
> The dullest or most noxious, should exist
> Divorced from good—a spirit and pulse of good,
> A life and soul, to every mode of being
> Inseparably linked.

Reading this we realise, with the immediateness of conviction, the equal, absolute value of all things, but when Wordsworth begins to *explain* this value, as giving an opportunity for others to do good by alms-giving, we are once more in the relative world, dubious and dim, the world of social amelioration. The Old Man as Wordsworth the poet sees him, is in the Absolute ;

> In that vast solitude to which
> The tide of things has borne him, he appears
> To breathe and live but for himself alone.

Wordsworth sees him and his ultimate death without senti· mentality, without regret.

> And let him, where and when he will, sit down
> Beneath the trees, or on a grassy bank
> Of highway side, and with the little birds
> Share his chance-gathered meal ; and finally,

> As in the eye of Nature he has lived,
> So in the eye of Nature let him die!

What we might call the life of Zen in extreme old age is expressed in a short but perfect poem, *Animal Tranquillity and
Decay.*

> The little hedgerow birds
> That peck along the road, regard him not.
> He travels on, and in his face, his step,
> His gait, is one expression: every limb,
> His look and bending figure, all bespeak
> A man who does not move with pain, but moves
> With thought.—He is insensibly subdued
> To settled quiet: he is one by whom
> All effort seems forgotten; one to whom
> Long patience hath such mild composure given,
> That patience now doth seem a thing of which
> He hath no need.   He is by nature led
> To peace so perfect that the young behold
> With envy what the Old Man hardly feels.

CHAPTER XXV

POVERTY

Just as in the case of death we saw that there was a pecu-liar but close relation between spiritual death (death of self) and physical death (bodily and mental dissolution) so there is an even closer relation between spiritual poverty ("Blessed are the poor in spirit") and actual, material poverty ("Blessed are the poor"). Christ went so far as to assert that for a rich man, the divine life was next to an impossibility.

"It is easier for a camel to go through the eye of a needle than for a rich man to enter the Kingdom of God." And when the disciples heard this, they were astonished exceedingly, saying, "Who then can be saved?" And Jesus looking upon them said, "With men this is impossible, but with God, all things are possible."

Other writers have taken a less extreme attitude; Marcus Aurelius declares that the good life can be led even by an emperor. Again in the *Saikontan* (菜根譚) we read:

The mark of nobility is to have nothing to do with power, reputation, wealth and rank; but the noblest thing of all is to have these and yet be unaffected by them.

　　勢 利 紛 華 不 近 者 爲 潔。　近 之 而 不 染 者 爲 尤。

Confucius, on the other hand, seems to agree with Christ:

To be poor without murmuring is difficult: to be rich without pride is easy.

　　　　子 曰、 貧 而 無 怨 難、 富 而 無 驕 易。

　　　　　　　　　　(論 語、 十 四、 十 一)。

for it is the broad, easy road that leadeth to destruction.   But perhaps before we go any farther it would be as well to define poverty and riches. By riches is meant superfluity; by poverty, less than the average man considers enough for comfort and well-being.   We may take the lives of Chômei, Bashô and Ryôkan as standards of the life of poverty.

Chômei tells us that at the age of sixty he built himself a one-room house near the river Kamo, a tenth of the size of his former dwelling-place, where he had lived about thirty years.

> I am now approaching my sixtieth year: the swiftly vanishing dew-drop of my life trembles on the very verge of the leaf: I make myself yet one more dwelling place.

> ここに六十の露消えがたに及びて、更に末葉の
> やどりを結べることあり。

This new abode on Mt. Hino, dwindling in size with the tale of his years, was only 10 feet square[1] and under 7 feet in height. The furniture: a small shrine, with pictures of Amida, Fugen and Fudô; on a shelf, some boxes containing poetry and music; a sô,[2] a biwa;[3] straw for a bed; a writing desk and a brazier; and last, but not least, a window.   Outside, the purple blossoms of the wistaria in spring, the green leaves of summer; in autumn the voice of the cicada, in winter the waxing and waning of the snow-drifts.

> In such a place there is no need to keep the commandments, for there is no temptation to break them.

> かならず禁戒を守るとしもなけれども、境界な
> ければ何につけてか破らむ。

Since I left the world, I have no envy of gain or fear of

---

[1] In imitation of Yuima's room
[2] A kind of *Koto*, or long harp.
[3] A lute.

loss. My life is in the hands of God; it is without desire
or loathing. I am like a cloud floating in the sky, I ask
for nothing, I reject nothing.

おほかた世を遁れ、身を捨てしより、恨もなく、
恐れもなし。 命は天運にまかせてをします、い
とはず。 身をば浮雲になずらへて、 たのます、
未だしとせず。

Poetry, music, art, religion — all in the compass of ten feet
square, — what is lacking here? We may perhaps answer,
"Love of mankind." In this respect Bashô and Ryôkan both
fully make up for any such deficiency on the part of Chomei.
See Bashô's delicate tenderness in the poem sent to Etsujin,
when thinking of his journey the year before:

> The snows of yester-year,
>   Which we together gazed upon,
>   Have fallen this year too?

(去年のわび寝をおもひ出て越人に贈る)

二人見し雪は今年も降りけるか 芭 蕉

with the underlying thought that the sameness or difference
of things, is in the eye, the heart, of the beholder.

In varying degrees of insincerity one may find this "love
of a hut" expressed all through English literature, with
Marvell's *Thoughts in a Garden,* Roger's *Mine be a cot beside
the hill,* Pope's *Happy the man whose wish and care,* and so on.
Even Wordsworth, in a late poem (*Ecclesiastical Sonnets, No.*
22) says,

> Methinks to some vacant hermitage
> My feet would rather turn—A beechen bowl,
> A maple dish, my furniture should be.

This of course is only one of the literary conventions, but years

before, he had written in *A Farewell,* when leaving for a two
months' holiday,

> Our boat is safely anchored by the shore,
> And there will safely ride when we are gone;
> The flowering shrubs that deck our humble door
> Will prosper, though untended and alone:
> Fields, goods and far-off chattels we have none:
> These narrow bounds contain our private store
> Of things earth makes, and sun doth shine upon;
> Here they are in our sight—we have no more.

This is in the true spirit of poverty.   The question now to be
answered is, what is the relation between Zen and poverty;
between poetry, religion and poverty?   One answer might be
that poverty is in the long run more simple, more "livable."
There is a humorous account, at the beginning of Bashô's *Oku
no Hosomichi,* of how he found his friends' parting gifts more
of a pain than a pleasure when he set out on his 1500 mile
journey.

> The bundle I carried on my thin, bony shoulders was
> the cause of my first discomfort on this journey.   I had
> intended to set off just as I was; however, — a *kamiko*[1] to
> protect me from the cold at night, a *yukata,*[2] a water-
> proof, writing materials and so on—all these things I had
> received from my friends as parting gifts, and I could
> hardly leave them behind, but they were necessarily a
> cause of discomfort and vexation all the way.

> 痩骨の肩にかかれるもの先づ苦しむ、ただ身す
> がらにと出立ち侍るを、 紙子一枚は夜の防ぎ、
> 浴衣雨具筆墨のたぐひ、あるは去りがたき餞な
> どしたるは、さすがに打捨てがたくて、路次の
> わづらひとなれるこそわりなけれ。

[1] Kimono made of white paper, prepared with persimmon juice, and
crumpled soft.
[2] Thin, cotton kimono for summer wear.

Another interesting example of the "livableness" of the life of poverty is given in the *Tsure-zure Gusa* (徒然草).

A man should be frugal, avoid all pomp and ostentation, own no treasures and desire nothing from the world. Few of the sages of olden times were wealthy men.

A certain hermit named Kyo-yu owned nothing whatever: even water he drank out of his hand. Seeing this, someone gave him a bowl made of a gourd. One day, he hung it on the branch of a tree, but the wind made it bang about and rattle noisily, so he took it and threw it away, and drank water out of his hand as before.

人はおのれをつつまやかにして、おごりを退けて、財をもたず、世をむさほらぬぞ、いみじかるべき。昔よりかしこき人の富めるは稀なり。もろこしに許由といひつる人は、身にしたがへるたくわへもなくて、水をも手して捧けて飲みけるを見て、なりひさごといふものを人の得させければ、ある時木の枝にかけたりければ、風に吹かれて鳴りけるを、かしましと棄てつ、又手にむすびてぞ水も飲みける。

Sometimes the inculcation of poverty may be a concession to human weakness, which finds the golden mean so difficult. Poverty then appears as a kind of universal Prohibition. Confucius says rightly,

I know why men do not walk in the Way: the clever go beyond it, the stupid do not reach to it. I know why men do not understand the Way: the virtuous exceed it, the vicious fall below it.

子曰、道之不行也、我知之矣、知者過之、愚者不及也。道之不明也、我知之矣、賢者過之、不肖者不及也。　　　　　　　　　　　（中庸、四）

But actually the sweetness and light of the Way of the Mean

comes from complete, absolute poverty, for as Milton says in *Samson Agonistes,*

> What boots it at one gate to make defence,
> And at another let in the foe?

Poverty appears again as a form of safety first, a kind of fire insurance by burning down the house.

> He that is down need fear no fall.

From this point of view the hermit's life is repudiated by Zen, and Chômei's life is rather that of Shin than of Zen.

There is something both deeper and simpler about poverty than the above explanations suggest.   Look at a very interesting poem (interesting, that is, in this connection, not intrinsically,) by Tennyson, called *The Lord of Burleigh,* which begins in a commonplace way enough.   The rich man pretends to be a poor painter, and marries the maiden in the village church.

> " I can make no marriage present:
>   Little can I give my wife.
> Love will make our cottage pleasant,
>   And I love thee more than life."

He then took her to a great mansion and told her it was their home.   She had wished to make him happy as a poor man's wife, but, though her heart misgave her, she made him a true wife,

> And her gentle mind was such
> That she grew a noble lady,
>   And the people loved her much.

But now comes the strange conclusion.   After giving birth to three children, she began to droop and fade, and at last *died from lack of poverty,* from the superfluities of life.   Her husband, looking on her, said, "Let her be dressed in the rustic clothes she wore at her wedding."

> Then her people, softly treading,
>   Bore to earth her body, drest
> In the dress that she was wed in,
>   That her spirit might have rest.

This illustrates Nerissa's saying:

> For aught I know, they are as sick that surfeit with too much as they that starve with nothing.

Dying for money—it is done every day; but to die from a kind of horror at the abundance of good things, what is the meaning of it? It lies, I think, in the fact that *poverty means closeness to nature.* Man is of the earth, earthy; of the water, watery; of the air, airy; of the fire, firey; and unless he remains in the closest possible contact with these elemental things, like Shelley he beats his luminous wings in the void in vain. Once this fact is grasped, we understand the true function of all literature, and especially poetry. The poems of Keats are solid blocks of poetry, those of Shelley poetical prisms and crystals, *at* which we gaze with delight, but those of Bashô and Wordsworth are windows *through* which we look with a feeling beyond joy or bliss, at the real world which we tread on, which we eat and excrete, breathe and grasp in our hands. This is the meaning of Ryôkan's poem:

> You say my poems are poetry?
>   They are not.
>   Yet if you understand they are not,—
>   Then you see the poetry of them!

誰か我が詩を詩なりといふ、我が詩はこれ詩にあらず
我が詩の詩にあらざるを知つて、初めて與に詩を言ふ
べし。

In other words, "If you think I am making some pretty poem for your delectation, you are mistaken and will never see the meaning of what I have written. Once you realise I am showing you myself, the nature of things, God, or whatever you choose to call it, then, and not until then, you understand the poetry of my poems." Wordsworth says (*Prelude* IV, 150),

> Gently did my soul
> Put off her veil, and, self-transmuted, stood
> Naked, as in the presence of her God.

When the soul is one with the thing, the poem does not, cannot stand between them. Longfellow wrote,

> Life is real, life is earnest,

and I do not know what he himself meant by these words, but from the point of view of Zen, it means that poetry is not iambic tetrameter or what not; it is reality conveyed to us in words, or rather through words, no, in spite of words, and when " we see into the life of things," we know that our life is reality, our life is poetry, and that these three are and always have been one.

What then is the function of poverty in life, reality, poetry? Poverty means the closest possible approximation of these three things which in our ordinary manner of living are separated. The following lines of Stevenson give us a clear idea of the value of poverty in our relation with nature.

> A naked house, a naked moor,
> A shivering pool before the door,
> A garden bare of flowers and fruit,
> And poplars at the garden foot:
> Such is the place that I live in,
> Bleak without and bare within.

*   *   *

> To make this earth, our hermitage,
> A cheerful and a changeful page,
> God's bright and intricate device
> Of days and seasons doth suffice.

Maupassant says in *Une Vie,* speaking of Jeanne's feelings after days out on the summer sea,

> Il lui semblait que trois seules choses étaient vraiment belles dans la création : la lumière, l'espace, et l'eau.

In the aesthetic realm, see the famous *haiku* of Ransetsu:

> White chrysanthemums,
> Yellow chrysanthemums,—
> Would there were no other names!

黄菊白菊そのほかの名はなくもがな

Commentators boggle over the meaning because they do not see the desire for aesthetic asceticism (forgive the uncouth phrase,) both in regard to the things themselves and the names of them. Wordsworth has a similar thought in the last lines of *Stanzas written in my Pocket-copy of Thomson's " Castle of Indolence."* The eccentric man and " that other Man,"

> There did they dwell—from earthly labour free,
> As happy spirits as were ever seen.
> If but a bird, to keep them company,
> Or butterfly sate down, they were, I ween,
> As pleased as if the same had been a Maiden-queen.

Again, in Bonchô's *haiku,*

> One long line of river
> Winds across
> The snowy moor.

ながながと川一すぢや雪の原

you have not got to "fill in the picture for yourself," any more than in Crome's landscape, *Moonrise on the Yare,* which is similar in spirit.

As for practical life, Patmore says in *Legem Tuam Dilexi,*

>   To have nought
> Is to have all things without care or thought,

which is in Kikaku's *haiku* so magnificently expressed:

>   The beggar!
>   He has heaven and earth
>   For his summer clothes.

乞食かな天地を着たる夏衣

More consciously, as a prayer for poverty of spirit, Bashô's,

>   Ah, *Kankodori,*[1]
>   My impermanence!
>   Deepen thou my solitude.

うき我をさびしがらせよ閑古鳥

The Japanese "sabishisa" has here a meaning very different from that of the English "loneliness," which suggests dreariness and spiritual discomfort, a solitary condition where it is impossible to love or be loved. The Japanese word in poetical usage has the meaning I have been trying to give to the word poverty.[2]

In the following lines by Siegfried Sassoon, the Western poet approximates very closely to the Japanese in his under-

[1] A species of cuckoo.

[2] This poverty, loneliness, Eckehart calls "Abgeschiedenheit," and in praising it above both Love and Humility and every other virtue, he says,

> Nun streift Abgeschiedenheit so nahe an das Nichts (空, the Void) dass es zwischen *Volkommener* Abgeschiedenheit und dem Nichts keinen Unterschied gibt.

standing of aloneness, though it does not represent the final
state of enlightenment.

ALONE

"When I'm alone"—the words tripped off his tongue
As though to be alone were nothing strange.
"When I was young," he said, "when I was young. . . ."

I thought of age and loneliness, and change.
I thought how strange we grow when we're alone,
And how unlike the selves that meet and talk,
And blow the candles out and say good night.
Alone . . . . The word is life endured and known.
It is the stillness where our spirits walk,
And all but inmost faith is overthrown.

In the following *haiku* of Bashô, we see the real thing.

> A paulonia leaf has fallen:
> > Will you not come to me
> > In my loneliness?

さ び し さ を 問 て く れ ぬ か 桐 一 葉

This was sent to Ransetsu, and expresses of course Bashô's
tender heart, and desire for the physical presence of his beloved pupil; but it also conveys, in the original, the meaning
that Autumn is here, the time when communion and union
with Nature comes almost of itself. If, at this season, it is our
own self which

> Warms in the sun, refreshes in the breeze,
> Glows in the stars, and blossoms in the trees,

we have attained that state of poverty, of loneliness, which
Bashô invites Ransetsu to share with him. Fellowship with
Nature in all its nakedness Ryôkan portrays in,

> The wind brings
>> Enough of fallen leaves
>>> To make a fire.

焚くほどは風がもてくる落葉かな

which Matsumura Keisuke, in his book *The Great Fool Ryôkan*[1], suggests is Ryôkan's unconscious alteration, through constant quotation, of Issa's

> The wind gives to me
>> Enough of fallen leaves
>>> To make a fire.

焚くほどは風がくれたる落葉かな

He further suggests that this slight difference has a deep meaning, Ryôkan having changed Issa's subjectiveness into his own objective attitude.   In any case, the meaning of both is the same as that of Marcus Aurelius when he says,

Nothing happens to any man which he is not formed by nature to bear,

that is, of course, so long as he receives what happens with poverty of mind.   We receive sensations of pleasure and pain,

But when these effects rise up to the mind by virtue of that other sympathy that naturally exists in a body which is all one, then thou must not strive to resist the sensation, for it is natural: *but let not the ruling part of itself add to the sensation the opinion that it is good or bad.*

When it does this, the original poverty is lost.   Rôshi says,

He that studies, gains something every day : he who follows the Way, loses something every day.

爲學日益、爲道日損。　(老子、四八)

[1] 大愚良寛、松村憲介著。

"Studies," means "collects opinions *about* things." In following the Way, we are not divided from them. Thoreau in
Walden, Stevenson in his phrase "Travel light!" have a
similar thought, but what Roshi is urging us to lose is such
things as self-respect, our immortal souls, our wish to live, our
pleasure in life, and so on. Of course, we shall get them all
back again, but changed out of all recognition. This is the
meaning of Christ's words,

> But when thou doest alms, let not thy left hand know what
> thy right doeth: that thine alms may be in secret, and thy
> Father which seeth in secret, *shall reward thee openly,*

which Suzuki finds antithetical to Zen. When we write poetry,
Ryôkan says, we are not to let the left hand know that the
right hand is writing poetry: this is to be our poverty-stricken,
childish, idiotic state of mind; and then are we not rewarded
openly? The poem is there for all to see! So it is with the
music of Bach: he never aims at beauty of sound or concord,
he has no purple patches or lucious, soul-fainting passages;
but does not his Father which heareth in secret, reward him
audibly? So it is in our daily life; our light cannot be hid,
men see it and glorify God.

Let us consider more closely the meaning of the statement
that "poverty means closeness to Nature." In the most thrilling, poetical, and profound words of the Bible, Christ says,

> Consider the lilies of the field, how they grow, they toil
> not neither do they spin: yet I say unto you that Solomon
> in all his glory was not arrayed like one of these.

Compare this with,

> One day the World-honoured One held up a flower before
> the assembled monks on Mt. Grdhrakuta. The whole con-

gregation made no response, except the venerable Kashya, who smiled at Him.

世尊、昔在靈山會上、拈花示眾。　是時、眾皆默然。　惟迦葉尊者破顏微笑。　　（無門關、第六則）

The important but usually overlooked part of Christ's short sermon, is the words " how they grow." The point is not the *beauty* of the flower, not the beauty of a Bach fugue but, *how it grows*. How does it grow? Neither Christ nor Buddha nor Bach attempted the task of explaining how it grows, for by its nature this is for all eternity and in all worlds to come, impossible. Buddha simply held up the flower, Christ held up the flower, merely adding the words, " Look at it! " Perhaps Tennyson was thinking of Christ's words when he wrote,

> Flower of the crannied wall.

It may be that Wordsworth remembered them when writing of the daisy:

> Sweet silent creature
> That breathest with me in sun and air,
> Do thou as thou art wont, repair
> My heart with gladness and a share
> Of thy meek nature!

Wither also was struck, not by its beauty, but by its simplicity, meanness, poverty, " loneliness."

> From every thing I saw
> I could some instruction draw,
> And raise pleasure to the height
> Through the meanest object's sight.
> By the murmur of a spring,
> Or the least bough's rustelling;
> By a Daisy whose leaves spread
> Shut when Titan goes to bed;

> Or a shady bush or tree;
> She could more infuse in me
> Than all Nature's beauties can
> In some other wiser man.

What is this instruction which Nature gives us? Bashô says
to his pupil Ensui,

> Yield to the willow
>   All the loathing,
>   All the desire of your heart.

もろもろの心柳にきかすべし

The so-called 'figure of speech' here is indeed profound. If
we explain it as meaning, 'Behave like the willow in not opposing the wind,' that is, act according to the circumstances,
it is excellent advice, but the poetry and the Zen have disap-
peared. Unless you and the willow are one, with nothing between you (here is the 'poverty,') unless life is running in you
as freely as in the willow itself, unless you realise that the life
of the willow and your own life are like the palm and the back
of the hand, inseparable and indivisible, you have no understanding of what Bashô means here.

Wordsworth gives the counterpart, the other half of the
tally, to "yield to the willow your likes and dislikes," in
Three years she grew in Sun and Shower. From Nature the
maiden shall receive law and impulse,

> And hers the silence and the calm
> Of mute insensate things.

> The floating clouds their state shall lend
> To her; for her the willow bend.

The willow bends for me, gives her pliancy to me. I yield my
heart to the willow, I give up my life to it. The willow and I

are one. There is no giving and receiving at all. Life appears there, in the form of a willow, here, in the form of a man.

There is another saying of Christ and a closely corresponding one of Buddha, which deserve to be studied here.

But I say unto you, Love your enemies and pray for them that persecute you, that ye may be the sons of your Father which is in Heaven, for he maketh his sun to rise on the evil and the good, and sendeth his rain on the just and the unjust.

The Tathagata recreates the whole world like a cloud shedding its waters without distinction. He has the same sentiments for the high as for the low, for the wise as for the ignorant, for the noble-minded as for the immoral.

如來の世を化するは晒雲雨の如く、着別なし。
貴も賤きも、賢も愚なるも、德あるも、德なき
も、如來は悉く同一の慈悲を以て之を視る。

The interesting point here is the reason Christ gives for loving our enemies. Instead of appealing to the inner consciousness, he gives a more easily comprehended explanation, namely, that in so doing we are following nature. But it may be objected (and this is a point of great importance,) that the poets and preachers use similes and analogies chosen from the gentler aspects of nature. Does not the sun scorch to death, and floods drown the good and bad with equal lack of discrimination? Do not the lilies of the field choke one another to death in their wild struggle for existence? This is true enough, but after all, not so staggering as it appears. In Zen this double aspect of life is expressed under the image of a sword, the sword that kills and the sword that makes alive. Nature is "red in tooth and claw," but so are the beneficient hands of the surgeon. What Christ and Buddha are urging upon us is not the cotton-

wool, milk and water life of abstract purity; they want us to
live fully *at each moment as it becomes our only possession,* to
take no thought for the morrow, to be like Nature, for

> Nature with equal mind
> Sees all her sons at play.

This "equal mind" is not indifference.   Indifference, enuui,
boredom are specifically human qualities, they are love's sad
satiety.   Lack of self, absolute poverty means you have all
things :

> Blessed are the poor in spirit,
> For theirs is the Kingdom of Heaven.

If you do not put your self in the way and block the view,
everything appears as it is :

> Blessed are the pure in heart,
> For they shall see God.

CHAPTER XXVI

ANIMALS

In writing about animals I feel that I am speaking of my life-line, for I came through Buddhism to Zen by virtue of my love for them. My love of animals is like Wordsworth's love of mountains, Bashô's love of the moon and cherry blossoms, but above all like Christ's love for men, for it embraces without effort or self-consciousness the most snaggle-toothed dogs, slit-eared cats, snakes, lice and bed-bugs, stopping short unfortunately at the intestinal worms, — but this is only what Lamb calls imperfect sympathies, due partly to the power of the association of ideas and partly to insufficient acquaintance (visual, at least) with the creatures themselves. What I propose to do in this chapter is to trace the connection, the living connection rather than the logical, between the love of sentient creatures and Buddhism, with its deliverance from evil, by enlightenment, from the illusion of selfhood, and Zen, with its abhorrence of hesitation and insistence on undivided, uninterrupted, whole-hearted, instinctive action. But before we do this, let us look first at the position of animals in ancient and modern thought.

The Greek attitude was that of modern times, with the addition of the sacrificial aspect of animals. Pythagoras, as is well known, was a vegetarian and taught the homogeneity of living things. The Romans, on the other hand, looked upon animals as existing entirely for man's advantage and treated them with cruelty, though there were many among the nobler

Romans who condemned the Games, for example Cicero. Plutarch, who was a moderate humanist, rejected the argument that animals were automata and relates several animal anecdotes. In Zoroastrianism, special care of God-created animals was taught, and animals also were apparently considered immortal beings. The slaughter of animals was allowed with an expiatory rite. In Mohammedanism also, kindness to animals is preached, and butchers have a formula of excuse, Bismillah, in the name of God. It is worth noticing that Baalam's ass, Jonah's whale, Abraham's ram, and Solomon's ant, are admitted to the highest heaven.

The Old Testament ignores animals except in so far as they have symbolic value in sacrifice. The New Testament is no better; in fact St. Paul quotes the Law of Moses as saying,

> Thou shall not muzzle the mouth of the ox that treadeth out the corn,

and then asks,

> Doth God take care for oxen? Or saith he it altogether for our sakes? For our sakes, no doubt, this is written,

and explains elsewhere that God is not considering the feelings of cattle, but only reminding us that clergymen and missionaries, who bestow spiritual things on us, should "reap carnal things," that is, receive a monthly salary and free house and coals.

The attitude of Confucius is even more indifferent than that of St. Paul, as is shown in the following well-known passage:

> Shi-kô wanted to omit the offering of a sacrificial sheep at the inauguration of the first day of the month. Confucius said, "Shi, you love[1] the sheep, but I love the ritual."

1 "Love" here means "are concerned about."

子貢欲去告朔之餼羊。　子曰、賜也、爾愛其羊、
我愛其禮。　　　　　　　　　　（論語、三、十七）

Also in the following:

> While Confucius was at Court, the Imperial stables were
> burnt down. When he returned, he asked, "Was any
> man injured?" He did not ask after the horses.

廐焚、子退朝、曰、傷人乎、不問馬。
　　　　　　　　　　（論語、十、十二）

But there is a very interesting passage in Mencius which I
quote in full for its intrinsic interest of psychological analysis.
King Sen of the Kingdom of Sai was speaking of virtue with
Mencius, who said to the King that he had heard the following
story of him from Kokotsu, his minister:

> The king was sitting on his dais in the Hall when a
> man appeared leading a bull past. Seeing this, the king
> said to him, "Where are you taking it?" The man an-
> swered and said, "It is to be used to consecrate a bell."
> The king said, "Let it go, I cannot bear its look of terror;
> it looks like an innocent man being led to the scaffold."
> The man replied, "Are we to omit the consecration cere-
> mony?" The king said, "How can we do that? Use a
> sheep instead of the bull."

王坐於堂上、有牽而過堂下者、王見之、曰、牛
何之。　對曰、將以釁鍾。　王曰、舍之。　吾不忍
其縠觫、若無罪而就死地。　對曰、然則廢釁鍾
與。　曰、何可廢也、以羊易之。

The king told Mencius that the story was true. Mencius
added that people thought he changed the bull for a sheep
from meanness, and said that this supposition was quite reasonable, for, after all, the sheep was just as much to be pitied as
the bull. The king felt rather non-plussed, and suggested that

perhaps it had been meanness on his part after all, and not, as he had supposed, feelings of pity for the bull. "No," said Mencius, "You really felt sorry for it.

> Your action was a kind of trick of goodness. You had seen the bull but not the sheep. So the ideal man in regard to animals, when he sees them alive, cannot bear to see them die. When he hears their cries of agony, to eat their flesh is impossible. For this reason he keeps far away from the kitchen."

是 乃 仁 術 也。 見 牛、 未 見 羊 也。 君 子 之 於 禽
獸 也、 見 其 生、 不 忍 見 其 死。 聞 其 聲、 不 忍 食
其 肉。 是 以 君 子 遠 庖 厨 也。 　(孟子、一、七、四)

Christ appears to have been almost completely indifferent to all the vast region that lies between the lilies of the field and the children of men. The only sentence into which we can read some consciousness of the existence of other creatures besides ourselves is,

> Are not two sparrows sold for a farthing? and one of them shall not fall on the ground without your Father.

But even this ends with,

> Fear ye not therefore, ye are of more value than many sparrows,

which, even if it were true, had been better left unsaid. Nevertheless it must be admitted that Christianity, by acting upon the cause (the heart of man) rather than upon the effects (cruelty to animals) has contributed much towards the decrease of animal suffering and the loving understanding of their manifold beauty.

The doctrine of "ahimsa," non-killing, carried to an extreme by the Jainas, who would not drink cold water because of the 'souls' in it, is found everywhere in the Hinayana texts

of Buddhism, but to a strikingly lesser extent in the Mahayana.
For example in the Hinayana *Brahmajala Sutra* (梵網經) we
are told not to kill ourselves, not to teach to kill, nor to find
means for it; not to praise killing, nor look upon it with
pleasure; not to kill by imprecation, nor to give our thoughts
to killing, or contrive opportunities and means for this sin.
That is to say we are to kill nothing living whatever.

> 若し佛子、若しくは自ら殺し、人を教へて殺さ
> しめ、方便して殺し、殺すを讃歎し、作すを見
> て随喜し、乃至呪して殺さん、殺の因、殺の縁、
> 殺の法、殺の業あらん。乃至一切の命有る者を
> ば故らに殺すことを得ざれ。

In the Mahayana sutras, however, such injunctions are com-
paratively uncommon, and in Zen itself they are unheard-of.
What indeed shall we say of the cat-killing Nansen, especially
selected and held up as a pattern and example in the *Mumonkan?* So with Kusunoki Masashige's son before his death in
battle at Shijonawate, when he went to his teacher of Zen,
Myôgaku Sôshun Zenji, and asked,

When at the cross-roads of life and death, what shall we do?

生死交謝之時如何。

the answer was not the Biblical "He who takes the sword shall
perish by the sword," nor as in the *Dhammapada*, "He who
seeks his own happiness in the suffering or death of others
shall not find happiness in the next world," (天地の生みにし
ものを、うちなやめ殺すが中に喜びを求むる人は、後の世
に樂みを見じ。(法句經、百卅一) but,

> Cut off both heads (of relativity) and the sword (of the
> Absolute) shines icy against the sky.

兩頭倶截斷、一劍倚天寒。

Yet this also is found in the *Dhammapada:* "If you give up both victory and defeat, you sleep at night without fear." (勝と負とを捨つる身ぞ、夜半の眠りのいと安き。(法句經、二百一) We thus seem farther off than ever from reconciling the warm love of all living creatures and the chilly trenchancy of Zen.

Animals enter English Literature in the 14th or 15th century with an anonymous poem on the cock.[1]   The Nature peace of Isaiah ("The wolf also shall dwell with the lamb, and the leopard shall lie down with the kid; the lion shall eat straw like the ox") and the beautiful fairy tale of Noah and his ark, must have had much effect on the minds of men, as also the animals in the stable at Christ's birth, but to poets the most attractive was the legend of the comforting of Christ by the animals of the wilderness.   In *Christ's Victory on Earth,* by Giles Fletcher (1588-1628) we have the following beautiful passages.   When Christ knelt to pray, the wild animals rushed to attack him,

But him their salvage thirst did naught appal,
Though weapons none He had for his defence,
What arms for Innocence but innocence?
    For when they saw their Lord's bright cognizance
    Shine in his face, soon they did disadvance,
And some unto Him kneel, and some about him dance.

*   *   *

Down fell the lordly lion's angry mood,
And he himself fell down in congies[2] low;
Bidding Him welcome to his wasteful wood.

[1] See *The New Book of English Verse*, p. 65:
        I have a gentil cock
            Crowyt me day;
        He doth me rysyn erly
            My matyins for to say.

[2] Salutations.

*   *   *

All the animals served him in their several capacities;

> If he stood still, their eyes upon Him baited,
> If walked, they all in order on Him waited,
> And when he slept, they as His watch themselves conceited.

Shakespeare seems to have disliked all animals, especially the dog, but like many other Elizabethans, for example, Drayton, had much interest in birds. From the 17th Century, Vaughan's *The Bird* is well worth quotation here:

> And now as fresh and cheerful as the light,
> Thy little heart in early hymns doth sing
> Unto that providence, whose unseen arm
> Curb'd them, and cloath'd thee well and warm.
>> All things that be, praise Him; and had
>> Their lesson taught them, when first made.

This is the teaching of Zen; that everything, even ourselves, had its lesson taught it when first made, that is, when it came into existence, and that to know what to do we must therefore "Enquire within." If you can't believe this, consider the lilies of the field, or even the stones:

> And though poor stones have neither speech nor tongue,
> While active winds and streams both run and speak,
> Yet stones are deep in admiration.

Wordsworth himself never wrote a line of more insight than this "stones are deep in admiration." It is the very voice of the stones themselves. Wordsworth only said that to

> Even the loose stones that cover the highway,
> I gave a moral life,

which is indeed a dismal failure.

Even so, why did not Christ say, "Consider the rats of the sewer, how they fight and squeal," or "Consider the bacteria of typhus, how they grow and multiply"? Why did not Buddha hold up, instead of a flower, a cheese-rind or an old boot?

> For each enclosed spirit is a star
> Enlightening his own little sphere,
> Whose light, though fetcht and borrowed from afar,
> Both mornings makes and evenings there

for centipedes, tapeworms, fungus and all the rest. The flowers and the moon are milk for babes, but when we become men, we must put away childish things, and take a look at our poor relations as they live by Zen all around us. Walt Whitman, who also has a great deal of Zen scattered through his writings, says,

> I think I could turn and live with animals, they are so placid and self-contained.
> I stand and look at them long and long.
> They do not sweat and whine about their condition,
> They do not lie awake in the dark and weep for their sins,
> They do not make me sick discussing their duty to God,
> Not one is dissatisfied, no one is demented with the mania of owning things,
> Not one kneels to another, nor to his kind that lived thousands of years ago,
> Not one is respectable or unhappy over the whole earth.

If our attitude to Nature, especially to animals, is false, nothing can be true to us or we to it. It is the sentimentality, that is, the falsity of nature poets, that moves Aldous Huxley to write, in *Wordsworth in the Tropics,*

> The Wordsworthian who exports this pantheistic worship of Nature to the tropics, is liable to have his religious convictions somewhat rudely disturbed. Nature, under a

vertical sun, and nourished by the equatorial rains, is not
at all like that chaste, mild deity who presides over the
Gemütlichkeit, the prettiness, the cosy sublimities of the
Lake District.

*   *   *

The jungle is marvellous, fantastic, beautiful; but it is
also terrifying, it is also profoundly sinister. There is
something in what, for lack of a better word, we must call
the character of great forests—even in those of temperate
lands — which is foreign, appalling, fundamentally and
utterly inimical to intruding man. The life of those vast
masses of swarming vegetation is alien to the human
spirit and hostile to it.

Huxley's criticism of Wordsworth and his followers is just;
they look on only one side of Nature, the birds and insects and
smaller animals, their life in the sunshine of the temperate
zone, utterly neglecting the monsters and swamps of Africa,
India and Equatorial America. This does not come from staying at home in England, for Nature is the same everywhere.
If Nature is as Huxley describes it in the Tropical Zone, it is,
as he himself says, "even in the Temperate Zone, always alien
and inhuman, and occasionally diabolic." The bacteria and
parasites in our own body are just as fantastic and sinister as
the cobra and the rhinoceros. But Huxley is no less wrong
than Wordsworth, or rather more so, and on his own ground,
for his mistake is mainly a logical one. How does Huxley
know that Nature is "alien," "foreign," "appalling," "inimical"? He *feels* it to be so, no less than Wordsworth feels that
Nature is our "teacher," and has no right to assert the validity
of one set of intuitions over another. What we have to do is
to find some larger truth that will include and reconcile the
two apparently opposing and contradictory lesser truths. A
hint of this is given in Huxley's reiteration of the fearfulness

and horror of Nature. Fear is often another name for hatred.
When Huxley says that Nature is inimical to man, he forgets
how inimical man (Huxley) is to Nature. As pointed out in another chapter, man complains that Nature does not care for his
sufferings, forgetting that he also cares nothing for the sufferings of Nature. In the same way, man ungraciously and un-
gratefully receives all that Nature gives him, but does nothing
whatever in return. Again, to a man afraid of dogs, that is,
who hates them, a dog is a fearful creature, only waiting for
the chance to fix his teeth into someone's leg. So with a tiger.
You may say, "But a tiger really is a dangerous, carnivorous
animal." So is a dog, if it is hungry enough, so is your own
brother, if ravenous enough. After all, we have only to read a
page or two of history to see that man is the most ferocious of
all animals. Plutarch and Gibbon are more terrible to read
than Darwin or Bates. There is no need therefore to go to
the jungles of Africa or the wilds of Borneo to disturb our
minds with thoughts of evil, suffering, death, the struggle for
existence. We are all bathed in it as in an invisible fluid, we
carry it with us wherever we go. The reason why the Temperate Zone produces nature poets like Wordsworth and Bashô
is a simple one, connected with the "poverty" discussed in
the preceding chapter. In the tropics there is so much life
(that is, life and death,) that we can hardly, in both a literal
and metaphorical sense, see the wood for the trees. In the
poem, *Black Season was it, Turbulent and Wild,* Wordsworth
has thoughts and impressions that could never have occurred
to a denizen of a jungle, and he actually gives thanks for the
"enmity" of all around him.

> Stern was the face of nature: we rejoiced
> In that stern countenance; for our souls thence drew
> A feeling of their strength. The naked trees,

> The icy brooks, as on we passed, appeared
> To question us: "Whence are ye? To what end?"

The same is equally true of a city, which is only another kind
of jungle, and this is why poets avoid it. It is so full of life
that it takes the genius of a Dickens, a Shakespeare, to grasp
it and reveal the poetical and religious meanings with which
it overflows.

The Chinese poets, with the honourable exception of Hakurakuten, seldom leave the conventional round of natural objects,—the moon, flowers, willows, nightingales, singing-insects
and so on. In Hakurakuten we have such poems as *The Government Bull* (官牛). The bull is hauling sand to spread on the
road so that the hooves of the horse of a High Official may not
be muddied. No one troubles about the bull, whose neck is
running blood (牛領牽車欲流血). There is the poem, *The
Wild Pheasant* (山雉), in which he compares the lives of the
wild animals with the domestic ones; the chickens and ducks
buy their gift of grain with the sacrifice of their lives.

既 有 稻 粱 恩、 心 有 犧 牲 患。

In the *Dog and the Falcon* (犬鳶) he rejoices in the freedom of
the falcon in the air, the freedom of the dog lying asleep in
the sun without rope or chain. Zen is freedom, and those who
are free, wish others to be free. Those who love animals and
have "freedom in their love," wish them to be free. This
comes out again in *Releasing a Migrant Goose,* (放旅雁), which
some boys had captured on the ice and were selling in the
city; also in *The Red Parrot* (紅鸚鵡), brought from Annam
and put in a cage because it was so beautiful and clever. All
kinds of insects interested him, and insect poems are many.
As with the Japanese poets, their voices penetrate deep into the

recesses of his soul, not, as in the English poets, drawing him
out of himself.

LISTENING TO INSECTS

Long is the night: unseen amid the gloom, the voices of
insects.

It is the gathering rain, the darkness of autumn.

Do they then dread that in my despair I shall sleep my
last sleep?

Their insistent voices deepen, they come nearer, and yet
more near.

聞　蟲

闇 密 蟲 唧 夜 綿 綿　　況 是 秋 陰 欲 雨 天
猶 恐 愁 人 暫 得 睡　　聲 聲 移 近 臥 床 前

Hakurakuten seems to have felt an unusual, and, if I may say
so, a very un-Japanese sympathy with fishes.   In addition to
the poem quoted before, look at the following:

RELEASING FISH

At dawn a servant brought a basket of spring vegetables.

Under the green parsley and bracken were two white-baits;

They uttered no cry but lay with their mouths open as if
gasping pity on each other.

Turning them out of the basket on to the ground, they lay
there more than a foot long, still lively.

Is it to be the fate of the carving-knife and chopping-
board, or are they to be eaten by ants and crickets?

He decides to set them free in the South Lake, and ends with
a playful but note-worthy remark:

Though I bestow this favour upon you, how far I am
from desiring anything in return;

Do not trouble to seek, on my behalf, among the mud and
sand at the bottom of the lake, for silvery pearls.

放　魚

曉日提竹籃　家僮買春蔬　青青芹蕨下　疊臥雙白魚
無聲但呀呀　以氣相煦濡　傾籃寫地上　撥刺長尺餘
豈唯刀机憂　坐見螻蟻圖　…　…　…　　…　…　…
施恩即望報　吾非斯人徒　不須泥沙底　辛苦覓明珠

This is the true attitude of religion, of Zen, of poetry, towards everything, and especially towards animals: to ask nothing from them, to give them all the freedom and happiness consistent with our own existence.

The typical attitude of Japanese poets may be exemplified by the following *haiku* of Kikaku, Bashô's often intractable, but here good and faithful pupil.

> Creep forward, O snail,
>   That we may gaze on you
>   As relish to our wine!

かたつぶり酒の肴に這はせけり

No theorising about the unity of life, no talk of "types and symbols of eternity," no pretence of liking uninteresting or disgusting things, no pathetic fallacy; simply the pleasure of drinking at home in the garden with his friend Yūgo, looking at the snail with its graceful form, its pretty shell and tender horns. Bashô, like Wordsworth and Hakurakuten, was inclined to the moral side of poetry, and in his well-known *haiku* of the cormorants, expresses his sense of the *lachrimae rerum:*

> The cormorant fishing-boat,—
>   How exciting! But after a time
>   I felt saddened.[1]

おもしろうてやがて悲しき鵜船かな

[1] See Miyamori's *An Anthology of Haiku, Ancient and Modern,* page 151, for a description of cormorant fishing.

Bashô does not tell us what made him sad. Was it pity for
the fish, for the cormorants forced to regurgitate what they
had swallowed, for the men engaged in such a labour of prey-
ing on the greediness of the birds, or for humanity in its endless desire and craving? The simplest and best answer is that
Bashô himself did not know. It was "tears, idle tears," and
that is all.

Issa's best known poem,

> Do not kill the fly:
> > See how it wrings its hands;
> > > See how it wrings its feet!

> やれうつな蠅が手をすり足をする

would seem affected or sentimental in another writer, but Issa
simply means here "Don't kill it: it's *alive!*" just like you
and me, as Blake also said. Issa wrote a very large number
of *haiku* on flies, fleas and lice, not from any affectation or
theory of the sacredness of all life, but for the best of all reasons,
namely, that he knew them so well and so intimately. These
poems are full of humour (for *humour is coterminous with life*)[1]
but entirely devoid of condescension. He writes of them, not
even as Johnson wrote of his cat Hodge, or Matthew Arnold of
his dog Kaiser, but as equals to himself.

> I'm sorry my house is so small,
> > But practise your jumping,
> > > Please, Mr. Flea!

> 狭くともいざ飛習へ庵の蚤

So far from pity being akin to love, they have no connection
whatever. Love is union; pity implies separation, or, worst of

[1] "Foolery, sir, does walk about the orb like the sun; it shines everywhere." (*Twelfth Night*, III, I.)

all, because the self is divided, self-pity. Love makes all things equal; and here we begin to see the relation of love of animals to Buddhism and Zen. An unusually (for Issa) difficult but very interesting and pertinent *haiku* is the following:

> Poor louse! I made it creep
> Upon the pomegranate that tastes
> Of my sweet flesh.

我味の柘榴へ這す虱かな

Even with Issa's own remarks preceding the poem, it still requires elucidation:

While thinking that crushing lice is a pitiful thing, and throwing them outside and starving them to death makes a melancholy sight, I suddenly called to mind Buddha's instructions concerning a mother-devil.

虱を捻りつぶさんことのいたはしく、又門に捨て
断食さするを見るに忍ばざる折から、御佛の鬼の
母にあてがひ給ふものをふと思ひ出して、………

The tradition referred to is this. A certain Mother-devil went about the country devouring, à la Grendel, the children of human beings. Hearing of this, Buddha gave the following counsel. "Get her son away from her by making him a Buddhist disciple and she will realise the anguish of losing children. If further she still retains a taste for human flesh, let her eat pomegranates, which have the same taste as human flesh." This same compassion Issa expresses in taking the louse and putting it on a pomegranate.

Thus we see that love of all living creatures which springs up naturally in our hearts, unless thwarted by instruction, custom, or self-love, is no more and no less than our Buddha-nature manifesting itself. Further, love, like knight errantry,

equalises all things, and this equality of all things, the absolute
worth and goodness of all that exists or happens, is what Zen
aims to make us realise in a practical, concrete way.   It may
be asked, "Is it a fact, then, that those who have come to a
fundamental realisation of the truth of Zen, feel a love for all
living creatures, beautiful and ugly, charming and disgusting?"
The answer will be, that though Zen gives the mind a general
spring-cleaning, cobwebs and dust still lurk in many corners
and crevices of the mind.   Again, as was pointed out before,
to Buddha after his enlightenment, sweet was still sweet and
sour still sour; for Christ also there was "that disciple which
Jesus loved."   The outside of our mind remains full of fears,
prejudices and cravings, yet not the same as before, because
deep down inside there is the consciousness that All is Good
without comparison or difference.   Or to put it in another way,
just as the hard horny hands of the young farmer do not become soft even though he falls in love with the gentle village
maiden, so the man who is insensitive to the affection and
charm of dogs, remains so after his enlightenment.   Only, the
use of his hard hands, the use of his hard mind, changes, since
in both, self has decreased in quantity and importance, and other
things correspondingly and inevitably increase in value and
significance.   What a strange emotion I feel when a man pats
my dog on the head and says, with a smile, "I don't like dogs
very much!"

CHAPTER XXVII

WORDSWORTH

The change that took place in Wordsworth as he passed from Zen through Pantheism to Orthodoxy, is almost unparalleled in the history of culture. The three periods of course overlap, but we are able, especially in *The Prelude* and *The Excursion,* almost to see the change taking place under our very eyes. In his earliest years, he tells us,

> The sounding cataract
> Haunted me like a passion : the tall rock,
> The mountain, and the deep and gloomy wood,
> Their colours and their forms, were then to me
> An appetite ; a feeling and a love
> *That had no need of a remoter charm*
> By thought supplied, nor any interest
> Unborrowed from the eye.

This is the true region of *haiku.* Words are many and the thing is one, but somehow it has got to be portrayed or suggested in words,—but as a unity, not after the post-mortem of thought, not after the dissection of the intellect. As an example of such a *haiku* we may take Kyorai's,

> " Yes, yes ! " I answered,
>   But someone still knocked
>   At the snow-mantled gate.

応々と言へど叩くや雪の門

or Bashô's, composed at Kyorai's house,

A cuckoo cried!
　　The moon filters through
　　　　The vast bamboo grove.

ほととぎす大竹籔をもる月夜

Wordsworth expresses an extreme case of this thoughtless,
almost senseless state, in *Personal Talk*:

　　To sit without emotion, hope or aim,
　　In the loved presence of my cottage-fire,
　　And listen to the flapping of the flame,
　　Or kettle whispering its faint undersong.

In these lines we can see Bashô sitting in his hut at Fukagawa.
Or another example, reminding one irresistibly of Bashô, the
last verse of *The Two April Mornings*:

　　Matthew is in his grave, yet now,
　　Methinks, I see him stand,
　　As at that moment, with a bough
　　Of wilding in his hand.

Again, in *Strange Fits of Passion Have I Known,* Wordsworth
says, as he rode towards the sinking moon,

　　My horse moved on: hoof after hoof
　　He raised, and never stopped:
　　When down behind the Cottage roof,
　　At once the bright moon dropped.

　　What fond and wayward thoughts will slide
　　Into a Lover's head!
　　" Oh mercy!" to myself I cried,
　　"If Lucy should be dead!"

Wordsworth leaves us with this mystery of the mind of man,
which selects, rejects, remembers, and associates according to
its own sweet will. Why did the visitor continue knocking

after Kyorai had answered "Yes, yes," and who was he, and what did he want? Why did Wordsworth's heart suddenly contract with unwarranted fear? Why did he remember Matthew at that particular moment? What was the connection between the voice of the cuckoo and the moonlight that stole through the leaves of the bamboo? These questions are out of place when one considers that the poems are the answers to them. We can say of these poems what Wordsworth said of those men wanting the faculty of verse,

> Theirs is the language of the heavens, the power,
> The thought, the image, and the silent joy:
> Words are but the under-agents in their souls.
> *(Prelude* XIII, 271)

They are like the sounds of the coming storm,

>   notes that are
> The ghostly language of the ancient earth.
> *(Prel.* II, 308)

In his early years Wordsworth's one object was to live

> The life in common things—the endless store of things,
> Rare, or at least so seeming, every day
> Found all about me in one neighbourhood.
> *(Prel.* I, 108)

He perceived with almost painful distinctness the shapes and forms of the rocks and plants and clouds, and his own character was moulded

> By silent unobtrusive sympathies
> And gentle agitations of the mind
> From manifold distinctions, difference
> Perceived in things.[1]   *(Prel.* II, 297)

[1] See *Formen des Lebens, Botanische Lichtbildstudien* by Dr. Paul Wolff (Langewiesche), for concrete examples of what Wordsworth means here.

When he looked at the lake,

> the calm
> And dead still water lay upon my mind
> Even with a weight of pleasure, and the sky,
> Never before so beautiful, sank down
> Into my heart.   (*Prel.* II, 171)

What he perceived was Existence, the existence of all things, animate and inanimate :

> I felt the sentiment of Being spread
> O'er all that moves and all that seemeth still.

But what he perceived was not something outside, something separated from himself.   *It was almost as if the object used his eyes to perceive itself,* or as he expresses it,

> Bodily eyes
> Were utterly forgotten, and what I saw
> Appeared like something in myself, a dream,
> A prospect in the mind.   (*Prel.* II, 349)

He could not find a single object in the whole universe, not a single thing

> Whose truth is not a motion or a shape
> Instinct with vital functions.   (*Prel.* VIII, 288)

All was Activity, as he looked with

> An eye
> Which, from a tree, a stone, a withered leaf,
> To the broad ocean and the azure heavens,
> Spangled with kindred multitudes of stars,
> Could find no surface where its power could sleep.

This reminds us of the Zen simile of Truth as an iron ball which we cannot take a bite out of.   The highest point in Wordsworth's youthful directness of insight into the life of

Nature is contained in the famous lines from *There Was A Boy*:

> Then sometimes, in that silence, while he hung
> Listening, a gentle shock of mild surprise
> Has carried far into his heart the voice
> Of mountain-torrents; or the visible scene
> Would enter unawares into his mind
> With all its solemn imagery, its rocks,
> Its woods, and that uncertain heaven received
> Into the bosom of the steady lake.

Farther than this, in regard to Nature, no man can go; but the problem remains, how can our bosoms become as a steady lake, to receive the uncertainties of our human life. That is to say, we must turn from Nature to Man.

Wordsworth's answer to this question is thoroughly in accord with that of Zen. Zen says, Act according to your essence of mind; in the words of the Fifth Patriarch:

> Perfect Enlightenment means spontaneous realisation of your Original Nature.

無 上 菩 提、 須 得 言 下 識 自 本 心。

(六 祖 壇 經、 第 一)

Wordsworth says,

> Come forth into the light of things,
> Let Nature be your Teacher.

Zen says, Look within! Wordsworth says, Look without! but there is no more difference here than in the case of Self-Power and Other-Power. Self-Power *is* Other-Power, because Self is Other. Looking at the microcosm *is* looking at the macrocosm, for one without the other is meaningless. "Where man is not, nature is barren." Wordsworth makes everything moral:

> To every natural form, rock, fruit or flower,
> Even the loose stones that cover the highway,
> I gave a moral life.   (*Prel.* III, 130)

Zen takes away from man even that which he hath not, his morality:

> "Forget the difference between a saint and an ordinary man!" said the (Sixth) Patriarch,

師 云、 凡 聖 情 忘。　(六 祖 壇 經、 第 八)

but here again, if you are not attached to the words, you will see the identity of the experience, a realisation of

> What an empire we inherit
> As natural beings in the strength of Nature.
> (*Prel.* III, 193)

Whether we ascribe morality to man and nature or not, does not matter, as long as we do not separate them qualitatively. How is it that Nature, external Nature, can teach us? Clearly, because of the continuity of the internal and external nature, so that we see

> the parts
> As parts, but with a feeling of the whole.
> (*Prel.* VII, 735)

As an illustration of this identity of inner and outer we have Wordsworth's beautiful lines, describing how, after spending a night in dancing, gaiety and mirth, he went out and beheld the rising of the sun, the waves dancing, the mountains shining, birds singing, labourers going forth to work:

> My heart was full: I made no vows, but vows
> Were made for me.
> (*Prel.* IV, 334)

In *The Tables Turned,* Wordsworth asserts, as from his own experience, something that has upset both the moralists and the poets:

> One impulse from a vernal wood
> May teach you more of man,
> Of moral evil and of good,
> Than all the sages can.

This is pure Zen, as we may see if we try to answer the question, "What can a vernal wood teach us?" The answer is, "It teaches us!" This annoys the moralist, who is at a loss without his book of words. It annoys the poet, because he does not want to be taught morality. In *The Excursion,* Book Four, Wordsworth expands this idea of the inarticulate language of animate and inanimate things. The poetic quality is low and the thought diffuse and thin, but it is worth quoting in order to attempt to convince intellectually those who have no intuition of its truth.

> For, the Man—
> Who, in this spirit, communes with the Forms
> Of nature, who with understanding heart
> Both knows and loves such objects as excite
> No morbid passions, no disquietude,
> No vengeance and no hatred—needs must feel
> The joy of that pure principle of love
> So deeply, that, unsatisfied with aught
> Less pure and exquisite, he cannot choose
> But seek for objects of a kindred love
> In fellow-natures, and a kindred joy.

In *Ruth,* Wordsworth shows the effect of tropical nature "to feed voluptuous thought" in a man without self-control and of vicious life, but adds, and I think justifiably,

> Yet, in his worst pursuits I ween
> That sometimes there did intervene

> Pure hopes of high intent:
> For passions linked to forms so fair
> And stately, needs must have their share
> Of noble sentiment,

that is to say, even where the effect of external Nature seems only to debase, it is actually mixed with good.

Now we come to a more painful part of our study of Wordsworth, that of the gradual disintegration of his poetical character. This was partly due to an inexplicable decrease in his intuitive powers and corresponding inspiration and out-put of real poetry, and partly the effect of the introspection and self-analysis to which he so rigorously subjected himself. We can trace, in *The Prelude* and *The Excursion,* the growth of a pantheism, a theoretical interpretation of his original insight, which ultimately destroys him. He tells us himself that he learned

> To look on nature, not as in the hour
> Of thoughtless youth.

The division of man and nature begins when we imagine things as they ought to be, not as they are. Wordsworth records his disappointment at the sight of the actual Mont Blanc,

> . . . . . . and grieved,
> To have a soulless image in the eye,
> That had usurped a living thought.
>
> *(Prel.* VI, 525)

He talks of how

> an auxiliar light
> Came from my mind, which on the setting sun
> Bestowed new splendour,

This is unfortunately in accord with his (later) peculiar definitions of the Imagination. In the 14th Book of *The Prelude,* he says,

> Imagination, which, in truth,
> Is but another name for absolute power
> And clearest insight, amplitude of mind
> And Reason in her most exalted mood.

This, though not very clear, one can hardly disagree with, but in a conversation, Wordsworth said,

"Imagination is a subjective term; it deals with objects not as they are, but as they appear to the mind of the poet,"

and this is positively dangerous, opening the way to all kinds of capricious and fanciful creations out of all relation with truth. What Wordsworth no doubt means by "objects as they are," is things not worked up in the mind of the perceiver, but in this sense, no such object can be represented at all. Again, in the Preface to the Edition of 1815, Wordsworth discusses at length the function of the Imagination. What he says is not so much wrong as it detestable, as Wordsworth usually is in his later prose and poetry. He states there that Imagination is a word

denoting operations of the mind upon those objects, and processes of creation or of composition, governed by certain fixed laws.

He then speaks of the mind, "for its own gratification," using various figures of speech such as metonymy, abstraction, hyperbole, but actually there is little difference between imagination and fancy in his definitions. I have already given my interpretation of what are called figures of speech and will now give a definition of imagination as the faculty was exercised by Wordsworth himself. *It is the power by which we become so united, – or better, by which we realise our original unity with persons, things, situations, so completely,—that we perceive them by simple self-consciousness.* This definition closely approximates to Wordsworth's own definitions scattered throughout the Preface to *Lyrical Ballads,* in which he says, for example, of poetry,

> Its object is truth . . . carried alive into the heart by passion: *truth which is its own testimony.*

The change from this definition to that of seventeen years afterwards, in the 1815 Edition, is the result of a change of attitude, to a state of mind which speaks of

> Ye Presences of Nature in the Sky
> And on the Earth! Ye Visions of the hills!
> And souls of lonely places!

> . . . . . the great mass
> Lay bedded in a quickening soul.

The very beginnings of this notion of presences and somethings and spirits Wordsworth notes in the First Book of *The Prelude.* At ten years old even, shades of the prison house of fear and discrimination had begun to close over the growing boy, for when he had done something wrong, he says,

> I heard among the solitary hills
> Low breathings coming after me, and sounds
> Of undistinguishable motion, steps
> Almost as silent as the turf they trod.

Instead of realising that this feeling was due to the illusion of separation between himself and nature, the seeds of this fatal division between man and the outer world, and later, between God and Nature, were allowed to spring up, until in *Tintern Abbey* (1798) he utters the beautiful lines,

> And I have felt
> A presence that disturbs me with the joy

> Of elevated thoughts; a sense sublime
> Of something far more deeply interfused,
> Whose dwelling is the light of setting suns,
> And the round ocean and the living air,
> And the blue sky and the mind of man :
> A motion and a spirit that impels
> All thinking things, all objects of all thoughts,
> And rolls through all things.

The loftiness of the thought, the truth of the details, the eloquence of the whole, must not blind us to the fact that there is
in this fruit the speck which rotting inward, slowly mouldered
all Wordsworth's poetry.   What is wrong with pantheism?
It is not that it is not true, it is rather that when expressed in
words it becomes false; it is that our minds are somehow un-
fitted to receive it.   When we say, "All is God, this book is
God, I am God," the very form of the thought, of the judgement, of the sentence, has in it

> the little rift within the lute,
> That by and by will make the music mute,
> And ever widening slowly silence all.

When we say "This is God," in our minds, the part is divided
from the whole.   Becoming aware of this, we assert with
dogged mysticism, "The part *is* the whole," but in the very
assertion of identity, the fatal separation is irrevocably there.
Thus Wordsworth says, the breach widening,

> The immeasurable height
> Of woods decaying, never to be decayed,
> The stationary blasts of waterfalls . . . . :
> The torrents shooting from the clear blue sky,
> The rocks that muttered close upon our ears,
> Black drizzling crags that spake by the way-side
> As if a voice were in them, the sick sight
> And giddy prospect of the raving stream,

> The unfettered clouds and region of the Heavens,
> Tumult and peace, the darkness and the light—
> Were like the workings of one mind, the features
> Of the same face, blossoms upon one tree,
> Characters of the great Apocalypse,
> The types and symbols of Eternity,
> Of first, and last, and midst, and without end.
>
> (*Prel.* VI, 624)

In 1800 Wordsworth had written,

> Jehovah—with his thunder and the choir
> Of shouting angels, and the empyreal thrones—
> I pass them unalarmed,   (*Recluse,* 786)

a passage that is said to have upset Blake so much that he fell
ill (the mystic out-mysticised for once!) but in the Fourth Book
of *The Excursion* (about 1809 or after,) Wordsworth makes full
recantation:

> One adequate support
> For the calamities of human life
> Exists – one only; an assured belief
> That the procession of our fate, howe'er
> Sad or disturbed, is ordered by *a Being*
> *Of infinite benevolence and power*
> Whose everlasting purposes embrace
> All accidents, converting them to good.

Twenty years after, in 1842, this doctrine reached its logical
and imbecile conclusion in one of the *Ecclesiastical Sonnets,
Forms of Prayer at Sea,* where we are told that the crew, saved
from shipwreck by God, are right to give solemn thanksgiving
for His mercy (but how about those who were drowned, or
died of thirst in an open boat?) and that English sailors will
always win naval battles if they ask God to assist them.

> Suppliants! the God to whom your cause ye trust
> Will listen, and ye know that He is just.

All this kind of thing comes from the intellectual separation of God and man and nature, a separation of man from Here and Now.   Wordsworth says,

> Our destiny, our being's heart and home
> Is with infinitude and only there.
>
> *(Prel.* VI, 604)

It is not.   Take no thought for the morrow, or for infinity or for eternity.   Take no thought for what will happen five minutes afterwards, one minute afterwards.   Blessed are the poor in spirit, now !   Namu Amida Butsu, NOW !

CHAPTER XXVIII

SHAKESPEARE

George Santayana in his *Poetry and Religion* has a chapter on The Absence of Religion in Shakespeare.

> For Shakespeare, in the matter of religion, the choice lay between Christianity and nothing. He chose nothing.
> He depicts human life in all its richness and variety, but leaves that life without a setting, and consequently without a meaning.

It will be quite clear to the reader by this time, that Santayana neither knows what religion is, nor does he understand Shakespeare. It is precisely this type of mind which cannot understand Bashô. Let me quote, without comment, from two books on Japanese Literature. Aston in his *A History of Japanese Literature,* tells us of Nô,

> They are deficient in lucidity, method, coherence and good taste. Still, they are not without charm.

Of *haiku,*

> It would be absurd to put forward any serious claim on behalf of Haikai to an important position in literature. ... Specks even of wisdom and piety may sometimes be discerned upon close scrutiny.

Dickins, in his *Japanese Texts* (2 vols. Oxford,) says,

> The modern literature of Japan, as such, is nearly worthless. Not a line of power or beauty, it is scarcely too much

to say, has been penned since the last monogatari was written.[1]

To return to Shakespeare.   In the Preface to *Bleak House,* Dickens quotes from one of the sonnets,

> My nature is subdued
> To what it works in, like the dyer's hand.

This is Shakespeare's Zen, his religion; his nature, his self, is subdued to what it works in, in men and women, in Nature, in all this mighty world of eye and ear.   We cannot find Shakespeare's "religion" for the same reason that we cannot find Shakespeare himself.   This is the meaning of Arnold's

> Others abide our question—Thou art free!
> We ask and ask—Thou smilest and art still.

Shakespeare is so fluid that he takes the shape of the human vessel he is poured into, and yet remains himself all the time; for example in Lady Macbeth's

> I have given suck, and know
> How tender 'tis to love the babe that milks me:
> I would, while it was smiling in my face,
> Have pluck'd my nipple from his boneless gums,
> And dash'd the brains out, had I so sworn as you
> Have done to this.

In Hamlet's cry when Polonius asks him,

> 'Will you walk out of the air, my Lord?'
> 'Into my grave.'

In Othello's

> O Iago, the pity of it, Iago!

1 This seems to mean, after the end of the Heian Period, 1186 A.D.

In Lear's

> No, no, no life!
> Why should a dog, a horse, a rat, have life,
> And thou no breath at all? Thou'lt come no more,
> Never, never, never, never, never!

—in such passages we see the Zen of Shakespeare, the thing as it is, the world as it is. While we also are immersed in such states of Mind, all the dogmas of religion and rules of morality dissolve away in the stream of life. As Bradley says in his *Shakespearean Tragedy,* afterwards

> we fall back on our everyday legal and moral notions. *But tragedy does not belong, any more than religion belongs, to the sphere of these notions.*

Of course, Zen itself is not enough to make a Shakespeare. We require also extreme sensibility, and power to express it, but the absence of self, of prejudice, of moral judgements, is the prime essential. Here again it is worth noting that this state of Zen, this God-like condition of mind does not imply absence of attraction and repulsion either in Shakespeare or the reader. It only implies lack of condemnation, lack of the apportioning of praise and blame. Good is good and bad is bad, but both are necessary—the acceptance of this is the secret of Zen, the secret of Shakespeare. If this acceptance is with the mind only, if it is half-hearted and with reservations, formal religion becomes necessary to fill up the meaningless blanks that our cowardice has made. We need a God to interfere, to rectify the balance, we need a future life to complete the defects of this one. But while we look at *Hamlet* or *Othello,* while we *are* Hamlet or Othello, God and immortality are useless encumbrances, not even necessary as stage effects.

If therefore we are asked for the Zen of Shakespeare we

can only point to the plays and say "There it is!" as intangible
as Milton's Zen, which we see reflected in the mind of Satan,
and which rolls through the cadences of *Samson Agonistes*.
Nevertheless, as Shakespeare, unlike Milton, was unencumbered
with the formal doctrines of the Church, we find all through
his plays, references explicit and implicit to the acceptation of
life, the freedom of selflessness, the equality of all things and
all men and all occasions, the here-ness and now-ness of Heaven
and Hell.

One of the most significant speeches in *A Midsummer
Night's Dream* is Helena's

> Things base and vile, holding no quantity,
> Love can transpose to form and dignity:
> *Love looks not with the eyes but with the mind;*
> And therefore is wing'd Cupid painted blind.

Zen means looking with the eye, the "quiet eye" of Wordsworth, the eye of him "who saw life steadily and saw it
whole," of Arnold. "Looking with the mind" means looking
through the distortions and discriminations of the intellect,
and indeed the whole play is an exposure of the absurdity of
Lysander's proposition,

> The will of man is by his reason swayed,

the fact being the precise opposite. Puck says, in amused
surprise at both the theories and practice of human beings,

> Lord, what fools these mortals be,

but Theseus, speaking for Shakespeare himself, sees deeper into this folly and gives the final word:

> Lovers and madmen ... apprehend
> More than cool reason ever comprehends.

When we have some understanding of Zen, ordinary phrases of Shakespeare become full of meaning, and profounder ones almost intolerably deep. For example, Cordelia says to her father,

> It is no vicious blot, or dishonour'd step
> That hath deprived me of your grace and favour;
> *But even for want of that for which I am richer,—*
> *A still-soliciting eye.*

We do zazen, not to get anything, but to throw away all we have and to throw away even the idea that we are throwing something away. "A still-soliciting eye." This is the precise opposite of Wordsworth's "a quiet eye"; it is *the* disease of the mind, to be always, incessantly, even in our dreams, demanding and desiring. When Lear gradually begins to realise that his attitude to his daughters should have been of a piece with that towards nature, he cries,

> I tax you not, you elements, with unkindness;
> I never gave you kingdom, call'd you children,
> You owe me no subscription,

and when he recovers from his insanity, brought on by the strength of his demands upon a world from which we are to ask nothing, he says meekly to Cordelia,

> If you have poison for me, I will drink it.

There is the same attitude of mind in Edgar's

> Men must endure
> Their going hence, even as their coming hither:
> *Ripeness is all.*

"Men must endure," this is stoicism, but "Ripeness is all," is a word of Zen; one can hardly get one's intellectual teeth into it. There is a similar passage in *Hamlet,* beginning, in the

same way, with the relative and ending with the absolute.
Hamlet says of death, not long before his own,

> If it be now, 'tis not to come; if it be not to come,
> it will be now; if it be not now, yet it will come:
> *The readiness is all.*

But "Ripeness is all" goes deeper. All we can say of it is that
Edgar understood it at the moment he uttered the words, and at
some moment or other we may do the same and repeat them.

In *King Lear* we have the following:

Lear: Dost thou call me fool, boy?
Fool: All thy other titles thou hast given away; that
        thou wast born with.
Kent: This is not altogether fool, my lord.

If only we can realise that we are born fools, if only we can
attain to this state of absolute foolishness, where everything
is good, we shall be like Sôshi's drunkard, who when he falls
out of a cart, though he injures himself, is not killed, because
he is not thinking of life and death, hope and fear, and thus is
in a spiritual condition of security. It is Lear's "cleverness"
that gets him and everyone else into trouble, but in compensation, how many things he learns and teaches us by his experiences. He finds that

> When the mind's free,
> The body's delicate,

that is to say, when we think about ourselves, we are deeply
conscious of our physical pains and pleasure, but if we forget
ourselves, the body too, becoming one with the mind, is hardly
aware of its pain and pleasure, cold and heat. How much our
happiness depends upon the condition of our minds, is shown
also in what Macbeth says,

> Present fears
> Are less than horrible imaginings.

Imagination, "looking before and after," increases our distress a thousand-fold, and though it may offer us a doubtful joy for the future, blinds us to the present good. Again, Lear says,

> The art of our necessities is strange,
> That can make vile things precious.

The absolute value of things is infinite; our minds, which change according to our circumstances, that is, our necessities, decide that things are vile or precious. Thus a man

> Must make content with his fortunes fit,
> For the rain it raineth every day.

The whole play of *Macbeth* is a dramatisation of Emerson's Essay *Compensation,* of the truth that justice is always done, instantly and irrevocably.

> He that hateth his brother is a murderer.
> The wages of sin is death.
> The Kingdom of God is within you.

These are the words written over the portals of the Hell in which Macbeth and Lady Macbeth writhe in anguish throughout five acts. Goethe says:

Beharren Sie nur dabei und halten Sie immer an der Gegenwart fest. Jeder Zustand, ja jeder Augenblick ist von unendlichen Wert, denn er ist der Repräsentant einer ganzen Ewigkeit. (*Gespräche mit Goethe,* 1823)

In Richard III we see Zen at work; no hesitation, no self-deception,

> Thy school days frightful, desperate, wild and furious,
> Thy prime of manhood daring, bold and venturous,

but there is something wrong somewhere; what is it? Richard
has separated himself from the rest of Nature, and in Wordsworth's phrase, we watch him

> to Nature's self
> Oppose a deeper nature.   (*Prel.* XIII, 200)

Thus, at the end of the play, he himself, for all his courage,
begins to whine:

> I shall despair.   There is no creature loves me;
> And if I die, no soul shall pity me.

He does not understand the true independence, loneliness,
poverty, which comes from complete union with nature,
with humanity.

In *Two Gentlemen of Verona*, Shakespeare writes,

> Were man
> But constant, he were perfect: that one error
> Fills him with faults.

This is the secret of the understanding of the character of
Iago, whose "motiveless malignity" puzzles the critics. It is
no more difficult to understand Iago than any other freak of
nature, such as a benevolent tiger; it is simply a question of
constancy, of perfection. Iago is not so much too bad, as too
good to be true. He is "der Geist der *stets* verneint." His
constancy, faultlessness, comes from his following Polonius'
advice, but mistaking "self" for his own character:

> to thine own self be true
> And it must follow, as the night the day,
> Thou canst not then be false to any man.

He is true to himself and therefore to others, in causing the
greatest amount of unhappiness to the greatest number of

people. There are, however, two flaws in this philosophy of life: first, that in this infernal utilitarianism, oneself also counts as one, and unhappiness, like curses, comes home to roost. Second, that just as, paradoxically, happiness comes from forgetting oneself and making others happy, so not less paradoxically and not less truly, pain comes ultimately from the pleasant task of inflicting pain.   In other words, the universe is not, as Arnold and Hardy thought, of "equal mind" in the sense of being dispassionate in the matter of good and evil, truth and falsehood.[1]   The scales are weighted, though ever so lightly, on the side of goodness and truth. Were this not so, how could we say, "Follow nature," "Know thyself"? Zen would become simply a participation in the Universal Suicide.

It is painful to watch Prof. Bradley floundering about in his endeavour to justify our admiration of Iago's Zen.   He quotes *Henry V*:

> There is some soul of goodness in things evil
> Would men observingly distil it out,

but then shows he does not understand this, by pointing out that Iago is not wholly bad.   Shakespeare is not saying here what he says in *All's Well that Ends Well,*

> The web of our life is of a mingled yarn, good and ill together.

He is not saying that we are all partly good and partly bad. There needs no poet to come from heaven to tell us this.   He

[1] Emerson, in *Unity*:
> A spell is laid on sod and stone,
> *Night and day were tampered with,*
> Every quality and pith
> Surcharged and sultry with a power
> That works its will on age and hour.

is saying that "there is a *soul* of goodness in things evil." Ripeness is all, directness is all. In both good and evil there is Goodness, if only men can forget their praising and blaming and see it as it flows, in its activity.[1] Let us admit it, Iago is inhuman, just as "gentle Jesus meek and mild" is inhuman, but not therefore impossible. But the constancy of Iago in evil is Goodness, just as the Satan of Milton is bad by his loyalty to his comrades and pity for his victims. It is only the simple but far-reaching fact that Goodness is on the side of goodness rather than badness, that is to say, the fact that evil in its own nature destroys itself,—that makes Iago a failure.

Shakespeare's profoundest thought about his own life is expressed in what Masefield calls "the noblest of his sonnets."

> Poor soul, the centre of my sinful earth,
> Fool'd by these rebel powers that thee array,
> Why dost thou pine within, and suffer dearth,
> Painting thy outward walls so costly gay?
> Why so large cost, having so short a lease,
> Dost thou upon thy fading mansion spend?
> Shall worms, inheritors of this excess,
> Eat up thy charge? Is this thy body's end?
> Then, soul, live thou upon thy servant's loss,
> And let that pine to aggravate thy store;
> Buy terms divine in selling hours of dross;
> Within be fed, without be rich no more:
> So shalt thou feed on Death, that feeds on men,
> And Death once dead, there's no more dying then.

The last lines, though in the witty Elizabethan manner, show Shakespeare's clear apprehension of the Zen truth that eternal

[1] Cp. what Friar Lawrence says in *Romeo and Juliet*:
> For nought so vile that on the earth doth live
> But to the earth some special good doth give;
> Nor aught so good, but, strained from that fair use,
> Revolts from true birth, stumbling on abuse:
> Virtue itself turns vice, being misapplied,
> And vice sometimes by action dignified.

life is to be gained by "feeding on death," that is, destroying death. How? By dying to ourselves once and for all, "selling hours of dross," thus entering into a timeless and self-less existence, "terms divine."

In conclusion, let us say that Shakespeare had a religion, a religion which could ask and answer the question which Macduff asked, when his wife and children were all murdered at one fell swoop:

> Did heaven look on,
> And would not take their part?

What is the answer to the question? It cannot be given in Yes, or No, because as the question is understood by most people, it has the same form as, "Have you stopped beating your wife yet?" But you may say, "You are only equivocating: answer the question, does Heaven care for us or not?" The answer is the plays of *Hamlet, King Lear, Othello, Macbeth,* for when we are watching or reading the plays, and even for a short time afterwards, before the glow has died away, we know the answer. But it is not Yes, and it is not No.

INDEX

INDEX

439

ZEN IN ENGLISH LITERATURE

禪と英文学

1942年12月29日　初版発行　　1993年4月25日　新装版発行

著　　者　R. H. ブ ラ イ ス

発 行 者　株式 北 星 堂 書 店
　　　　　会社

代表者　山　本　雅　三

〒113 東京都文京区本郷駒込3-32-4

検印省略

Tel(03)3827-0511　Fax(03)3827-0567

THE HOKUSEIDO PRESS

32-4, Honkomagome 3-chome, Bunkyo-ku, Tokyo 113 Japan

◇落丁・乱丁本はお取替いたします。